Advance Praise For

The Seven Secrets
of Learning Revealed

"Read this book! *The Seven Secrets Revealed* is for anyone who wants to learn more in less time using less energy with increased memory and creativity." - **Mark Victor Hansen**, co-creator, *#1 New York Times* best selling series *Chicken Soup for the Soul*® and co-author, *The One Minute Millionaire*

"*The Seven Secrets of Learning Revealed* is an outstanding contribution to our expanding knowledge of the operations of intelligence and how learning takes place. No teacher or student should be without this book."- **Larry Dossey, MD**, Author: *Healing Beyond The Body, Reinventing Medicine, and Healing Words*

"This is the Day and Age, when everything will be made known. Here is a book that shows how to reveal this inner knowledge, through true education from the Latin word *"educare"* meaning to lead out of you, all that lies deep within. This book by Laurence Martel is a *"Must Read"* showing you how to use your hidden talents, *"The Genius Within You."* - **Alexander Everett**, Father of the Human Potential Movement and founder of Mind Dynamics, Inward Bound and more recently, Spiritual Dynamics.

"Larry Martel has had remarkable success in using the seven secrets with elementary school children, high school students, and beyond. Now, others can benefit from the great wisdom contained in his book."**General David C. Jones**, former Chairman, Joint Chiefs of Staff, and Chair of Americorps

"I enjoyed reading the *The Seven Secrets of Learning Revealed*. 'Seven Secrets' is full of inspiration, interesting facts, and an abundance of sources for further research." **The Honorable Senator William Brock**, former U.S. Secretary of Labor

" ...it **is** exactly the type of book that will win your heart, energize your soul, and make you feel **great** about teaching and learning!"
- **Professor Rita Dunn, Ed.D.**, Director, Center for the Study of Learning and Teaching Styles, St. John's University, N.Y.

"Every century there comes along a couple of books that revives the soul of education. A must read for those who administer and work directly with kids in education..." - **Christopher Eaddy, Ph.D.**, author of ***The Greatest Teacher and Quantum Wisdom*** and State Director, N.C. Governor's Support our Students Program of the N.C. Department of Juvenile Justice and Delinquency Prevention

"...outstanding as a resource for teaching and learning. Everything you ever wanted to know about the latest, newest discoveries about the human mind, brain and heart can be found within the pages of this book... Whether you are a parent or student, teacher or community leader, the realities described can help you understand and work with your own relationships. This book is a keeper." - **Liz Kiai**, Director of Curriculum and Instruction, Leilehua High School, Hawaii

"A must read for all educators concerned about the negative classroom impact of high stakes testing. This book refreshes and extends our knowledge base of why teaching the "whole" child is critical to higher performance."- **Joe Peel, Ed.D.**, Director Wake County, N.C. School District Wake Leadership Academy

"An important and inspirational book for all superintendents and other administrators seeking to reform the learning process, especially as it relates to individual students..and how teaching should take place in the classroom." - **Robert F. Kelly, Ph.D.**, former Superintendent of Schools in New York, California, Pennsylvania, Virginia and Ohio

"Dr. Martel brings together the latest knowledge about how we learn and how we can structure learning environments. Teachers in Hawaii who have implemented these ideas have reported immediate and positive results...all the information we need to transform our system of education to one where everyone is successful..."**Jim Williams,** President, Royal State Trust, Honolulu, Hawaii

"*The Seven Secrets of Learning Revealed* is a wonderfully practical user's guide for getting the most out of your own brain AND improving your relationships by **better understanding** the brains of others, especially your loved ones…AMAZING!"- **Abby Braune Rohrer**, Founder, Self-Rescue™ System

"Quality Leadership in business, education, community and family life is made possible by building quality 'relationships'. Dr. Martel clearly lays out the Seven Secrets for Success in this groundbreaking book on learning and performance."- **Wayne Alderson,** founder and president Value of the Person – Theory R Leadership Consultant for Corporate America

"Dr. Martel takes a lifetime of learning research and summarizes the 'secrets' for the rest of us. And the secret is that there is no secret. Learning is a definable and predictable outcome of the utilization of the many gifts of human intelligence that we are just beginning to identify and comprehend…" - **Gerald Gochenour, Ph.D.**, former Director of Technology Education for State of Ohio and former high school principal

"…Psychology, medicine, science and technology have advanced, and Dr. Martel has successfully applied these new sciences to a new vision for learning. You will enjoy the benefits of this book. - **Anees A. Sheikh, Ph.D.**, Psychologist, Department of Psychology, Marquette University

"…The book encompasses so much more than a mere seven secrets. Packed with information, both practical and theoretical, it is an educator's guide that can become a cherished resource book…the book reaches out to educators and parents with its myriad of ideas and love for education." - **Renee Fuller, Ph. D.**, Psychologist; creator and founder of Ball-Stick-Bird Publications

"From the perspective of a former State Senator, what Dr. Martel presents in the *Seven Secrets of Learning Revealed* is an opportunity to dramatically improve all children's learning performance through the use of limited resources."**George F. Disnard,** former New Hampshire State Senator and Chairman of the New Hampshire Senate Education Committee

"The reader is forewarned ... the 'secrets' contained in this book are not communicated in whispers, rather they are sounded as a clarion call to reinvent our educational system and methods. Dr. Martel....confronts us with our own freedom and capacity as learners, inviting us to choose personal accountability for our own development, and for that of others in our community. He has filled these pages with his extraordinary fervor, keen insights, gentle wit, and deep compassion for every individual..." - **Joe Braidish,** Director, Kelley Executive Partners, Indiana University

"A book that should be part of every educator's library. The use of any or all of the strategies offered by Dr. Martel will result in children learning more efficiently and more joyfully. The "eighth secret" is that the application of these *seven secrets* has already produced remarkable results in classrooms throughout the United States. Share this book with others!"- **John R. Grassi, Ph.D.**, Professor of Graduate Education, Vice President of The Alumni College, Cambridge College, Cambridge, MA

"Having had first-hand experience as a high school principal with the concepts and strategies included in this guide, I heartily recommend *The Seven Secrets of Learning Revealed.* This collection of practical and effective tools should be required reading for anyone devoted to instructional improvement. Dr. Martel helped make a difference for teachers and students in my school."- **Rick Butler,** Director, Professional Leadership and Organizational Development and former High School Principal, Springfield, Ohio.

"An extraordinary read. The information is both practical and profound. Teachers, mentors, and parents alike gain real strategies and new knowledge which can be immediately applied. His discussion on the seven intelligences alone is worth the read."- **Christopher Grant**, Chief Strategy Officer, Envision U, Inc.

"Impressive in its scope and depth, fascinating in its balance between scientific observations and research and practical applications, Laurence Martel's book provides the direction and exciting tools to better understand how we learn and then how we can apply these strategies . . ."
- **Elizabeth Schiever**, Director, High School Financial Planning Program, National Endowment for Financial Education

"Larry once more turns tidbits of information into gems of knowledge in *The Seven Secrets*. These secrets are knowledge and knowledge is power. Teachers must now find the courage to apply these secrets in the classroom. We must all find the courage to implement some of these secrets in our daily living. **- Jesus Martinez**, Director, GANAS Education Consultant and scientist, Sandia National Laboratories.

"… The more school staff and parents have access to these Seven Secrets, the more they gain information power to make changes. I believe the application of these Seven Secrets of Learning are critical concepts needed by educators today, especially those personnel working in low performing schools."**- Margaret K. Grater, Ph.D.**, Consultant, Partnership Academy Assessment Center and Grater and Associates

"…Imagine having all students maximize their learning potential regardless of learning style, ability, or disability. …packed with leading-edge, research-based approaches that deliver clear results and ignite the inherent ability of those who teach and those who learn".
-Debbie Smith, Peak Performance Consultant, Mobile Team Challenge

"This work has allowed the door to be opened from the barriers of the cage of traditional education, allowing chemistry students and the teacher to FLY FREELY in the Chemistry lab and classroom with joy and excitement for learning." **- Leo Wood,** former High School Chemistry Teacher and Regional Director, Southwest Coordinator, Math/Science Programs, National Academy of Integrative Learning, Inc.

"…a wonderful resource for all educators.…Dr. Martel's research will reaffirm what you have always known in your heart was the right way to teach. We hope all educators will take time to read this book and practice the strategies provided. To quote a passage from the book, 'Good, better, best, never let it rest; until your good is better and your better is best!'…" **- North Carolina Association of Educators -** Center for Teaching and Learning 2003

"Thank you for taking the time to develop and compile this information that has the potential to transform the educational system in our country and uplift the self-worth of our youth."**- Jamilla Canady,** Spelman College Acting Dean, Continuing Education

The
Seven
Secrets
of
Learning
Revealed

What Your Teacher Never Taught You,
Because Your Teacher Never Knew

Dr. Laurence D. Martel

03 04 05 06 HH 10 9 8 7 6 5 4 3 2 1
Printed in the United States of America
ISBN: 0-9715739-8-0
Library of Congress Control #: 2003108989

Requests for permission to make copies of any part of this work can
be made to:

National Academy of Integrative Learning, Inc.
P.O. Box 5784
Hilton Head Island, SC 29938

Published through Cameo Publications, LLC for
Dr. Laurence D. Martel, President
National Academy of Integrative Learning, Inc.
http://www.intellilearn.org

Cameo Publications, LLC
PO Box 8006
Hilton Head Island, SC 29938
1-866-372-2636
publisher@cameopublications.com

FOR MORE INFORMATION

on how you can obtain training products and research, materials, or to request a seminar, please contact Dr. Martel at the following address:

Laurence D. Martel, Ph.D.
President
National Academy of Integrative Learning, Inc.
PO Box 5784
Hilton Head Island, SC 29938
phone: 843-686-4050 fax: 843-686-4519
www.intellilearn.org
martel@intellilearn.org

Additionally, Dr. Martel provides keynote addresses for national and international organizations and is available for your community group or parent or student organizations to speak on a variety of issues related to improved learning performance.

Dedication

Most books are a labor of family involvement. Having taught me so much about raising children and grandchildren, I dedicate this book to my four children – Lauren, Brantley, Quincy and Matthew, as well as to our grandchildren Spencer, Mary Piper, Mason, Lara, Faith, Madison and "new baby about to be," along with our daughters-in-law, Rebecca and Libby.

This book also serves as a tribute to my wife, Mary, who for nearly forty years has lived through and tested all the ideas, from our first moments together, while struggling in our first years of parenthood and teaching, on to establishing a clinic for head injured, stroke and dementia patients and on to our role as caretakers for our own aging parents and now as grandparents. All of our family and friends have enriched us with the meaning and blessings of family loyalty and love which you will find imprinted throughout this book.

LDM

The
Seven
Secrets
of
Learning
Revealed

What Your Teacher Never Taught You,
Because Your Teacher Never Knew

Dr. Laurence D. Martel

About
The Author

Dr. Laurence D. Martel, President of Integrative Learning Systems and Chairman of the nonprofit National Academy of Integrative Learning, Inc., is perhaps the nation's leading developer of research and systems for the study of learning and retention within corporations, schools and government agencies throughout the world. These include corporations like Eastman Kodak, Intel, Xerox, Shell Asia Pacific, Alcan, Gulfstream Aerospace, and Keene Industries in Liberia. In addition to medical colleges, universities, public schools and government agencies in the United Nations, Brunei, Liberia, Singapore and the Philippines have brought Dr. Martel's work to their shores. Dr. Martel's broad experience as a College Trustee, State Commissioner, Company President, University Faculty Member, Department Head, Researcher and Community Service Board Member have helped formulate his "Science of Learning" concept, delivered through the National Academy of Integrative Learning, Inc.

The National Academy of Integrative Learning, Inc. is a nonprofit organization working in cooperation with several colleges and universities, among which are Syracuse University; Antioch University; Oklahoma State University; Institute for Telecommunication; Georgia Southern University; and Spelman College. The main goal of the Academy is to drastically increase learning performance by training teachers and trainers in new educational techniques. This includes the systematic implementation of effective training services, seminars, products and programs as the centerpiece to strengthening the workforce, increasing economic prosperity, revitalizing schools and facilitating community regeneration.

From 1987 until 1990 he was director of the Center for the Study of Learning and Retention at Syracuse University, disseminating the only U.S. Department of Education endorsed system for reducing attrition in higher education. The goal was to train faculty and staff to improve the quality of the undergraduate experience and to significantly reduce attrition. From that platform, he launched the first full-time daytime college program for prisoners in Auburn Correctional Facility and led the initiative to obtain state tuition grants for financially disadvantaged, part time adult students. The successes in outcomes have ranged from the Onondaga Reservation in New York through to the Apache Reservation in New Mexico; to Harlem and the Southside of Chicago; to the bayous of Louisiana and the rural communities of Hawaii.

On a national and international basis, he conducted research, faculty training, curriculum and materials design, policy development, and graduate education at Syracuse University. He was also assistant professor in the College of Human Development and adjunct faculty, teaching professional ethics and applied epistemology in the Philosophy Department.

Dr. Martel was an original member of the Walt Disney Design team for the "Celebration" school, brought in by leading community designer, Mr. Charles Fraser. He was a founding member of the Board of Advisors of the Institute of Telecommunications at Oklahoma State University and a consultant to the United States Department of Energy, The United States Air Force and the United States Junior ROTC Programs. In addition, Dr. Martel has been a personal coach to several corporate executives, helping to develop "learning organizations."

Dr. Martel was a State Commissioner and Chairman of the New York State Parks, Recreation and Historic Preservation Commission, which founded the Empire State Games and the Urban Cultural Park concept, under the leadership of Governor Cary and Orin Lehman, State Chairman of the Office. It was Dr. Martel who introduced the name change of the State Agency, which later was enacted into Law, to include, "Historic Preservation," reflecting the comprehensive nature of that state agency and recognizing the value of all of its employees.

In another policy role, he was also instrumental as a Board Member of the United Cerebral Palsy Center for enhancing adaptive use of technology to learning among cerebral palsy clients. Dr Martel founded a private clinic for patients suffering from head injury, stroke, and dementia in cooperation with physicians at Upstate Medical Center.

Dr. Martel is a senior faculty member in the graduate studies in education and business and is the author of more than twenty major academic publications (ranging from Forbes Magazine to Family Circle Magazine to the American Society of Quality) with an orientation toward advanced learning methods, including the book, *School Success: The Inside Story*, (co-authored), along with this book: *The Seven Secrets of Learning Revealed.*

He received his Ph.D. in Philosophy of Education in 1979 from Syracuse University. Dr. Martel lives in Hilton Head Island, South Carolina with his wife, Mary. They have four children and seven grandchildren.

B y what measure of gratitude can one express the deep appreciation for all who have contributed to the creation of this book?
Former teachers, students, colleagues, friends and family are
too numerous to fill the space available here to say: "Thank you, from
the bottom of my heart!" You know who you are and if you read these
words, know that I am speaking to you personally in thankful gratitude
for our journey together.

Everyone needs maps in life to guide them in paths of success.
And maps come in different sizes and kinds, all the way from "treasure" maps to the hand written words on a note pad, indicating the
direction and location of your destination. Another kind of map is the
analogy or the "story" structure to provide insight and guidance. This
book is filled with maps of all kinds, provided by many people to help
you with your purpose and direction. I'd like to acknowledge some of
those map makers.

To paraphrase Sir Isaac Newton, who turned the world of science
around in his day, "If you, dear reader, see further as a result of reading
this book, it is because you stood on the shoulders of giants." And that
is exactly what has happened in my life. I have been blessed to be
lifted up on the shoulders of many giants in a wide variety of fields of
expertise, from science and medicine to theology, from day care management to corporate transformation.

This book is woven by the thread of the great and enduring principles of life that have been shared with us through many Scriptures
from the many different religions of the world and, expressed in the
Golden Rule. And this Rule has been acknowledged by people all over
the world and in many faiths as being taught by the great Master teacher,
Jesus of Nazareth. I have attempted to stay faithful to His messages of
truth and integrity and of love and kindness throughout the voyages in
these pages.

You will travel a long way before you will find a greater friend of
children, parents and teachers than Dr. John Grassi whose intellect,
passion and compassion appear as footprints throughout this book, and
for that we stand taller.

The Walt Disney Company brought the nation's leading architect
of planned communities, Mr. Charles Fraser, to help them build the
"Celebration" community in Florida. Mr. Fraser asked me to join him
with a small team, including Dr. Larry Rosen, a professor at Stetson
University, to create the "Celebration School" as a centerpiece to the
community. Many of the Secrets in this book were presented to the

teachers and administrators of the Osceola County School and their enthusiasm was so high that the board shifted its indecision to a vote in favor of permitting Disney to create and build an innovative public school at the outset of the project.

Former Eastman Kodak Executive and CEO of James River Corporation, UK, Robert Ward taught me most of what I know about the world of "Quality" in business and contributed to the evolving perspective I have written about in this book on "The human side of quality." When he was head of Quality at Kodak, he influenced the leadership, including the Vice President of Manufacturing, Dr. Ron Heidke, to fund our research and implementation of many of these Secrets at Kodak. The implementation of many of the strategies in this book helped Kodak turn around its Black and White Film Division and go on to save $20 million dollars over a three-year period. The company then helped fund the training of about one thousand public school teachers where employees had children in school.

Superintendent of Schools, Dr. Robert Kelly, is one of the top leaders of education in America. Wherever he provided leadership for a school district, ranging from Fairfax, Virginia to Utica, New York, his unswerving focus was on "children's achievement" and the improvement of teachers and systems to support the classroom. It was Dr. Kelly who paved the way for school reform in New York, leading the N.Y. State Legislature to enact legislation which supported several schools that appear as case studies in this book. The effort to fund a statewide initiative was led by State Education Chairman, Senator James Donovan, and rigorously supported by long time friend of equal educational opportunity, Mr. John Graziano of Albany, New York. Superintendent Dr. Janet Aikele launched a system-wide implementation in Idaho which resulted in a two-thirds reduction in special education referrals in the district.

The Honorable Adelaide Sanford, Deputy Chancellor of the New York State Board of Regents, saw the results of our work and introduced the components of this book to the Black and Puerto Rican Legislative Caucus in N.Y. As a result, with a small grant and teaming up with the School districts across the State of New York, several of the secrets of this book were implemented from the inner city of New York City to the farmlands of Oswego. The research from these schools, as well as from the Chicago Guggenheim Elementary School, was independently validated by the N.Y. State Board of Education for statewide replication. Former Regent Emlyn Griffith, a Welsh descendent, was always steadfast in supporting these innovative processes to empower parents, teachers, administrators and students. The government of Wales has translated one of my co-authored books into the Welsh language to obtain many of the secrets contained in this new book.

After recommending the use of the "fun-filled" processes contained in this book, Dr. Jesus Martinez was chided by his serious fellow scientists at one of the nation's leading science facilities, the Sandia National Laboratories. Nevertheless, Dr. Martinez persisted, along with Dr. Larry Salgado and Dr. Janise Baldo-Pulaski, leading to significant contributions to the 500 teachers throughout the public schools in New Mexico. So successful were we that two Belen, N.M. Public School teachers, Janet Jackson and Arlene Garcia, won U.S. Presidential Awards for their exemplary achievements with middle school students as a result of implementing the *Secrets* they learned at Sandia during a teacher seminar – the same *Secrets* you will read about in the pages that follow.

George Smith, whose works to develop the personal skills of people of all ages, has been a strong supporter and friend to the principles in this book, along with our mutual colleague Stefan Neilson, developer of "Winning Colors" and other communications conflict resolution books for students, adults and families. You can contact them through the Appendix E - Resources.

I wish to thank the dedicated people at the several foundations which have stepped up to the plate to support the innovative solutions to learning provided in *The Seven Secrets of Learning Revealed.* The Joyce Foundation in Chicago, The Avon Foundation in New York, The J.M. Huber Foundation of New Jersey, The Intel Foundation in Arizona, The Panasonic Foundation in Texas, The Rapides Foundation in Louisiana, The Eastman Kodak Foundation in Rochester, N.Y., The Albertson Foundation in Idaho, The State University of New York Research Foundation, The Trust for Emergent Education in Hawaii and The Anthony Robbins Foundation in California are contributors to our efforts described in this book to make successful learning more possible and readily available to families and school children. A special expression of gratitude to Peter Francis, Chairman and CEO of J.M. Huber Corporation, Hicks Waldron, former Chairman of the Avon Corporation, Frank Vullo of Eastman Kodak Company, Sally Anderson of the Albertson Foundation, Jim Williams, Executive Director of the Hawaii Trust for Emergent Education and Maureen Kilkenny, Executive Director of the Anthony Robbins Foundation.

The men and women of the military have utilized these processes to improve learning across their training divisions. The Air Force improved its Quality Leadership training with the Secrets in this book, thanks to Col. Colleen Turner, Ph.D., and Director of the quality program at the U.S. Space and Missile Center, Col. James Hegland.

One of the best-kept secrets in the United States is the JROTC Program across nearly 1500 high schools. Sparked by the leadership and foresight of The U.S. Army Cadet Command, Bureau Chief Donna Rice took the learning concepts and strategies to the field instructors, along with the U.S. Air Force, under the guidance of Col. Brian King, impacting the improvement of literally thousands of student cadets across the United States. A special thanks to the retired military personnel who have trained to become public school JROTC instructors and who have steadfastly committed themselves to the citizenship development of young people through this exceptional program enacted by Congress in 1916. Congress should give itself a standing ovation for funding and supporting this important national treasure. Thanks also to Donna Rice, John Shultz and his team, including Ed Tillett, at American Management Services, who produced our award winning CD on the secrets in this book.

Ginnie Moore at Shawnee State University in Portsmouth, Ohio led the way to cultivate the Secrets in this book for "Tech-Prep" students, with significant results in improved teacher and student performance in both the rural and urban areas along the Ohio River. State Director of Technology Dr. Jerry Gochenour, High School Principal Rick Butler, Middle School Principal Larry Nickels and Elementary School Principal Marnie Gochenour built a new vision of possibilities based on solid data in Springfield, Ohio, showing remarkable improvements in student achievement using the processes you will read about. Marnie's school, The Kenwood Elementary School, went from "poor performing" to win the Ohio Governor's "Best Practices" Award three years following implementation of these strategies.

Perhaps the most highly decorated researcher in American innovations in education is Dr. Rita Dunn of St. John's University. She has had more doctoral students win national and international awards than any other. Based on the Model of Learning Styles developed by Rita and her husband, Professor Ken Dunn, Ed.D., more children have avoided failure and flourished as a direct result of their leadership, enthusiasm and solid research approach. The world is a better place because of them and their work, which you will review in this volume. Thank you Rita and Ken for all you have taught me.

A nationally recognized consultant on "Leadership," Rod Hairston conducts the training seminars for the Anthony Robbins Foundation's "Discovery Camp" for youth from around the world. From the time we met, Rod and his colleagues Chris Grant and Julie Hairston who runs the EnVisionU Company, have been tireless in supporting the efforts described in this book. With a "eureka" insight, Julie helped me shift the subtitle to its current message.

My youngest son Matthew and his wife Libby designed the Cover and the logo at the Chapter headings and also formalized the graphics based on the drawings by Leo Wood, a top chemistry teacher in the United States and trainer in the processes discussed in this book. Brantley, our eldest son, is an artist and drew the flag draped behind the "Angels of Inspiration." Our daughters Quincy and Lauren gave feedback on various segments of this manuscript, as did my wife Mary.

A word of gratitude for my friend Leo Wood, who is not only an award winning band director and exemplary musician, but is one of the top science teachers in the world. His students at Tempe High School rose from 54% passing with C grades or better in Chemistry to 93% passing with C's or better by using the key concepts and strategies contained in the Secrets. His dropout rate tumbled from 28% to 6%. Leo has been an inspiration over the years and a critical player in the evolution of the successes reported herein.

I want to acknowledge the dedication and support of Ms. Phyllis Driscoll who read every word, along with preparing the first drafts of this manuscript to the final details of its layout. In addition, many of the case studies you will read about emerged from the planning and preparation she provided.

To Dawn and David Josephson at Cameo Publications of Hilton Head Island, S.C. I am indebted for the supportive, gracious and professional guidance from start to finish in the publication of this project. Also to Wayne Carter, my brother, for his dedicated support in video production, documenting the dramatic success presented in case studies.

How many friends does it take to write a reader focused book? The answer is one - if he is Ray Cooper. Ray has been an outstanding "guide at the side" to make this a better book.

Finally, I am so grateful to the children, families, teachers and administrative leaders from across the globe, from Harlem to the Apache Reservation in New Mexico; from Europe to Liberia in West Africa; from Singapore to Brunei and on to Hawaii. They all are in this book as an expression of how achievement, success, meaning, value and purpose can flourish in the context of love and kindness.

ANGELS OF INSPIRATION

Leo and Ursula L. Martel	New Hampshire
Norman and Virginia Gibbs	New York
Norman and Maureen Gouldin	Connecticut
Arthur Langan	New York
Dee Dee Bennett	Idaho
Margaret Willoughby	Ohio
Stan Meyerson	New York
Sandra Kim	Ohau, Hawaii
William Crook, M.D.	Tennessee
Clem Hartley	Ohio
Cinda Fisher	Arizona
Cliff Bailey	Kuaii, Hawaii
Lynette Yeager	Ohio
Andrea Carlson	Idaho
Edward "Pete" Wood	Arizona
Morgan Doughton	Washington, DC
Philomena Grassi	New York

CONTENTS

CONTENTS

Foreword

Two decades ago, when American industry woke up to the shock of foreign competition, particularly in manufacturing, many people, including myself, had been studying and highly involved with the new thinking "High Performance Work Systems." We had major reservations as to whether we could ever become competitive again. Higher labor rates, organizational restrictions, environmental and human protection requirements, less government support, etc. were real challenges that we had to offset, fast.

Only one solution appeared possible: "Total Involvement." Every member of any business, organization, or family had to have the opportunity, capability, and desire to develop and contribute his/her unique talents. This started with top management. To quote one of the most outstanding CEOs of the time, "*I*, I repeat, *I* must learn, teach, and model the improvement programs, and this process must cascade down through the entire organization."

With the recognition of the importance of learning, it was obvious that huge investments in time and money were required to determine, create, and provide the training programs that were necessary to truly make the employees world class. This reflected upward all the way to the CEO, with each function providing unique responsibilities and support to the operational level. Everyone would have to be involved with a rededication to expanding personal capability through learning, teaching, and modeling excellence and quality. It was quickly apparent that a revolution in training and learning methods would be essential to accomplishing the goal.

This book represents the start of the turnaround for American business, education, and personal learning. ***The Seven Secrets of Learning*** was in its early stages twenty years ago, but it was the only process we found for Kodak that indicated the potential to dramatically streamline the speed and quality of all training and learning. The initial trial investment and scope were sizable. However, very quickly, the results we achieved were amazing at all the levels of Eastman Kodak. In the intervening years, the enhancement of understanding and improvements in expediting total training and learning efficiency in business and education has been further improved.

The Seven Secrets of Learning provides a comprehensive yet easy to understand guide on what this process is all about. Today, it is far more important that business leaders, educators, public policy leaders, and parents exercise their unique responsibility to learn, teach, and model learning excellence and ensure that it is cascaded throughout their entire organization, whether that is a business, classroom, or family.

In addition to my experience at Eastman Kodak and James River Corporation, I have also witnessed my family's growth in learning, as well as educational improvements in my church, my community, and other public organizations as a result of using Dr. Martel's processes and strategies for learning more in less time with higher achievement. As a result of the successes in every category, I highly recommend this book to all who are interested in continuously improving their quality of learning and their quality of life.

Robert M. Ward
Former Division Director of Quality, Eastman Kodak Company and CEO, James River Corporation, UK Division

Introduction

Welcome to ***The Seven Secrets of Learning Revealed***! This is a survival guidebook for your journey into the secrets of learning. Its purpose is to empower you to release the energy of your mind and heart for greater success, health and happiness. This new knowledge as well as strategies, tactics and tools will help you, your family, co-workers and community cope with the challenges which face each of us today.

The world needs many things right now and if you took a poll, I am certain that a book about education, training, or learning would not be selected as one of the top priorities. Today's world is filled with case after case of ecological disasters from the chainsaw massacre of the rain forest, to water and air pollution and on to the global warming phenomena. Couple this with an alarming population explosion which is migrating to global urban centers where millions are starving, unable to feed themselves and survive. In the face of these issues, a book about education seems trivial.

Nor would a book about teaching and learning emerge as a priority, since the bookstores are filled with a variety of volumes, ranging from school reform to building "learning" organizations. All seem to have an emphasis on the structure, function and outcomes of the education system, with the hope of increasing the results by re-arranging the chairs on the deck of the education ship of state. And where research proves that a particular model of improvement does work, there is no nation-wide market either for the distribution or the advocacy of such proven models. In fact, in several states, public officials view advocacy as a conflict of interest.

Believing that our schooling system is another *"Titanic,"* others have jumped ship altogether. For instance, Charter Schools abound, along with home schooling as alternatives to a seemingly deaf institution we call "the education system," which is neither hearing nor reading the lips of a nation's call for improvement in learning for all of its people. Just look at Michigan's growth in Charter Schools and their performance, as well as the enrollment in home schooling in North Carolina. The trend is growing, paved partly by the voucher and "parent choice" initiatives. Despite such experiments, the overwhelming majority of the children in the United States *are* enrolled in the traditional school system, whose record over the past seven years includes nearly twenty gun shootings in school classrooms, involving elementary, middle, high school, and college students.

Blind to the significant economic and cultural shift from an industrial society to an information economy, state policy makers and school administrators throughout the United States are still clamoring for higher performance by inspecting the outcomes. Just take an inventory of the state proficiency tests across the country, as well as the proliferation of standards. Seemingly justifiable as a strategic intervention, no significant gains in children's or adult's learning performance has occurred as a result of inspecting the outcomes of the system, since the first *Nation at Risk* Report nearly twenty years ago. The single-minded focus on measuring and monitoring outcomes ignores the processes that produce high results. The United States, for example, is woefully far behind other nations in benchmarks such as Standardized Test Scores in areas of reading, math, science, writing and communications. Pointing to marginal increases in SAT Test Scores is like looking for your lost car keys under a streetlight, just because that is where you can see. There is no correlation between SAT Test Scores, or for that matter Valedictorian status and personal, professional and economic performance in later life.

The knowledge, skills and values required in our information economy demand that we rethink the very nature of learning in our personal lives and in our society. And that is precisely what this book intends to help you do. The issue in front of us is less about education, nor is it about school reform. It is about survival!

And this book is about survival through learning as a national priority and core competency in the information economy. ***The Seven Secrets of Learning Revealed*** changes the way we think about learning as a necessary condition to personal health, wealth and happiness, as well as national economic growth and survival.

We cannot continue to increase our population and allow outmoded, educational systems, including the TV influence, to "dumb down" citizens whose competence is less than the preceding generation. Our information economy requires more than a "dutiful" labor force or "fighting" army; it requires the highest standards of personal learning competence for a life of creativity, inventiveness, problem identification and problem solving. And today's workforce and military require no less. If any society continues to fail its people by providing "old" models of the factory school model, it will have to emigrate skilled and knowledgeable talent from other countries, as President Abraham Lincoln did in the early 1860's, and as the United States now does for its medical staff and shortly, I project, for its teaching force. The State of Hawaii has already projected a 40% shortfall of teachers and administrators by the year 2006. Moreover, one third of the children in the United States live below the poverty guideline, with little hope of climbing out without success in learning.

Several segments of the population are increasingly disenfranchised without achievement in learning. At the University of Georgia, for instance, only 1% of its enrollment is from African-American males; while the incarceration rate in Georgia is 50% African-American males. One of the fastest growing segments of the construction industry is in prison construction. Locations for new prison construction are selected based in part on the fourth grade and below reading levels, as there is a direct relationship between reading performance and incarceration.

Indeed, the United States is a *nation at risk*, requiring us to rethink learning in America. However, the educational development in America has been an experiment of evolving "at risk" accommodation.

For example, Cambridge, Massachusetts is the place where the first legislation was enacted a long time ago to create the first public education initiative called "The Massachusetts Bay Act of 1641." At that time, the early Puritans were concerned about the "old deluder Satan" and the neglect of parents in teaching children to "read and write the scriptures."

Nearly a century later, in Virginia, Thomas Jefferson introduced his version of a public education Act called "The General Diffusion of Knowledge" and wrote to the Members of Virginia Legislature that "If a nation expects to be both free and ignorant, it expects what never was nor ever shall be." Whether the "deluder" was Satan or the lack of an educational system, Jefferson and his fellow framers of this Democracy believed that a society of free people cannot exist under the tyranny of ignorance and intolerance. Nor, for that matter, can a family, community, organization or corporation thrive when there is a pervasive disregard for learning, knowledge, creativity, problem solving and the diversity of people's learning styles. Moreover, as the population continues to age, it will take more people at higher levels of productivity than previous generations to support the aging population of retirees. This doesn't mean working in more jobs (some people have three jobs just to make ends meet) it means working smarter to produce more and better results.

After another hundred years, and back in Boston, Horace Mann grew up in poverty and was "sponsored" to attend Brown University where he graduated with honors. Instead of practicing his career in the legal profession, Horace Mann dedicated his life to the development of a public education system that would replace the "one room" schoolhouse and provide children of all families, rich and poor, with the opportunity for a free and public education. This became the "class and grade" system, which we now experience in every community. It was intended to provide the "social balance wheel" of society's gaps in wealth and culture among a flux of new immigrants, and provide the engine to educate the population in knowledge and skills to produce the future generation of wealth upon which society depends.

During this past century, John Dewey was one of five members of a group that met regularly at Harvard College. They were to become known as the Pragmatists. William James, George Santyana, Josiah Royce and Charles Sanders Pearce were pioneers in their fields ranging from psychology to mathematics and philosophy. Dewey was the one among them who was concerned with education and the fate of the Democracy. He wrote extensively in his book "*Democracy and Education*" about the importance of creating well-educated, young citizens, who could prosper as self-reliant citizens. This was called the "progressive era" of education and Dewey said that "education is too important to leave to the educators."

Today, although the focus has shifted away from "citizenship" and economic development to both "standards based curriculum and standardized exams," not much has changed in the criticism of parents, particularly if you read the condemning articles in newspapers. In fact, reading the newspapers from across the nation leaves little doubt that the poor performance of children in schools is in a state of crisis. Nearly one-third of the nation's children live below the poverty guidelines and the concept of "*equal educational opportunity*" has vanished from the landscape of educational policy. Low reading ability, low math scores, low analytic reasoning and weak communications skills are barometers of a "nation at risk." And the technology and learning gap is widening between rich and poor and among minority populations.

This "risk" has been previously stated in terms of economic opportunity that is increasingly restricted to those who participate in continuous learning and professional, career or skill development. Technology has drastically changed the landscape of the workforce and job market leading many to claim that the future of any country is not what grows from the ground, but rather what grows from the mind. The failed promise of the American education system has become almost a cliché, so pervasive is the evidence of accelerating decay. Several years ago, the President's Council on Education underlined the depths of our predicament in a report whose grimly appropriate title was *A Nation at Risk*. Little has changed since then. Among other indicators cited:

√ Over a million youths drop out of school each year.
√ About 23 million American adults are functionally illiterate.
√ Another 47 million are borderline illiterate.
√ In addition to those who are illiterate in basic verbal and mathematical skills, many more are technically illiterate.
√ At least 75% of today's workforce will need retraining by the year 2000.

It would be difficult to overstate the dangers of this slippery slope, in either the human, corporate or national dimensions. In the first instance, sizable segments of our youth leave school, whether prematurely or on time, without the skills needed to live and work in the real world. Many are being institutionally frozen out of the technological marketplace. This phenomenon applies across the whole society, but is especially acute among our minority population. Perhaps worst of all, many of our young people have been so soured by their experience in today's classrooms that the joy of learning has all but died for a lifetime.

Businesses, in turn, are finding it more difficult to find new employees with the requisite skills and/or values to perform many manufacturing, administrative and service functions. Many companies have resorted to remedial education along with task training, and some have even provided financial support to school systems to help improve the skills of prospective employees.

These stopgap corporate measures may provide some limited, temporary improvement, but they can't rectify the underlying systemic weaknesses that created the problem in the first place. It is doubtful that our country can reverse the erosion of our national competitiveness in an increasingly international economy if we continue to educate our 21st century youth with 19th century methods.

Since 1641, the educational policy debate has focused on transferring the knowledge, skills and values necessary to preserve, yet improve the culture. Along the way, literally thousands of books were written forecasting what should be done to educate the young. So, why another book?

This book is different in that it reveals the **Seven Secrets of Learning** that can turn our country, or any nation into a **Nation of Promise** by following the strategic insights and strategies that empower people to learn how to learn, learn how to choose, learn how to relate and learn how to create. This book will guide you along the path of successful learning, in accordance with the **Seven Secrets** and embracing seven key principles or *"corecepts"* (core concepts). These core concepts emerge throughout the **Seven Secrets** and are:

1. "THE MESSAGE RECEIVED IS THE MESSAGE SENT!"

This is the *"First Law of Communications"* identified by Marshall McLuhan. It anticipates that you might have the most well thought out message, teaching style or curriculum. However, if the message you wish to have sent is not being received the way you want it to be perceived, then you must pay attention to the receiver.

2. "YOU GET MORE OF WHAT YOU REINFORCE!"

This is the *"First Law of Psychology"* introduced by the Behaviorists. If you can hold onto anything the Behaviorists brought into this world in the last century, it was this principle. Indeed, building redundant systems that reinforce the knowledge and skill you wish for people to learn is critical. Thus, having a useful framework like the Theory of Multiple Intelligences provides a schematic of at least seven intelligences through which to present information and skills, reinforce, reflect and review that information and those skills and create higher performance than the "one size fits all" mode of traditional learning pedagogy.

3. "ANY ACT OF LEARNING IS AN ACT OF CREATING!"

This is a first principle, which is derived from research in brain sciences and neurocardiology. When people learn new and difficult information, whether it is knowledge, beliefs or skills, the act of learning is *not* a simple "transfer." New information requires the making of new connections with knowledge, beliefs and skills. When this occurs, a change in physiology takes place, including the increase of chemicals associated with improved memory. This connection making is an act of creativity within the learner's brain, heart and body systems, and is often accompanied with an "aha" reaction that we have all experienced.

4. "DIVERSITY IS A CAPACITY!"

The motto of the longest surviving Democracy is *"E Pluribus Unum."* In the last century, we understood it as meaning "one out of many," where the focus was on the "one." The actual Latin translation is "out of many, one" where the emphasis is on the "many" who make up one unity. Diversity is a key to capacity building and this has been proven over and over from science and medicine to literature and invention. It takes different people thinking and doing different things to make challenging competition and to make improvement. We are smarter together than we are independently as individuals.

5. "OUR STRENGTH IS IN OUR CONNECTEDNESS!"

No man is an island, although plenty of people feel helpless, alone and abandoned. The history of human progress is filled with examples, both on a personal basis and on a group basis, that the strength of the individual or the organization is as strong as its weakest link. A renowned scientist, Buckminster Fuller was noted for his scientific discoveries and inventions. Among his inventions was the geodesic dome, which had no interior walls for support and which used the strongest structure known on this planet, the "tetrahedron." The tetrahedron gains its strength from the connections of the components, not just in the material used. Thus, even in the world of physics and chemistry, we see that linkages or connections strengthen the structures of things. The same holds true for human beings.

6. "STUPIDITY IS A LEARNED BEHAVIOR!"

This is a very serious principle. When I first formulated it, I was astonished at the reaction from university professors, school administrators, corporate executives, employees and teachers. The statement seemed counter-intuitive. However, they were surprised because our cultural assumption is that some are "smart" and some are "dumb." And it is the business of education to sort out who is who and which is which.

7. "EVERYONE IS BORN A GENIUS!"

This key corecept draws heavily on the "Pygmalion" research at Harvard University and elsewhere around the world. The Pygmalion studies show that what people in authority (supervisors, administrators, teachers, parents) or what people engaged in learning, achievement, performance or health recovery *"think"* about their chances of success will influence the outcomes. People who think students will fail will experience failure among those students. What you expect of people and your anticipated outcomes will affect outcomes.

Embracing these seven "corecets" *The Seven Secrets of Learning Revealed* will enable you to release the energy of your mind and heart for greater success and happiness. Each chapter reveals a particular secret that amplifies the importance of these core concepts.

Finally **Chapter One** reveals a fresh new perspective about learning as a miracle in human growth and development. **Chapter Two** identifies how that growth is expressed in uniquely different and diverse ways in each individual. In **Chapter Three**, you will learn about breakthrough brain research that helps us learn more in less time with enhanced memory. You'll also learn how to grow your brain, regardless of your age. **Chapter Four** uncovers a major secret in modern medical research about the heart's capacity to enable the brain to learn better with advanced memory and creativity, along with increased health and reduced stress. **Chapter Five** shows that you have at least *ten* (10) distinct intelligences, which is eight more than our society measures in tests or values in conduct. **Chapter Six** discloses the environmental hazards that degrade or interfere with high results, learning and hardiness. **Chapter Seven** puts it all together in a validated Model, called *The IntelliLearn® Model* for implementing High Performance, Achievement and Success in your community.

Good luck with your journey in reading this book and may *The Seven Secrets of Learning Revealed* uplift and strengthen you and your family in the path of the "Miracle of Learning."

Laurence Dean Martel
Hilton Head Island, South Carolina
June, 2003

ACTION ITEM: Although space is available throughout this book for you to make notes, I suggest that you
buy an inexpensive journal to keep notes as you proceed. I also suggest that you buy some colored pencils
so you can make notes in this book or in your journal.
Use different colors for different things you want to remember,
as the different colors will help to reinforce various aspects to
the book's message. In addition to the mindmaps that appear at
the front of each chapter, feel free to create your own
"mindmaps"(see **Chapter Five** under the section on spatial
intelligence), as well as the "mind maps" at the beginning of
each chapter. Consider this a coloring book for your mind! After all, this book is designed as an "operator's guide" for your
brain, your heart and your happiness. I will coach you through
a process of several "action items" that will encourage you to
consider, reflect and act on the information presented to you.

Remember: You get more of what you reinforce.

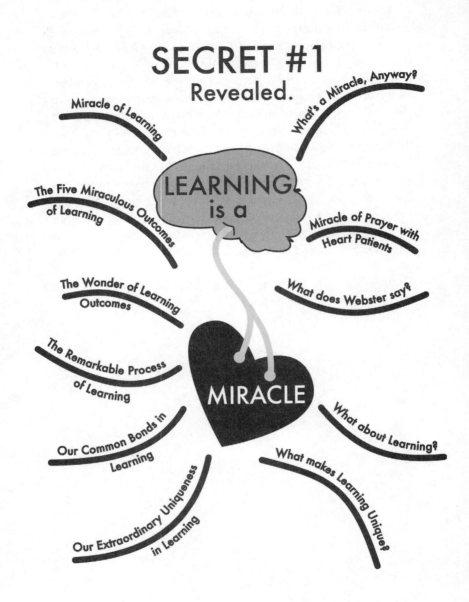

SECRET #1
Revealed.

Miracle of Learning

What's a Miracle, Anyway?

LEARNING is a

The Five Miraculous Outcomes of Learning

Miracle of Prayer with Heart Patients

The Wonder of Learning Outcomes

What does Webster say?

The Remarkable Process of Learning

MIRACLE

Our Common Bonds in Learning

What about Learning?

What makes Learning Unique?

Our Extraordinary Uniqueness in Learning

Chapter One

Secret #1
Learning is
a Miracle

By recognizing this fact, you can take advantage of your mind power and heart energy for greater success at home, at work, and in balancing your life

In what ways are *you* smart?

For most people, that question seems a bit strange and even difficult to answer. After all, throughout the traditional educational system, we've been answering two primary questions: 1) "Who here is smart?" and 2) "Who here is dumb?" The issue of "smartness" or "dumbness" has always been black and white, with no gray area in between. You are either one or the other, and once labeled, there's little opportunity to change course.

Why is this so? Because the majority of people take learning for granted. They think learning is something that "just happens" and that there is one "right" way to learn. Therefore, anyone who doesn't learn the presented concepts (whatever they may be) gets labeled with a learning disability or as a slow learner. Because of this mindset, we fail to see learning for what it really is – a miracle. And the miracle of learning is the key to unlocking your dreams and happiness.

What's a Miracle, Anyway?

Before we can go any further into how and why learning is a miracle, we must first establish the basis for what a miracle is in general. Miracles occur every day, and you can probably remember some of them taking place in your own life. Perhaps those miracle stories changed you or the lives of your family.

I remember one miracle story that happened when I was at Syracuse University conducting research on learning. A small group of us founded a clinic for head injured and stroke patients to provide rehabilitation with innovative approaches, including tapping the emotional intelligences of the patients to help them recover from brain damage.

One day we met Michael, a young man who lived in a nearby community. Three months before, Michael had crashed his motorcycle into a tree, nearly killing himself. He suffered multiple head injuries and his prognosis looked bleak. The medical team informed him that he would likely have limited recovery and might never work again.

Prior to the accident, Michael had been an outstanding mechanic and had dreams of owning a garage. When I met him, he could remember nothing about auto mechanics and had physical tremors requiring that he walk with two canes. It was even difficult for him to hold a pencil. When I told him that he could re-learn what he once knew, Michael was hesitant. He revealed that he had hated high school and wanted nothing to do with classrooms.

Despite his hesitation, we built a positive relationship and I taught Michael how to use the Apple IIe computer, which had a typing tutor software package with it, and I gave him an old typewriter so he could practice the keyboard at home. He liked working with his hands and he vaguely remembered taking a typing class in high school. He remembered that he liked that class. With that, he worked on SAT test preparation material and increased his eye-motor coordination through reading. And upon our advice, Michael enrolled in a Tai Chi class to further improve his coordination skills.

Within six months, Michael was able to walk without a cane and the tremors reduced significantly. He gained memory in every area, except auto-mechanics, about which he remembered nothing. His SAT test preparation exercises greatly increased his vocabulary and language expression. Two years following his accident, with encouragement from his family, Michael was specially admitted as a vocational rehabilitation student at a community college. While a student, Michael got a part time job as a swim therapy assistant for the nursing home residents.

Five semesters later, Michael's family and his fiancé watched him proceed in the college graduation ceremonies and receive his Associates degree in physical therapy. After graduating, he was promoted to full-time at the nursing home, got married and continued to soar on a new path in life. Everyone, including the medical team, felt that Michael's recovery was a miracle. So did Michael!

The Miracle of Prayer With Heart Patients

In another instance nearly a decade ago, Randolph Byrd, M.D. conducted a double blind study (a scientifically rigorous research design) of patients who were to undergo heart surgery at a hospital in San Francisco. Three hundred and eighty-two (382) names of patients were fed into the computer, and half of them were randomly assigned to "prayer groups" from around the globe. No one on the medical team knew about the study, and no one, including the researchers, knew for whom the strangers in the prayer groups were praying. Also, since the prayer groups consisted of various individuals representing different religious groups, no one knew what prayers or incantations were offered. All the prayer groups knew were the name of the patient, the heart condition, the procedure to be given and the date of the operation.

The result was considered a miracle. The patients who received prayers from strangers improved in every category over the group that received no prayers. Recovery rates, length of stay at the hospital, infections, and tracheotomies were significantly better statistically for the patients for whom strangers prayed. Also, the morbidity or death rate was lower for the "prayed for" group. It appeared to the scientific community that prayer generated the miracle of divine intervention among these heart patients. In addition to this study, there have been several other studies that have been documented by surgeon Larry Dosey, M.D. in his book *Healing Words: The Power of Prayer and the Practice of Medicine.*

What Does Webster Say?

When we define a miracle, we often use words like "wonder," "amazement" and "spectacular" to describe the event that seemed miraculous. These words convey the splendor of these unusual events, which happen either in direct relation to divine intervention or by an unexplained natural happenstance.

The dictionary gives us two definitions of the word "miracle." The first definition is "an extraordinary event manifesting (revealing) divine intervention in human affairs." For example, a miracle of divine intervention might come from the example of the heart surgery patients in Randolph Byrd's study or from *The Bible* when Jesus fed the multitude or when Moses received the Commandments. More ordinary might be the moment of birth, which occurs every day in hospitals and huts around the world. When the baby takes its first gasp of air, family members gather with smiles and gratitude, exclaiming that a "miracle" has occurred in the birth process. Although routine and natural, there is always the sense of divine intervention in this new life

The second definition involves "an extremely unusual event, thing or accomplishment." An example of this sense of the word "miracle" might come from Michael's recovery. Another example might be Roger Bannister, who was the first human being on record to run the mile in under four minutes. Although others eventually broke his record, his original performance could be referred to as the natural, yet unexplained, sense of the word "miracle."

In addition to the examples provided, you might have heard someone say, "Can you believe that Bill hit his thirty-first home run in one baseball season? Why, that's a miracle!" Or, "I am really happy that Randy graduated from high school. With his grades, it was nothing short of a miracle." We have also heard people say things like, "Polly really had a troubled pregnancy, and her newborn is a true miracle story." And some of us have certainly said, "It would take nothing short of a miracle to change that person's mind."

 ACTION ITEM: Think about some events that you have deemed miraculous in the past and write your reflections down in your journal or in the margins of this book. What happened? Why was it a "miracle"? How did the miraculous event alter your perceptions or knowledge base? What did you learn from this miracle?

What About Learning?

Now that we have a better grasp of the word "miracle," what could be so miraculous about the act of learning? Does learning stand the test of being a miracle? After all, learning seems to be a quite ordinary act that takes place every day in every culture and at all age levels. Is learning an outstandingly unusual event? Is there divine intervention? According to the dictionary, learning simply means "to gain knowledge, comprehension, or mastery through experience or study." This definition describes the ordinary garden variety of human experience.

Learning is the extraordinary process, uncommon in all of nature, that we have been endowed with, which permits the possibility for us to move from the selfish, humdrum of daily routine to the potential of unfolding our dreams and uncovering our unique purpose on this earth. Without active learning, the potential for us to improve and contribute to others would be marginal. At every level of society, people with a restricted or limited opportunity to learn, as well as those who simply choose not to learn, are reduced to alienation, fear, threat, intimidation, loneliness, abandonment, self-absorbed pity and narcissism. The Buddhist religion claims that the first noble truth is "Life is suffering." A key principle of Christianity is that "love conquers all" and alleviates all suffering. Consequently, the business of living is the activity of continuous problem solving – and that requires the pursuit of knowledge and skills through active learning.

As a specific example of overcoming suffering and the miracle arising from learning, consider the story of Helen Keller who, although deaf and blind, learned from her teacher Ann Sullivan and became a worldwide inspiration, author and speaker. Thus, an ignorant person can learn to know; a skeptical person can learn to believe; a selfish person can learn to selflessly serve others; an incompetent person can learn to develop talent and perform with excellence. History abounds with stories of people who were lost in their purpose, only to miraculously discover the meaning of their lives by learning fresh new perspectives and skills. It was through "learning" that their lives changed.

Our individual ability to perceive and process information from the world around us is a direct result of our capacity to utilize strategies, tactics and tools and to learn from the external world in order to comprehend the world "within" us. The Latin expression *"experientia docet"* means *"experience teaches all."* Indeed, experience provides a basis from which to learn, comprehend, survive, control, love, empower, laugh, fear, reflect, contemplate, create, imagine, invent, relate, expand, grow, choose and act – totally based on our learning from that experience, regardless of whether it is direct personal experience or an indirect, vicarious experience through the lessons and stories we hear from our parents, grandparents or teachers. I believe this is what the modern philosopher and educational reformer John Dewey had in mind when he coined the phrase "Learn by doing."

The miracle of learning, however, keeps ever present the potential and actual sense of humility in the pursuit of knowledge, wisdom and love. The old axiom that "the more you learn, the less you know" speaks volumes to the personal experience people have on their journey toward self-fulfillment and purposefulness. As we become more focused on our purpose, our talents and contribution in this life to our family, our community and our planet, there is a natural shift which I call taking the trip from *"ego"* to *"colleague-o."* The diminished "selfishness" is exalted to "selflessness" in the execution of our purpose and our contribution of teaching and learning to others. Scott Peck wrote in his book *The Road Less Traveled* that every human experience is an opportunity for "teaching and learning." Conversely, to the degree that we are inhuman to others, we neither teach nor learn in the sense of positive growth and development, but instead regress to a lower level of racism, bigotry, genocide and other crimes against humanity.

We have the capacity to imagine a future different from today and the creative capability to invent that future. According to the noted psychiatrist William Glasser, M.D., we all are genetically programmed to pursue five distinct outcomes in our daily lives, each of which varies from person to person depending on his or her perception. We all seek: (1) to survive; (2) to obtain power and control; (3) to find love and friendship; (4) to achieve freedom; and, (5) to have fun. Dr. Glasser has written several books about his theory and clinical application of it, in which he says that you and I are programmed at a "cellular" DNA level to pursue these five wants and needs in our lives. These five are the measures against which each of us define our own personal *"quality world-view."*

The miraculous human mechanism that permits us to obtain the "quality world-view" is our human capacity to learn. If you limit or disenfranchise a person from "learning," you disconnect him or her from life success and the attainment of the five wants and needs in his "quality world-view." If you enhance the capacity to learn, you increase the likelihood of personal success, thus ensuring fulfillment by pursuing and achieving one's purpose.

In reality, our ability to learn is directly related to our ability to live. In order to survive, obtain power and self-control over our environment and ourselves, enjoy love and friendship, maintain freedom from harm and freedom to create, and engage in fun, we regularly draw upon those processes of learning which are familiar to us, as well as those which we uncover as we experience the world.

Learning is the gift we have been given. Think of it as an inheritance of an old family house. At the top of the house is an attic in which there are numerous treasures that have been stored away for years. This treasure chest is readily available to us – all we have to do is ascend the attic stairs and explore what is there. But far too many people never make it above the first floor. Also, although it doesn't have to be as difficult for people as it often is (as this book reveals in its truths), making the journey itself requires the decision to take the trip. And, as with any worthwhile journey and despite the joy, beauty and fun along the way, it takes effort and time to take the journey to the attic, and many people succumb to the artificial barriers or the obstacles created by an outmoded educational system, or just don't take the initiative to even explore. For us as individuals, "learning" is like the "stairway to the attic." If you take the time and effort to constantly and persistently make the journey into the wide range of learning processes and capabilities, then life's blessings will unfold before you as you gain clarity and focus on your dreams, your vision, your purpose and your direction toward personal happiness, wisdom and fulfillment.

Or you could consider another analogy. Imagine that each person is born on a mountaintop, under which is a rich, gold mine. Access to that gold mine, however, requires the awareness that it is there, within the earth, and the skills and tools to excavate the riches that are below. In this sense, one could say that we are all born with a "Gold *Mind*," waiting to be harvested through the processes of learning.

What Makes Learning Unique

When we look past the surface of learning, we discover that the "gift" of learning, the uniqueness of learning, the common bonds of learning, and both the "processes" and "outcomes" of learning are what make it remarkable and unexplained. Certainly, we are able to describe what we think happens in the learning process, but we have not satisfactorily explained "why" learning occurs the way it does or "how" innovative and new outcomes arise from learning, such as creativity, scientific invention, and problem solving.

As mentioned earlier, each of us was born with the gift of "learning." This gift is something we receive when we are born, continue to develop as we grow and are able to give to others as we travel through our path in life. In fact, learning is the only thing I know of that you can give to others while personally growing in the process of giving it away – a miracle of its own kind.

Think about it…when you give the gift of learning to another person, you not only pass along valuable knowledge, skills, beliefs or information to him or her, you do so without ever losing any of the information you've just given away. Think about all the books that have been written, all the video documentations produced and all the scientific and practical inventions that have been created as a result of knowledge transfer. You gain in the process of giving, especially if you give out of love, dignity and trust in the effort to build relationships. An old Chinese expression captures this insight: "If you teach something once, you have learned it twice."

Our Extraordinary Uniqueness in Learning

Another unusual event that makes learning a miracle is that all people learn differently from each other. They have different *learning styles*, a term coined by award winning researcher Professor Rita Dunn.

Every human being is born different from every other human being. That is a biological fact. Just as no two snowflakes are the same, no two people are alike, including identical twins. For example, look at the fingers on your left hand. Gaze at your fingerprints. No one else on the planet has the same fingerprint as you. No one has your voiceprint. No one has the "iris" print in your eye. No one has your barefoot print. No one learns quite the way you do. You are unique. What can explain that miracle other than divine expression?

The ancient philosopher Plato believed, as well as other notable philosophers and theologians since 500 B.C., that each of us is born with a unique purpose, much like our individual fingerprints. As we attempt to leave that mark in our life, we proceed through our unique path on this earth to uncover that purpose before our journey ends. I have found that people who are troubled with self-debasement and alienation have often stopped learning and evolving toward purposeful fulfillment. Instead, they have fallen into a rut of self-satisfaction inside the comfort and convenience of their "victimization." It takes continuous learning to develop a commitment and compassion for growth in purpose.

Through the continuous process of trying to better understand ourselves, our families and our communities, we unfold and discover our purpose and meaning and identity. This discovery process is called "learning," which builds our capability for self-growth and contribution to others. That capability (which is often called "learning style") is unique to each of us, although we share common patterns of our unique learning process with others.

While we can describe how this process works, as you will discover in **Chapter Two**, we are uncertain as to "why" each person learns differently. It would seem to be more rational if we all learned the same way, as in the concept of "one size fits all." Unfortunately, it's this "one-size" philosophy that has contributed to the calamity and misfortune of many students who have fallen victim to the educational administrations and policy makers who subscribe to it. However, when we organize new and difficult information in accordance with how people learn best, significant increases in performance occur in all kinds of environments.

For example, "in June of 1987, only *25 percent* of the mildly-handi-capped students in Frontier's Central High School District in Hamburg, New York had passed the State Competency Tests to receive diplomas. During 1987-88, the *year* that learning style-based instruction was introduced, that number increased to *66 percent.* During 1988-89, the *second* year, *91 percent* of the Special Education high school students were successful. Indeed, that year, a greater ratio of handicapped students passed the State Competency Tests than regular education students."[1] That is a jump from 25 percent to 91 percent passing state examinations, after only two years of implementing strategies unique to how people learn differently from one another.

Our Common Bonds in Learning

Even though we are all unique, we are also alike as humans and set apart from other living beings. We use symbols and language to communicate, tell stories and record history. We invent tools and use them. We set goals and initiate actions to achieve them. We establish communities in which diversification of labor and function frees people for recreation, leisure and rest. We laugh, have fun and enjoy humor through abstract jokes and puns. None of this would be possible without the miracle of learning.

Aristotle, the Greek philosopher, maintained that the chief purpose of human existence is the pursuit of "happiness." For Aristotle, "happiness" (The Greek word is "eudaimonia" which translates to "happiness.") meant being possessed by a good or benevolent spirit, which he believed kept you in a state of joyful blessedness. This is much like the "state of being" that medical researcher Candace Pert describes at the chemical level in her book *The Molecules of Emotion,* which is discussed in **Chapter Three**. Moreover, in his profound book *Power vs. Force*, David R. Hawkins, M.D., Ph.D., reveals a scale of human States of Being (or consciousness) ranging from "shame" (with a low value of 20) to higher level "love" (with a value of 500), on to an ultimate level of "enlightenment" (whose value extends from 700-1000). Anything below 200 is life depreciating, leading to an antagonistic and disappointing existence. Above 200 is a potential for the feasible, the hopeful, the meaningful and the complete in one's pursuit of happiness. Only through learning do we develop the necessary skills and dispositions to ascend the ladder of consciousness to achieve levels above 200. And for those who dwell in ignorance of their problems and of themselves, they tend to be "energy vampires" disconnecting the fabric of the world around them, often inflicting misery and abuse to themselves and others in the wake of their clouds of despair and despondency.

What does this have to do with learning? It is through the process of *"learning"* that we can move from "humiliation, blame and despair and scorn" to higher energy levels of "forgiveness, understanding, reverence and bliss." Imagine the countless stories of men and women in history who have shifted the patterns in their lives, evolving from humiliation and anger to trust, love and serenity. The character "Scrooge" in the Charles Dickens' famous *A Christmas Carol* is but one example.

As another example, British sea Captain John Newton was a successful merchant in the dehumanizing slave trade. During one of his trips from Africa, a storm nearly swamped the vessel. All on board feared for their lives. Captain Newton prayed for his life, with a commitment that if he lived, he would change his evil ways as a slave trader. Well, the storm blew by, sparing the Captain and crew their lives. Captain Newton returned to England, attended seminary, and became an Anglican priest. He then led the movement to abolish slavery in England in 1779, after which he wrote the Hymn, *Amazing Grace*, whose first line summarizes Captain Newton's transformation: *"Amazing Grace, how sweet the sound, THAT saved a wretch like me!"* That song summarizes Newton's "ah-ha!" moment.

When filled with chemicals called "endorphins," the human body is in a state of euphoria (eudaemonia) and happiness. Endorphins are the chemicals required for us to experience "joyfulness." Indeed, whenever we are learning and a positive outcome occurs, the "Eureka!" or "Ah-ha!" moment we experience is the result of the release of endorphins in our bodies. This is the body's natural "joy" drug that spurts into several systems of the body whenever we learn something new and make new connections with existing information or skills.

Can you remember a time when you giggled and laughed as a result of learning something new? Or do you recall looking into a child's excited face as he or she mastered a new concept or task? That excitement is nature's way of rewarding you for learning, with a little squirt of endorphins to encourage you to keep going, growing and improving to keep you learning. This only occurs under conditions where fear, threat, intimidation and put-downs are absent. Environments that provide such things as certain colors, classical music, balance, joy, peace, as well as a sense of kindness and patience foster an endorphin release. Likewise, the opposite conditions – fear, threat, intimidation and putdowns – produce adrenaline and cortico-steroids to be released in the body, which limit learning and memory and create a fight or flight response. (See **Chapters Three and Four**.)

The Remarkable Process of Learning

In addition to the gift of learning, the uniqueness of learning among people and the common defining characteristic of what it is to be human are the mysterious "processes" of learning. The remarkable processes of learning allow us to speak of the "miracle of learning" despite the tendency to take learning for granted as an ordinary everyday experience. For example, we all take the act of walking for granted as a normal human function, but walking on the moon is considered a miracle.

Remember that the process of learning is the ability to "make connections" between existing experience and new information. If we don't make the connections, we don't learn, often leaving us destined to repeat mistakes or experience hardships and adversity in our lives. When people don't make the connection, they often say, "I just don't get it!" And when they do make the connection, they say, "Now, I've got it!" (along with a little squirt of endorphins).

Any act of learning is an act of creation in the learner's brain, nervous system and memory system. This unique process of learning, by itself, is an unexplained and remarkable event – a miracle of the human experience. Although many theories exist, no one has satisfactorily explained the process of creativity and the making of connections and memory. Thus, the "miracle of learning" is much like the miracle of the human heart cells that form to beat on their own. No other cells do this, and most cardiologists describe this as one of the "miracles" of science. It happens every day, yet it is unexplained as to how it happens. Even if it could be explained, it's doubtful that it would be considered any less of a miracle.

The Wonder of Learning Outcomes

As well as the "processes" of learning, consider the "outcomes" of it. As a result of creating, inventing, problem solving and making new connections, the human learner becomes a changed person with new knowledge, new beliefs, new capabilities and a new identity. The process of "creation" of these and all new things is, itself, a miracle, despite its daily occurrence. It is undoubtedly a mystery unexplained by science or nature.

While memory and remembering what you learn is critical to learning, no one has explained the mystery and miracle of memory. Although ordinary, when it happens, it is an extraordinary event that has led to the creation of unusual outcomes, such as the invention and development of penicillin, the pasteurization process, nuclear medicine, computer technology and the Internet – things we have all heard of, used, or experienced at one time or another. For example, Christian Bernard imagined what others thought impossible, namely the transplant of a human heart. Today, many years after the first heart transplant, there are nearly two thousand such procedures performed each year in the United States alone. And today, a half dozen mechanical hearts have been implanted successfully, taking Bernard's dream of "heart transplant" to a previously unimagined level.

Any act of learning, then, is an act of creating something entirely new or modified out of the current experience or knowledge base. It is both unusual and divine in both senses of the word "miracle" in that it grows, enhances and extends the ordinary person through the act of creating, which mirrors what theologians call the divine process of creation and evolution.

 ACTION ITEM: Think about a time when you learned something new and difficult in a group setting – whether in a classroom setting or maybe in a family setting, where someone like a parent, a teacher or a supervisor was teaching you something new, such as how to program the VCR or how to play "Monopoly." Think about how you learned and about your own learning process during that time, as well as how others present perceived your learning process. Did others in the group learn differently than you? What specifically was different and what was alike in the process, and what kind of outcome did each person have? Write your observation down in your journal.

The Five Miraculous Outcomes of Learning

The five miraculous outcomes of learning enable us to grow, develop and transform our lives in our journey toward personal fulfillment. These five results of learning contribute to transforming your current reality into a future state that is different and better than today. These learning outcomes which are learning "to know," "to believe," "to perform," "to be," and "to serve," are different from one another in scope, focus, and verification, but they reinforce and support each other. When we advance in one, we often strengthen another in the process. Unfortunately, our tendency in our families and in our institutions of "schooling" is to take these five categories of learning for granted as something that is common, usual and ordinary.

Learning and its five life-sustaining outcomes, though, are far from usual and ordinary. And rather than take learning for granted, we need to treat learning like a treasure that we can increase as we continue to learn and improve in our capabilities to both experience the world and to express that experience to others. Without learning and the five outcomes of learning processes, we can not enjoy life in its optimal state of quality and excellence.

1. Learning **"to know"** with certainty and truth

Aristotle wrote: "All people, by nature, seek to know." That is, each of us seeks knowledge, and we seek others to validate the truth of our knowledge. In this regard, we find three kinds of knowledge, which have different ways of learning and verifying the truth. First, there is factual knowledge, where empirical facts give validity to a statement. In this realm, what is true today may be false tomorrow. For example, it is true that my glass of water is half-filled. In ten minutes, it could be true to say that my glass is completely empty, although earlier it was half-full. In this world of factual knowledge, things change as the facts change.

The second kind of knowledge is value knowledge. This is the realm of morality and is the business of ethics that deals with good and evil. Some would like us to believe that ethics and values are like "facts" or manners that either change over time or change relative to whose interpretation is being held. However, values and ethics stand the test of time and are irrefutable, regardless of the time and interpretation. For example, slaughtering innocent women and children is evil. This was always true (including in Herod's time with what the world knows as "the slaughter of the innocents," as well as in our own time where, despite the conditions of war, soldiers were convicted of war crimes in the Mei Lai massacre). People often subscribe to different values, just as they subscribe to different magazines. But simply because people choose or are brainwashed into subscribing to genocide (as evidenced in anti-democracies like Nazi Germany and Rwanda, Africa) does not make genocide any less or more evil.

The third area of "to know" is in analytic knowledge. We might call this "definitional knowledge," since what we know is determined by the meaning of our language. For example, the princess is always the daughter of the king and queen (even in fairy tales). We choose to verify this knowledge by deeming it either true or false, depending on the meaning attributed to the words we use. This area of knowledge is critical to human communications, conflict and peace, in that how we understand has everything to do with meaning. Each of these three kinds of knowledge can assure our confidence from high probability to certainty.

2. Learning **"to believe"** with faith and value

Every culture tells stories to explain the moral basis for all living beings. Through these stories, legends, folklore, myths, etc., we learn the difference between "good" and "evil" in a stable manner.

3. Learning **"to perform"** with work and production

All societies carry on the "work" for survival in a variety of ways, from aboriginal tribes to modern nations. In addition to people being understood as "homo sapiens" (man as big brain), humans have also been defined as "homo fabre," which means "creator, inventor and fabricator." Even atheists acknowledge a God of which they deny existence. That God as a creator and fabricator is understood in most religions. Some people subscribe to humans being "created in His image." Despite a person's theological view, no one can escape the fact that we all create and make both things and processes to produce and work in order to provide for our survival.

4. Learning **"to be"** with meaning, purpose and identity

Hamlet's question "To be or not to be?" impacts everyone. How do you act, with what authority, and toward which purpose? How will you gain meaning in your life and fulfill your responsibilities? Remember that no person is an island, nor is anyone known solely by his or her community. The old adage that "it takes a village to raise a child" requires that someone build the village and pass it on to younger generations. Although some inherit their station in life, living out that position is a personal choice.

5. Learning **"to serve others"** with love, joy, peace, goodness, patience, humility and kindness

We all seek to survive and be self-satisfied. Yet, part of that need is to have love and friendship. Thus, part of our complex makeup includes the capacity to learn to give, to share and to empathize with others. We indeed express love as well as require it for ourselves.

Be aware that these five miraculous outcomes of learning, knowledge, and skill are not innate. We must learn, grow and develop in each category to gain capability for the journey toward personal and community enhancement. As you take the journey of continuous learning and improvement, keep in mind the following homily I learned as a child:

> *"GOOD, BETTER, BEST,*
> *NEVER LET IT REST;*
> *UNTIL, YOUR GOOD IS BETTER*
> *AND YOUR BETTER IS BEST!"*
>
> *Ursula A. Martel*

These few poetic lines illustrate that only through a commitment to the "miracle" of learning do we soar above the natural tendencies of limited self-interest, self-satisfaction, and self-absorption and transform our nature to more noble levels of human conduct, appreciation and performance.

 ACTION ITEM: Take the five results of learning above and make a list as it applies to your life. Answer these questions:

    1. What do I know for certain and how do I know it?
2. What do I believe in and what is of value to me?
3. What are my gifts and talents that allow me to perform and produce?
4. What gives me meaning and identity?
5. What are examples of my contribution to others in my family and in my community?

The Miracle of Learning

So, is learning a miracle? *Yes, it is!* For it provides the extraordinary capacity to change our perceptions of the world and to provide the possibility for us to imagine and create a future that is different and improved. This miracle provides us with the possibility of changing the world by transforming the quality of life for us and those around us.

All humans have in common the five categories created by Dr. Glasser that require us to learn in order to achieve our perceived sense of survival, power, love and friendship, freedom and fun. We cannot develop any of these without the process of human learning and the five outcomes of the learning process. In the remaining chapters of this book, you will discover and explore those different processes for learning which enable each individual to learn more in less time with increased memory and creativity.

The First Secret Revealed

Learning is a miraculous process, is necessary to a person's success, and enables people to unlock their dreams. As a result of both its mystery and wonder, learning is one of life's miracles that we must treasure and harvest rather than take for granted.

But realizing that learning is a miracle is only the first step. In order to gain a more complete and useful understanding of how you can optimize and utilize the miracle of learning in your life, your family and your community, you might wish to turn to the next chapter, where The Second Secret Two awaits to answer questions that will unlock your learning potential. *"How do I learn best?"* and *"In what way am I smart?"* are questions whose answers reveal the uniqueness about you and every other learner with whom you relate. That knowledge, by itself, has helped millions gain significant increases in unfolding the miracle of learning and achievement.

ACTION ITEMS: (Please complete the following):

1. Write a brief vision statement about yourself as a learner, including the Glasser categories. State the "current reality" that exists for you now, and then identify the "future state" of what you would like in your "quality" world-view. Also note the things you want to stop doing to be a better learner that will lead to the "future state," as well as those things you feel you must "start" doing that will lead to the "future state." List the things you're currently doing that you want to continue to do and that will help you achieve your "quality world-view" or "future state." Keep this vision statement in your journal or in this book and refine it as you grow through reading this book and putting the ideas, strategies and tools to work for you.

2. Identify and write the name of someone you admire as a "learner." List three characteristics of that person that you can model and emulate in your behavior. Plug in the first initial of that person's first name in the following acronym and carry it with you. "WW_D," meaning, "What Would (your mentor) Do?"

3. Create and write an "affirmation statement" that you can repeat often to yourself and that supports you as a learner. For example, "I love learning new things and I enjoy the benefits that learning brings me." Repeat your statement at least six times a day.

4. Make an observation about something in your life that appears ordinary, like birds chirping, and write a note about what you see in it that is a miracle.

5. What is your "quality world-view?" Make a list of the five Glasser categories and write a sentence that expresses your wants and needs in each of the five categories listed above. Then make a note about how learning something new can help you in each category.

References

[1] Dunn. Rita and Andrea Honigsfeld and Laurence D. Martel, *Learning-Style Characteristics of JROTC Cadets and Instructors: Implications for Training and Instruction*, Virginia: Department of the Army, 2001.

SECRET #2
Revealed.

The Learning-Relating Styles Map

We're All Different

Joy of Diversity

Mapping Yourself

Visual Learner
"I SEE what you mean."

Auditory Learner
"I HEAR what you are saying."

Kinesthetic Learner
"I have a FEEL for that."

Print-Oriented Learner
"I READ you loud and clear."

Group-Process Learner
"I need to SHARE this with my friends."

Chapter Two

Secret #2
Your *Unique* "Learning Style!"

An amazing new discovery about "how you learn best" and "how you relate to others" will help you learn more in less time with increased memory

Everyone has a "comfort zone" when it comes to learning. What's yours? Once you find out where you are on the "Learning-Relating Styles Map," you can not only learn better, but you can also resolve differences between those around you and form closer relationships.

Differences among family members abound. For example, a wife may squeeze the toothpaste tube from the middle, while the husband rolls the tube from the bottom. Frustrated with each other's "style" for squeezing the tube, they may "compromise" and buy the pump. This is just one simplistic example that has few consequences. But chances are that if you do something one way, your spouse, child, or significant other does the activity a totally different way. Husbands and wives in particular are often totally opposite in several different ways in perceiving and communicating information. (And by the way, this has nothing to do with either Venus or Mars.)

Similarly, if one child in your family needs bright light to do her homework, chances are that another child will go around the house shutting the lights off and insisting that he needs dim light to study. Children, too, in the same household are most likely to be opposite in several ways when it comes to learning, relating and communicating, which takes us all out of our comfort zones. This concept also applies to co-workers, as well as teachers at school.

These differences often lead to anxiety and anger among family members, and sometimes create family squabbles and conflicts. They also create conflict at work, as well as at school, or in any realm of your life. For example, at a conference on family studies in Ohio, I asked over three hundred people (all of whom said they had family member problems): "How many of you like to do things the right way?" Everyone raised a hand. I then asked: "Whose way is the right way?" They all burst into laughter, realizing that we judge our spouses and children from our own perspective and our own way of doing things. One of the conference participants, Mary, said her mother used to say to her: "I told you ten times and you still don't get it!" and her father constantly said to her brother, "What do I have to do, draw you a picture?" In Mary's family, as with all of our families, some people don't process information by listening, and others *do* require a picture to understand what's being said.

We're All Different

Thales, the father of Western philosophy, was renowned for his scholarly pursuits. However, he had so little practical wisdom that he would easily fall into the well in the city square! What does this prove? Just because someone is book smart doesn't mean he or she is smart in other ways. Today, people who are strongly competent in their practical ability can pursue training in vocational schools; unfortunately, not all towns have vocational alternatives to their academic high schools. Also, unfortunately, our society affords less status to those who are vocationally trained than students who graduate from academic institutions, although the same society cannot function well without the contributions of such individuals. (Ironically, the plumber and electrician who currently are helping to build a new house I am constructing make more money than my grandchildren's schoolteachers in our state.)

Think about your own school experiences. When you were in class, did you ever feel bored and restless listening to lectures? Perhaps you thought that there must be some other way to learn about a subject aside from just having to listen to someone talk about it? Though the subject may have been interesting, it may have seemed that you couldn't "get your hands on the material." You couldn't "get a feel" for what the teacher was talking about. It was hard to "see" what she meant. If you tried to ask another student for help during the lecture, you may have been sent to the office for disrupting the class or cheating.

Learning is as much a part of being human as having fingerprints. And just as our fingerprints are unique, so is our preferred learning style. The fact is that no two people learn in exactly the same way. Educators have studied many individuals in all walks of life, and their research indicates a wide variety of ways in which people learn and process new information. They have found that each person has a unique focus, application of learning, and a manner or *modality* of learning that is tailor-made for taking in new information and thinking about it. Despite advances in theoretical and empirical research about learning, there are different schools of thought about intelligence, all of which has value to our purpose. I call these scholars "Diversity Theorists," since they all depart from the prevailing public policy of a single view that each of us has a "single intelligence" measured by the I.Q. Test and its national and state standardized test derivatives.

Harvard Professor Howard Gardner, who is one of the most compassionate advocates for the improvement of children's success in learning and cognitive development, formulated his Theory of Multiple Intelligences in his book *Frames of Mind*. His theory explains learning and behavior in terms of all people having seven intelligences, instead of the two favored by our I.Q. centered culture. Everyone has these intelligences, claims Gardner and his research colleagues at Harvard University, but no two people have them developed or expressed in quite the same way (see **Chapter Five** for a full discussion, along with useful strategies for implementing this Model of Instruction).

In addition, Professor Robert Sternberg, a researcher at Yale University, and author of the book *Successful Intelligence* developed the *triarchic intelligence theory* to explain the various ways in which people think and express their talents. His theory states that humans have three levels and application of intelligences that function with a different focus:

√ Academic performance (book learning)
√ Sense of self-preservation (intuition)
√ Practical ability to get things done ("common sense")

Modern science has a lot to tell us about the workings of the brain and how we learn. In addition to Professor Sternberg at Yale and Professor Gardner at Harvard, a number of other award winning researchers, most notably husband and wife team Drs. Rita and Kenneth Dunn, www.learningstyles.net have identified important differences in the way people process new information. For example, do you learn best by hearing something told to you, or when you read it yourself? Is there a reason some people are better at understanding graphs than others? What do you do while absorbing new information? Do you drink coffee, seek out sunlight, seclude yourself? Do you like to sit up straight in a chair as you learn, or recline in a bed? Whatever your answers, chances are no one in your family will give the same response.

Understanding the various learning styles is the first step toward improving your child's ability to learn and to solve problems (as well as yours, too!). The more different models of learning you explore, the more in-depth understanding you'll have of what makes you, your spouse, your employer or your child tick as a problem solver.

You may be surprised at what you find out about your learning modality or the learning modality of others. That's because most of us have suppressed many of the things we want to do while learning for such a long time that we don't even think about them any more. I recall a particular engineer in a training seminar at the Sandia National Laboratories. She was among several scientists and engineers enrolled in our seminar on the *IntelliLearn*® processes which include "learning styles" identification and implementation. She held back tears, claiming that if she had only known about learning diversity while in college, she would not have had to struggle to adopt a mode of learning which was unnatural and uncomfortable for her. Agreeing with her, the former Director of Recruitment for New Engineers at General Electric, Ned Herrmann, told me about his challenges at Cornell University in pursuing an engineering curriculum with a concert violinist personality. Until he became familiar and comfortable working within his style of learning, he was less productive. You might enjoy his book, *The Creative Brain*. However, research has shown that all learners do better when they're working within the framework of their unique learning style. Once you know the areas in which learning works best for anyone in your world of influence, you can gain some insight into what to do to increase your own, your child's or your boss's learning potential and make the concept of "Multiple Intelligences" a reality that works in everyone's favor at home, in school, or in any learning situation.

The Joy of Diversity

Each of us has a "right way" to learn that is comfortable for us. Unfortunately, this often causes arguments and bickering between people. Rapport and trust erode when we get annoyed at family members or coworkers, because *they* do not relate the way *we* do. They tend to disconnect us from our comfort zone, which for us is the place where we do well and feel good. Fortunately, each of us can improve rapport, harmony and closeness within the different worlds in which we live by recognizing the diversity in how each person acts and behaves. These learning differences are not unique quirks of personality. They are identifiable differences that you can assess, identify, acknowledge and use for your personal and professional strategic advantage.

To improve the dynamics in your family and work life, you should have answers to specific questions:

1. How do YOU learn, relate and communicate?
2. What is YOUR best way of doing things?
3. And how do YOUR family members and others relate and communicate best?

You can answer these questions by completing the "Learning-Relating Styles Map" contained in this chapter. The map contains seven "road signs" that can change and improve your relationships with family and others with whom you interact. The seven "road signs" include: 1) Time of Day, 2) Senses, 3) Grouping, 4) Light, 5) Sound, 6) Mode, and 7) Brain Dominance. When you learn about each of these road signs, you will find new ways to improve rapport, trust and affection, and become a more close-knit, happier and healthier family member and team member in the rest of the areas of your life.

These "road signs" are known in education as "learning styles," according to Rita Dunn, Ed.D. of St. John's University in New York and Ken Dunn, Ed.D. of Queens College in New York. The Dunns have had six children together, written a dozen books and taught hundreds of graduate students. As parents and educators, they found their family interaction drastically improved when each member understood everyone's "road signs."

How exactly do these "road signs" work? Here's an example: consider the first "road sign": Time. Everyone in your family and workplace has a best time of day when it is optimal for them to communicate and perform tasks, such as homework. If your worst time is early morning, and that's your spouse's best time, you are likely to have quarrels and anger at breakfast before the day gets started. Later, regret sets in. Unfortunately, the cycle might continue the next day and each day thereafter. This contributes to hostility, anxiety, frustration and dysfunction. You can change this with the knowledge from the "Learning-Relating Styles Map."

Consider another example. The second road sign is Senses, which determine our best way for processing information. If you have a child, spouse or employee who does not understand well by listening, this person will be criticized with such blaming questions as "Don't you ever listen?" You must recognize that verbal communication is not the best way to reach this person. I've seen two visual learners talk at each other without taking a breath and constantly talking over the other person, often completing the other person's sentence. Do you do that?

Such behavior often creates resentment and withdrawal, since people feel the lack of respect for not being heard. The "Learning-Relating Styles Map" will help you sort this out when problems in your family and in your world of relationships arise from different processing senses.

As a final example, consider the third "road sign": Grouping. This relates to whether you do best alone or with others. Perhaps you have had your feelings hurt because one of your family or friends prefers to go off and do certain things alone, rather than together with the family or work group. Or, you might have a family member who can't seem to do anything alone and always needs a buddy along. Some of our family and associates are "loners" and some are "lonesome." Finding out where you stand can avoid a great deal of conflict and hurt feelings and can, indeed, bring you closer with others through this knowledge.

A few years ago, I consulted with a well-known Fortune Fifty corporation. Top management was initiating "work teams" through which individuals would perform their work. But their plan was not working out well at all. We gave the employees the "Learning–Relating Styles Map" and found that the majority of employees were most comfortable working alone – not in teams. We restructured the teams to become support groups for individual performance and to be a sounding board for the entire group. It worked and performance skyrocketed.

Mapping Yourself

One reason you need your own personal map of "Learning-Relating Styles" is to handle anxiety, anger, conflict and tension. This can be difficult, as psychologist Judith Sills, Ph.D. noted. She wrote that she and her husband shared everything, including raising the children, paying the bills, going on vacations and portable phones. But this kind of togetherness in a family can create "suffocation," requiring private time to avoid choking. Her antidote is a "balance between family interaction and privacy time." In other words, take a time out.

Stephen Covey, author of the book *Seven Habits of Highly Effective People*, agrees that "We all need a 'pause button' to *choose* our responses." "Time outs" and "Pause buttons" are helpful to cool us off, but they do not give us the framework for acting more lovingly and positively toward others in our family who see the world from a different viewpoint. The Map will provide the road signs for you to see where the differences in your family foster or inhibit family connectedness.

Another reason to find where you are on the Map of Styles is that most of us are not aware of our spouse's relating style, those of our children, or those of the people we relate with every day. All we know is that they don't approach things the way we do, which sometimes drives us mad and dissolves personal or family rapport. In other situations, we get angry or develop a poor attitude toward another person out of our own ignorance about how that person functions best.

A study of children and their parents by two professional educators, Tom Debello and Richard Guez of East Setauket, New York, showed that parents are not likely to know how their children learn and relate best; furthermore, there was an inconsistency in how students viewed their learning style and how parents thought their children learned. The parents in the study didn't have a clue about the road signs. They were also surprised that these road signs made a difference in how children get along with one another and how they relate with parents. In addition, parents didn't know each others "relating style," although they knew very well that they had different ways of communicating and doing things. These findings also apply to people in the workplace, teachers and students in the school place, and the general world of relationships.

According to John Grassi, Ph.D., Vice President of Cambridge College in Cambridge, Massachusetts, visual relaters and learners tend to talk rapidly with short breaths, while using expressions like "See what I mean?" or "Get the picture?" It is difficult to get a word in with visual relaters since they talk so rapidly and often interrupt and finish other people's sentences. (An example would be newscasters Barbara Walters, Brian Gumble or O'Reilly.)

Auditory relaters speak with a slower pace than visuals, and the sound of their voice resonates, as they like to hear themselves talk. They often use words like "How's that sound?" or "Do you hear what I mean?" (Newsperson Walter Cronkite is an example of auditory.)

Tactile/movement relaters seldom speak, and when they do it is with great difficulty because they have to "feel" what they are saying in order to process the information. Other people often finish their sentences or offer words, as they are slow to "get it out." They want to know if you grasp what they say or if you get the feel for what they think. (Movie character Forest Gump is a good example of tactile/movement.)

If visual learners do not *see* it, they don't get it (they need pictures, mind maps, and written notes or drawings); if auditory people don't get the *sound* of things, they miss it (you have to get them to repeat what you said and say what they agree to do); and if tactile/movers don't have a *feel* in their bodies, they don't get it (have them act out what they want to say with their bodies in a charade fashion or draw doodles or diagrams. They need to be physically engaged). This applies in your family, in your work place and in all of your relationships with people.

Once you have a better understanding of your modality or the modality of a co-worker, spouse or child, you can help him select learning experiences that can benefit him the most. Choosing the right learning experience can have an effect on your life or your child's whole life, because it can mean the difference between success and failure. To give you a picture and a "feel" for how the "Learning and Relating Styles Map" will help you, some additional examples of learning modalities and road signs are provided below. As you read, listen carefully to determine how close any of these are to yourself or family members.

"I See What You Mean!" – The Visual Learner

This is the type of person who, when taking in new information, likes to see a picture, a mind map, a graph, or any other type of illustration or set of symbols of what is being learned. The visual learner enjoys it when the coach goes to the chalkboard and uses drawings to explain each football play to the team and enjoys the graphs and illustrations in the text books, the maps used to explain the route to a friend's house or a party, or the picture symbols on international road signs.

"I Hear You!" – The Auditory Learner

Auditory learners understand best by listening. Such people often like to sit quietly and take in everything that's being said, a lot like the bartender or counselor who patiently listens to all his client's problems. Often such people make good friends, because their listening skills may be outstanding. They enjoy lectures and can spend hours with audiotapes. Listening is a skill that comes naturally to the auditory learner, while others may have to practice it. Music and words, alone or together, may be what such a person enjoys most.

"I Really Have a Feel for That!" – The Kinesthetic or "Movement" Learner

This is the forgotten learner, the one who wants to "get physical," perhaps an athlete who is brilliant on the field but unsuccessful in math, science and English, or the teenage girl who wants to spend all her time with horses. Too little attention has been given to people who need to "walk through" the material. Perhaps they can best feel the experience of living in an ancient Egyptian city on the Nile by taking part in a play that dramatizes the flavor of such a life. On the other hand, they might need to walk through a problem in mathematics to "feel" the difference between addition and multiplication.

Often a person with a strong preference for this modality may have an excellent sense of direction and a deep feeling for how the body works. Some of our greatest scientists, Einstein and Edison, for example, were geniuses whose learning was primarily kinesthetic. Unfortunately, traditional education provides little opportunity for such people to move about "inside" the information.

"I Read You Loud and Clear!" – The Print-Oriented Learner

This is the modality of the person who, in school, was always reading a book, and occasionally may have had one confiscated during class. Such students often enjoy school because they read well and remember what they read, which helps them retain information for tests.

Because there's a great deal of useful information to be found in books on just about every subject, print-oriented learners can educate themselves almost entirely by devouring books. For them, there's no better way to learn, and learning from books is exciting and fun because it's like a trip away from home. It may mean, however, that they don't get enough exposure to the social aspects of learning. This chapter should be very helpful in expanding their horizons.

"I Need to Share This with My Friends!" – The Group Process Learner

Have you been in classes where talking was regarded as cheating? Remember how it felt to discuss schoolwork and questions with your friends when you were allowed to do so? If sharing ideas and experiences with others has always been especially appealing to you, you may be a group process learner, the type who likes to have discussions and seek out others' opinions on issues of importance. The recent emphasis on cooperative learning helps such learners get what they need more often, because schools today are more apt to divide students into small groups for projects. It is helpful for children who prefer this learning modality to form study groups and share ideas and processes with friends to get the most out of them.

Which modality is best for you? Your child? Your spouse? Your supervisor? Does your child or spouse respond to one of these modalities in particular, or does more than one seem to describe her? If she identifies with one alone, you've probably identified her modality correctly.

Fortunately, the "Learning-Relating Styles Map" is available to you and your family and will provide you new knowledge and confidence to build better attitudes toward one another by recognizing and respecting these differences pointed out on the map. Remember to ask yourself as you approach the road signs: "How does each of these relating styles help or hinder me in all of my relationships, especially my family closeness, rapport and trust?"

After you take the Road Map Test, observe yourself and others closely, particularly members of your family. You'll find new possibilities for better communication opening up as you observe how differently you, your spouse, or your child learn and solve problems.

Some of the elements on the Map are physical and social, while others are environmental and psychological. Read the Map and mark the appropriate answer that best applies to you. Use a pencil or colored pen unique for you, since you will want other family members to read this chapter and determine where they are on the map as well. You might want a different mark for each family member. The rank order is from 1 to 9, with 1 being worst for you and 9 being best for you. Feel free to copy this section of the map for other members of your family to read and complete. Then, together, you can compare and contrast learning preferences and their variety among the family members with the aim to improve communications, understanding and empathy.

The "Learning-Relating Styles Map"

Road Sign # 1: *Time of Day*. This is a period in the day that is best for you. Some call it our Circadian Clock. Recognizing this road sign can improve cooperation, discipline and communications. Are you an early morning person or are you one who prefers mid-morning? Perhaps afternoon is your best time or maybe you "kick in" and are at your best in the evening?

Many of us drink pots of coffee (which is hazardous to your health, by the way – see **Chapter Six**) to wake up in the morning and to get going because we are not alert in the early morning. When you have conflicts and arguments with family members and others, it might well have to do with the stress associated with your worst time of day. For example, a recent *Family Circle Magazine* Child Survey found that the hours between 5:00 and 7:00 p.m. to be the most stressful time of day. That's when many people are tired and hungry, when homework is supposed to be done, and when nerves are frayed. Well, the fact is that for many, this simply is *not* our best time of day and we generate conflict and stress since it is our worst time of day. We drag people down, who might otherwise be up. If you have tension and stress in your worst time of day, create a positive attitude by repeating the affirmation that, for example, "I enjoy 5:00 to 7:00 p.m. and love each of my family and enjoy the energy I have during this time." Change your routine by taking a walk right when you get home to gain a fresh new perspective. If 5:00 to 7:00 p.m. is your best time of day, then encourage others you relate with to change their frame of reference or the spiral of tension will continue as a habit.

Rank your best time of day when you do new and difficult things successfully. (Circle each with a number from 1 to 9 – one being the worst and nine being the best):

Early Morning: worst 1 2 3 4 5 6 7 8 9 best
Mid Morning: worst 1 2 3 4 5 6 7 8 9 best
Afternoon: worst 1 2 3 4 5 6 7 8 9 best
Evening: worst 1 2 3 4 5 6 7 8 9 best

Road Sign # 2: *Senses.* These are our physical attributes of perception and communication. Most of us prefer one or another of the senses in order to communicate, learn and remember. It is often the way we "get" information the best. And our way is usually different from others. For example, how do you like to remember things and how do you like to have information presented to you? Rank the senses according to how you prefer to learn and remember information. It is okay if you rank them equally since that simply means that you don't have a preference and can learn and remember in a variety of ways.

a) Visual Preference - You have this if you like to see things, perhaps reading or seeing pictures, charts and diagrams. You prefer this to verbal directions. (circle one)

Visual   worst 1 2 3 4 5 6 7 8 9 best

b) Auditory Preference - You have this if you like to hear things and remember what is being told to you. You might like to listen to audiotapes or listen to people talk to gain information. You enjoy listening. (circle one)

Auditory   worst 1 2 3 4 5 6 7 8 9 best

c) Tactile/Movement - You have this if you don't easily sit still when you communicate, learn and remember. You like to touch things, doodle or sketch things. You enjoy activities and materials that you can manipulate. Also, you don't like to sit very long and you stay active and do better when you can move around. You enjoy using the whole body and might get bored listening or reading without being able to fiddle with things and get up and move. (circle one)

Tactile/Movement   worst 1 2 3 4 5 6 7 8 9 best

Tiffany Wood, a recent Tempe, Arizona high school graduate and now college student, received top grades in math courses. But her third grade teacher told her parents that she had a "math-disability" and that if she didn't listen and follow directions written on the board, she would continue to fail third grade math. Tiffany did not learn best by auditory or visual instruction. This created anxiety and stress in the family because both her mother and father had faith in Tiffany, despite the teacher's rigid criticism. What were they to do?

Well, Tiffany and her dad, Leo Wood, who is a nationally recognized teacher of Chemistry and Biology, and currently the Science and Math Director for the National Academy of Integrative Learning, Inc., knew how talented the eight year old was and knew that tactile/movement activities, along with songs and games, could communicate to Tiffany multiplication facts and other basic math we all need later on in the upper grades. Tiffany used gallon milk jugs to add fractions of water together, hop-scotched addition, played a bingo game for multiplication, and handled cut up geometry figures from cereal boxes to learn fraction addition and subtraction. The self-esteem of this now "A" college student might have been forever lost to math-phobia had she not had the tactile/movement activities at home. If the Wood family did not have the road signs on the Learning-Relating Styles Map, they might not have been able to manage their child's success.

Little wonder that in the *Family Circle Magazine* Child Survey many moms and dads cited managing their children's behavior as a major stressor. In fact, parents ranked kids' not listening as the form of misbehavior that pushed their buttons most, followed by arguing, fighting with siblings, lying and not cooperating.

Young children and many teens tend to be more tactile/movement oriented and seldom hear or see what you want them to do, such as cleaning a room. Find out their best mode. For visuals, have them make banners or posters to be on visual display as reminders of household chores or rules. For the auditory, have them write a poem or a song that includes the things they should be doing. Put it to music and record it with an inexpensive recorder. For the tactile/movement persons (including parents and children) have them go through the motions physically with a blindfold. Perhaps they could mime making a bed or doing the dishes or homework, creating a physical connection to the task or responsibility that we usually communicate about through verbal commands. Use all of the processing modes and you will find greater communication and encourage others in your family to recognize the strengths of others rather than limiting themselves to their way of communicating and relating.

Road Sign # 3: *Grouping.* This is a social preference that might well improve our appreciation and affection for others, including mother-in-law and distant uncle, as well as "the boss." Do you like to be by yourself and work alone, or do you prefer to work in pairs or in a team? Indicate below your preference for grouping.

a) Self – This is when you prefer to work or be alone when doing challenging tasks. Other people distract you, and you seem to concentrate and solve problems when you are alone. You enjoy privacy and get more done by yourself. (circle one)

worst 1 2 3 4 5 6 7 8 9 best

b) Pair – This is when you like to relate with another person or a partner. You get more done and can build on another's ideas. Your interaction with another person gives you the support to get things done. (circle one)

worst 1 2 3 4 5 6 7 8 9 best

c) Team – This is your relating style if you prefer working or thinking in a group. You find committees or task groups and teams easy to get things done. You'd rather not do things alone or in pairs. (circle one)

worst 1 2 3 4 5 6 7 8 9 best

Often when learning or improving, we "go it alone." If you are a solo person or one of your family is, then go ahead and carry out your pursuits in a self-directed way. But don't hurt other people's feelings by making them feel like you either don't care or don't want to belong. Explain your learning/relating style, and ask for some privacy. On the other hand, if you like to work in pairs, you will most likely do well if you work with someone else. Many children don't do their homework because they have to do it alone. Some of your family and friends might need to function with a buddy or a pal. So when you set them on tasks and they have to work or do homework alone, they just won't function as well as if they had someone else around. Others just prefer teams or small gatherings and need the company of a breakfast or dinner family gathering. Obviously, people who prefer to work alone seem aloof and those in pairs seem inseparable, while those who enjoy group activity long for togetherness.

It is hard to build family or work team closeness and rapport if one person likes to do things in a private study or garage apart from others, while other family or team members enjoy time doing things in pairs or as a family unit. Seldom do we get a compromise on this, unless we understand that this is not a personality defect, but rather is a relating style. When we fall in love and decide to get married, generally we don't even see these different preferences until much later. Then we seek to change the other person toward the way we like to do things.

Find the best circumstance and develop appreciation, but also have time when everyone in the family or work team gathers together to discuss this and other issues that lead to appreciation, affection and cooperation.

Road Sign # 4: *Light.* This is an environmental influence that affects many of us; but for others it depends on what they are doing. Some of us don't function at all unless we have bright lights, while others need dim light to get things done. When our four children were growing up, I noted that among the six of us, two needed bright light to function; two required dim or natural light, and two just didn't care about the issue. One of our daughters leaves the lights on in the rooms she most often frequents. I go around turning them off, not only to save energy, but also because I like a dimly lit house. This difference could lead to an unspoken negative attitude or hurt feelings if we didn't communicate our preferences and respect for one another. I enjoy natural or dim light so much that people who come by my office jokingly comment that they don't wish to disturb my taking a nap, even though I am thoughtfully reading a book or writing.

In opposition to dim incandescent lights and natural light, which often create a calming effect, fluorescent lights can create hyperactivity in people and keep them energized. Since we often blame others for not having the light the way we want it, understanding light preference can increase our empathy and support for others in our family and reduce our criticism. And where there is a genuine conflict, as in the case of conserving energy, we can gently arrive at compromises without either blame or shame.

If you are less than a three on this scale, you prefer or require dim light to do your best, whether it is cleaning the house or running your office. If you put more than 6, you prefer or require bright light to do your best. Other members of your family will vary and you will want to encourage the environment that is best for them, whether at home, work or in school. An answer of 4,5, or 6 signifies that it depends on what you are doing or it just does not matter for you. In any case, if you are under fluorescent lights, whether bright or dim, get rid of them. Change the bulbs from fluorescent to "full spectrum" lights, which research has proven have a positive effect on your physiology and performance. (See **Chapter Six, "Light"**)

Where are you on the light scale? (circle one)
> **Light**   **dim** 1 2 3 4 5 6 7 8 9 **bright**

Road Sign # 5: *Sound.* This is also an environmental influence that, when you recognize it, can improve your appreciation and support for others. Maybe you like music or sound in the background and can remember someone criticizing you or asking you to turn down the radio or TV. Perhaps you feel you can't function unless there are no competing distractions from the TV or radio. "It's too loud!" or "It's not loud enough!" are frequent household expressions that are often followed by "What's wrong with you?" These expressions are usually meant as "put downs," mean spirited remarks or arguments.

Some of us do especially well with music, noise or sound in the background, while others of us need quiet. Still, for others, it depends on what they are doing or it simply does not matter. You may have a child who insists on doing homework with the radio on or a husband who can't hear you over the music. Take the time to find out what preference each family member has and provide an opportunity to discuss this issue. Then, develop time and strategies in your home to enable people to feel respected and honored for how they process information best. This does not mean that everyone does "her own thing," but it does mean to back off from making wrongful assumptions about your family members. Creating an opportunity for each to express one's self and seek compromise as full participants in the family makes for respect and rapport in the family dynamics (As a further reference, read *The Mozart Effect* by Don Campbell or John Ortiz's *The Tao of Music*. Also, see **Chapter Six, "Sound"**).

Chances are this road sign applies to you and members of your family. (circle one)

Sound   **music** 1 2 3 4 5 6 7 8 9 **quiet**

Road Sign # 6: *Mode*. We all have heard the phrase "variety is the spice of life." Well, for some of the people we relate with that is true, and for others it is not. Some of us prefer stability and others prefer variety. This affects how we plan for vacations, how we shop for groceries, what we wear for clothes and how our children study.

If you prefer predictability and few changes, you most likely prefer stability. A routine and schedule helps you be more successful and you are comfortable with consistency. You might use a daily planner. Has anyone in your relationship world been called a "stickler" for routine? Maybe your husband or wife seems boring because of a desire for routine. It is easy to judge, blame and make negative comments because people don't like the way we enjoy either routine or variety.

On the other hand, if variety is your spice of life, you might get bored with routine, requiring schedule changes often. Change is something you thrive on, and you enjoy new ideas and ways of doing things. Or you may know someone in your household or someone in your world of work who is always spontaneous, wanting to do things on the spur of the moment. When conflict occurs, you can avoid hurt feelings and bad tempers by understanding this important road sign. (circle one)

Mode   **variety** 1 2 3 4 5 6 7 8 9 **stability**

If you circle 4, 5, 6, your need for variety or stability probably depends on what you are doing. You can go either way, with variety or with the same routine. Usually you will act as the mediator between others in your family.

Make a list of each family member or person at work and recall arguments about trips, vacations, doing household chores or playing family games. When you do, identify who creates the argument by being too rigid about routine or who starts a crisis through the need for spontaneity. Having such a list gives you a predictor to help one another back off and compromise toward family harmony and cooperation. By knowing where you stand, you can enhance communications and develop new appreciation for those who vary from one another in mode.

Road Sign # 7: *Brain Dominance* - Left Brain/Right Brain. You've heard the story of the woman who couldn't sleep because she was off $0.37 in balancing the checkbook and exclaimed: "I must be a left brain person!" or the case of the man who kept forgetting where he left his car keys and gave the excuse: "Well, I guess I'm a right-brained person." Despite such stereotyping, each of us uses both sides of the brain. However, members of your family or fellow workers might behave more from one than the other.

Left brain oriented people like things in a step-by-step sequence. They like facts, details and specific directions. They tend not to fool around or joke about things and they focus on getting the task at hand done. "One thing at a time" is best, and they prefer outlines. They put Christmas presents together by first reading the directions and counting the parts. TV commercials like Smith Barney's "We do things the old fashioned way" appeal to these people. This person parks the car at the first available spot, regardless if it is two blocks from the destination. Often within the workplace or family dynamics, a "left-brainer" could drive other non-lefties crazy by the almost neurotic demand for precision, orderliness and detail. Understanding where you are can allow you to be more even tempered and result in less anxious approaches to family communication and harmony.

A right brain preference enjoys the whole picture and the meaning and purpose of things. They might start in the middle, at the end, or the beginning of a book, depending on their intuition. They have several projects going on and enjoy many different areas of interest. "Right-brainers" are laid back on details and like to come to their own conclusions. They put Christmas presents together by setting the directions aside and jumping right in (if you've been around awhile, you've learned not to throw the directions away). TV commercials like the Nike "Just do it" strike a chord with these people. This person pays little attention to the first parking spot and drives right up to the entrance of the destination, usually finding an open spot to the amazement of others in the car. Often completely out of harmony with the left brain preference, this person is spontaneous and doesn't care if the checkbook balances as long as it is close. Also, this type has many unfinished projects going on at once, which will be done "someday." (circle one)

Left Brain 1 2 3 4 5 6 7 8 9 Right Brain

The "right brain dominance" relating style could be a frightful burden to the left brainer, often fostering anxiety, anger and depression. Also, "left brain dominance" relaters can have a negative impact on communications and relations if it is domineering. And, although we each have characteristics from each side, there are individuals in our families who are more or less one sided or the other. Get a reading on brain dominance for each of your family members and you will see why there is often conflict, stress and tension. New perspectives that explain the differences in your family members' preferences can give you all an edge on improved communications, harmony and happiness. When people communicate more effectively and have greater harmony and happiness, they increase their health and hardiness as well. Another useful brain dominance indicator is available for you in **Chapter Three.**

ACTION ITEMS:

1. Ask yourself, "What is the best time of the day for me to learn?" Then, make arrangements to do this consistently at the best time for you. Note that this might not be the best time for concentrating for others.

2. Ask and listen to others about their comfort in room design for learning. This will be different for each person. Some will want a formal hard chair and table and others will do better in a soft chair.

3. Find out if you learn best under bright light or dim light, and then make the appropriate adjustments. Remember that this might not be the way others like to learn best. Do not force your style on others. In either case, you can learn better under full-spectrum lighting rather than under fluorescent lights.

4. If you are a parent, in all the things you do to support your child, include visuals, listening and hearing activities and body movement exercise in any learning episode.

5. For more information on research pertaining to Learning Styles and Dr. Dunn's work, refer to- www.learningstyles.net

The Second Secret Revealed

There's no need to positively identify for all time what your or your spouse's and child's learning strengths are. They may, in fact, fluctuate from time to time. What's important is that you help others form the habit of exploring alternative ways of doing things, so they can select from several possibilities for any study task. With time, they'll get progressively better at selecting approaches to studying or problem solving that work particularly well for them. This is necessary because so many of us have come to believe there is only one right way to do a given task – usually the way that it was first presented to us in school or on the job.

These models are not meant to complicate your effort to improve your ability or anyone else's ability to learn. On the contrary, they are meant to help you recognize your tremendous power to learn. They describe potential and abilities that your family members and friends possess right now. Over time, as you work with these various sources of insight about learning, you'll develop a much deeper appreciation of how your mind works. This is empowering, because it helps you understand and take advantage of your uniqueness as a learner.

Now that you know where you are on the MAP of "Learning-Relating Styles," have other family members or people you relate with read this chapter and indicate their preferences to obtain a profile of your family or a profile of your work team. Then you can compare and discuss the differences that have an impact on your communication, discipline, cooperation and expressions of affection with the goal of improving mutual understanding and rapport.

But don't be surprised if you find your family and friends in two or more categories. That means they may want to use several different approaches to understanding and learni ng about new things. In fact, it's not a bad idea for everyone to do this, because we can all benefit by strengthening the different learning modalities, even those we do not prefer to use. This is what my friend, colleague and mentor, Dr. John Grassi, calls becoming a *"comprehensivist,"* which helps you do the right thing at the right time under the right circumstances. One definition of intelligence is "what you do when you do not know what to do." Being a *comprehensivist* gives you an advantage of acting in accordance with greater wisdom. For further information, results, and strategies on implementing "Learning Styles," refer to **Chapter Seven** and the Appendices.

"E Pluribus Unum" means *"Out of many, one."* It is the motto of a nation based on diversity as a capacity within a common framework of a Constitutional consensus. How we recognize, honor and celebrate the diversity in our personal relationships can give us a more mindful basis for communication, harmony, cooperation and love. Acknowledge and celebrate the many differences that make a difference in the quality of your life and the quality of the lives of those with whom you relate. This does not mean that you compromise on first principles of ethics or justice, nor does it mean blind relativism where "anything goes!" What it does mean, among other things, is that the quality of your life is a function of the quality of the relationships you establish and nurture. And that is determined, in large measure, by the extent to which you permit your brain to function at its best. The secret of how you can use your brain more effectively, with a new owner's manual for your brain, is revealed in **Chapter Three**.

SECRET #3
Revealed.

The Story-Telling Brain
The Brain Organizes and
Remembers in Stories

The Quadra Brain

Why study the Brain?

Brain Structure & Function

Brain "Spurt"
Development -
A Time for all Seasons
and Brain Growth

Who thinks about
the Brain?

Chemical Brain
"How you Feel
determines
how you Think"

YOUR BRAIN
and YOU.

The Brain as a
System

The Brain Geography
"A Brain Map"

Enriched Brain Grows -
How to Grow your Brain's
Power and Strength

The Holographic Brain
"The Brain Picture"

Split Brain and Gender

The Triune Brain - "Three Brains in One"

The Split-Brain Idea
Two Brains working together in your mind

Three layers must work together

Chapter Three

Secret #3
Your Brain and You

Use the new knowledge about your brain to your advantage and empower your mind with proven ways to achieve higher success.

D id you know that you have three separate minds in your brain? Did you know that you could either grow or shrink your brain? Did you know that *how* you think could create either toxins or healing chemicals in your body? Such is the power of the remarkable human brain. Current brain research reveals that the human brain has the power to dramatically improve our thinking, learning, and performance, as well as to increase our memory, health, and happiness. That's why having an understanding of how the brain works is the third secret in giving you the edge in learning, health and happiness.

Current brain research provides us with a useful map of brain geography, which tells us about the structure and function of our learning behavior. So in order to tap into your true learning potential, you need some foundational knowledge about the brain. This new knowledge can help all people be more successful in providing a learning advantage for themselves, their family members and their fellow workers.

Why Study the Brain?

Knowing how the human brain works can help ease lots of life's stressors. For example, is your child stressed out from school? Is your boss always yelling at your colleagues when dealing with challenges at the office? Are you unsure what to do to help your kids learn? Do you get frustrated that your spouse or one of your children learns in a different way than you do? Do you get panicky under pressure?

Don't despair! Unfortunately, no one ever received an owner's manual for the brain and how it operates. What we need is a special kind of "operator's guide" for the brain that can help people understand how the brain is structured and how it functions. This understanding will help you learn how to help your brain work better for you. This is important, because our brains are more effective when the geography and processes of the brain system are put to work *for* us – especially for thinking and learning success.

You might think that you got along just fine in the past without knowledge of the structure and function of the brain. So why is it so important now? Indeed, it is true that you can drive a car without understanding the principles of combustion and the operating processes of the engine and the transmission. However, understanding the structure and function of the automobile could give you a better opportunity to get more out of the car and keep it from wearing out, as well as create optimal performance for the life of the car. And, you might have a greater appreciation for the automobile.

Similarly, having a working understanding of the structure and function of the brain can help you choose the right strategies, tactics and tools that will give you optimal performance as a human being. It can also provide you with knowledge about those habits and behaviors that can inhibit, retard and stunt your growth and happiness. The use of such knowledge and skill can lead you on a personal path of continuous improvement; a journey of mental, physical and spiritual growth; as well as guide you toward health, happiness and abundance

An Understanding of Brain Structure and Function is Critical for Your Brain

Today we must process more information and do it more quickly to keep up with our careers, our children, our relationships and our personal growth. A number of research studies show that the high-speed life of our families is challenging for even the youngest of our children. For example, the Fordham University Social Policy Institute claims that our nation's social health is the lowest it has been since 1975. With over 84% of families having both parents working outside the home, it is difficult to handle work responsibilities and provide the emotional support, attention and love children need. Toffler called our times "Future Shock," since the time horizon for change is immediate. In order to avoid the personal and community disintegration of ignorance, we must develop knowledge and skills that maximize our capacity to learn more in less time and with greater memory.

Living in a democracy, whether we are parents, employees, leaders, students, or children, requires personal and community learning and education. Therefore, the practical understanding of the brain structure and function is critical. The scarecrow in Frank L. Baum's well known children's story *The Wizard of Oz* told us that "if we only had brains, we could accomplish just about anything" (including conferring with the flowers). Well, you and all the people who surround you at home and at work do have brains. But having a brain and using it effectively are two different things.

While humans do have brains, so do lots of other animals. But animals can't think, at least not the way humans can. Nor do they have the ability to communicate their thinking to others. "Thinking" is what defines us as a species, as well as "acting" on that thinking. And how effectively we think and act upon our thinking defines our personal destiny. Humans can think and that's what they uniquely do. Some do it well and some do it poorly.

It is on this issue of "thinking" that French philosopher Renee Descartes launched the questions of modern philosophy. In a world of doubt, Descartes wondered if there was anything about which he could be certain without a doubt. After doubting everything he could, he realized that he could not doubt that he was thinking. Therefore, he concluded, *"cogito ergo sum,"* which means literally, *"I think, therefore I am."*

Descartes was the first Philosopher to define "thinking" as the defining characteristic of being a human being. It is true that Aristotle wrote that "the unexamined life is not worth living" and that knowledge is supreme. But Descartes elevated the *process* of thinking to another level of value and importance.

Not only are we "thinking" beings, as are some other animals, but also we have the unique potential to use thinking to transform human nature for our family, our community and ourselves. This is one of the paradoxes of being human: namely, we want to both live in our nature and to rise above our nature. For instance, it is quite natural for us to fight one another in groups or families. Witness the gangs or warring factions in any country, as well as the family rivals like the feuding "Hatfields and the McCoys" or Shakespeare's families in *Romeo and Juliet* – the "Montigues and Capulets." Only through human thinking and inventiveness could governments be created out of clans and tribes to establish rules, regulations, rewards and punishments to permit people to go beyond their nature and act with civility, if not with love and kindness. And it is that process of thinking that strengthens and improves us through a greater understanding of the structure and function of the brain.

Who Thinks About the Brain?

The people who study the structure and function of the brain are called *neuroscientists*. In recent years, technology has enabled neuroscientists to peer into the brain to get a better picture of its structure and function. However, we are far from any complete description or explanation of how the brain works, what makes up the mind, and what enables us to remember. We still have much to discover. As important as the strides have been within science, however, very little of this research has been translated into useful theories and strategies for practical learning and education.

According to leading brain researcher Paul MacLean, M.D., "On the basis of what the brain knows of itself, it is the most complicated and remarkable instrument in the known universe. It is therefore surprising that in this age of machines and computers we give so little thought to educating ourselves about the structure and function of the brain."[1] In fact, in the world of educators, legislators, and corporate executives, very little is known about brain research and its value to help improve the quality of life for every individual. The entire subject is outside the conventional wisdom of traditional educational policy research agendas.

Only recently have medical schools utilized current brain research to improve instruction of medical students. Using what we know about the brain to improve the brain's performance has generated positive results in medical education, from EMT training at Booth Memorial Hospital in New York to medical staff training in Guided Imagery Processes and Healing. At the Medical College of Georgia, I consulted with Dr. Thomas Nosek on a project to create a computer graphics course in Anatomy and Physiology that could supplement the traditional "lecture" course. Evaluations from the students showed that they loved the computer CD and recommended that it replace the lectures altogether. Also at the Medical College at Upstate New York, several key principles outlined in this book were used to help medical students increase their satisfactory course completion rates. Physicians have used some of these principles in their strategies for preparing for their relicensure examinations.

Psychiatrist Daniel Amen, M.D. courageously set a new standard for mental health improvement by using brain scans to measure and monitor brain activity during psychiatric treatment for a wide range of areas from "panic attacks" and "mood disorders" to schizophrenia in order to determine the effectiveness of therapy, whether behavioral, pharmacological or a combination of the two. Using new technology which allows a 3-D picture of a patient's brain before, during and after treatment, Dr. Amen has been able to chart progress toward a normal image and healthy behavior. This gives the medical team, for the first time, clear evidence of the improvement of function, while observing positive changes in structure. Dr. Amen has a Web Site that not only demonstrates his theory and practice, but also connects you to other important brain research and resources - www.brainplace.com .

The Brain as a System

Ask anybody where the location of "thinking" is and, usually, they will point to the head. However, when we speak about the structure of the human brain, we will want to acknowledge all the players in the central nervous system (CNS), including parts and processes outside the skull. This includes the spinal cord with all of its nerves extending to the surface of the skin. The skin and the muscles are "sense" receptors of information processed by the different parts of the brain. The eyes, ears, nose and mouth all interact with different brain structures to process and interpret information from the external physical and social world. Even those energy field receptors, which process information and put us on alert before we are consciously aware, are considered part of our CNS. Many different models of the brain attempt to explain some aspect of the thinking process.

   With this vast information available, I have selected several "Models of the Brain" that are particularly useful in assisting us in understanding the structure, organization and function of the brain. Keep in mind that the goal here is to improve your thinking, learning and performance. The purpose of this book is to take you through an overview of the brain so you can have a new way of looking at yourself and others in order to maximize your personal success. It is not intended to be a primer in anatomy and physiology. The book, *The Brain*, by Richard Restak, M.D., is my recommendation to you for further study of the anatomy and physiology of the human brain.

Brain Geography – A Brain Map

These concepts refer to the specific identification of brain function in terms of specific locations in the brain. Functions such as verbalization, logical performance, and visualization dwell in specific regions, localities or canals in the physical brain. Major functions seem to have their own street address within the brain. Knowing this fact alone provides us with an increased sensitivity and, perhaps, motivation, to develop those parts of the brain.

During 1936-1960, Dr. Wilder Penfield conducted delicate brain surgery on patients at McGill University in Montreal, Canada. As a neurosurgeon, Dr. Penfield conducted his surgery by administering a local anesthetic, allowing the patient to remain conscious. When he stimulated various areas of the patient's brain with an electrical probe, reflex responses were elicited, including muscle twitches, sounds, smells and emotions. This supported the view that memory was stored in localized regions of the brain.

What was most surprising to Dr. Penfield's research team was the consistent response from probes above the temporal lobe where very specific memories were recalled about incidents long forgotten or never before recalled. The minute detail of recollection was like a video replay available to the mind. This led Dr. Penfield to conclude that every data element ever perceived at the conscious and sub-conscious level is imprinted in the brain in memory.[2]

What does this teach us? Most important is that we must be careful how we treat one another, especially our children and grandchildren, as we might be laying down an infrastructure of "fear, threat, intimidation and put-downs" as opposed to a network of memories of love, kindness, joy, peace, comfort and confidence. What you say and do can leave a legacy long after you have departed this world. Some psychologists argue that mental health problems are trans-generational because of the behavior that is set in motion by parents, grandparents and so on.

ACTION ITEMS:

1.   If you have to discipline your child, don't wait until later. Act immediately, focusing on the behavior and reinforcing your love for that person, but not the behavior.

2.   Put colorful word strips around the house and on the refrigerator that reflect the value of positive speaking and no put-downs. Also, have phrases such as "I love the feelings of learning and enthusiasm" on banners strategically placed in the house. You can teach a child anything by having it printed on a banner above the kitchen clock.

3.   Use the "Good and New" technique. Develop a daily ritual of asking: "What is good and new about what I learned to-

day?" Each family member can answer the question, making a game of this to see what each person can express from the events of the day. If someone says: "Nothing!" ask about one thing that was learned and if there could be something "good and new" about that. Don't give up on developing the habit of reflecting on or relating things that were "good and new" to the process of learning (see **Chapter Five**).

The Holographic Brain – The Brain Picture

Although locality of brain function has been well established, there is still a genuine ambiguity about particular functions and activities having more than one address or more than one home throughout the regions of the brain. Karl Pribram, M.D., the father of neuroscience, advocates a Holographic Theory of brain function. His research has indicated that although certain functions of the brain are associated with a region, in some sense that function seems to be interconnected in an integrated circuitry with the rest of the brain, like an escape tunnel or a butler's stairwell in an old house

For example, children with a left hemispherectomy (having one side of the neo-cortex removed) do develop speaking ability and other left-brain functions over time. The earlier the operation, the better the recovery. People with right hemisphere damage (where emotions are controlled) learn to control the mood swings associated with right hemisphere insult.

Pribram's Model of the brain asserts that although there is clear evidence of dominance of function (speech is processed in the left hemisphere of the neo-cortex) and localization of function (vision is processed in the rear of the brain in the visual-cortex), there is a sense in which all functions are accessible through different routes. His model was drawn from holographic photography that builds upon wave interference patterns from two laser beams focused upon an object. If you look squarely at the photographic plate, you can only see waves. If you shine a laser beam through it, you see a three-dimensional image. If you were to cut the photographic plate in half, discarding one half, and shine a beam of light through that remaining half, the entire object appears as before, but slightly degraded or fuzzy. Cut the half in half again, and there is a three dimensional representation, but more blurred.[3]

The practical point of this Model of the Brain is that, in some sense, the various brain functions are embedded in all parts of the brain. Thus, when learning and thinking are to occur, it is helpful to have a variety of pathways into the brain for perceiving, processing and providing output for thinking, problem solving and creativity. Diversity of input to the nervous system, including art, music, drama, diagrams, interpersonal interaction, and personal, private reflection can, therefore, enhance the processing of new knowledge and skills, increase memory and recollection, and finally create lasting and improved performance.

The Triune Brain – Three Brains in One

A very useful Model of the Brain uncovers the three minds in your brain – the thinking mind, the feeling mind, and the "fight or flight" mind. Dr. Paul MacLean of the National Institute of Mental Health developed this Model of the Brain to both describe brain structure and explain different functions. When Dr. MacLean discovered the three-mind brain, he named it the "triune" brain, or the "three in one" brain. Each of the three minds in the brain has a different structure and function that *does* affect our learning and behavior, depending on which brain is in charge or is operating. And you can learn strategies that can help you control which brain state you are in.

This theory provides an explanation of the development of the three layers of the brain as it forms *in utero* and as it has evolved over millions of years. In a way, the Triune Brain Theory views the operation of the brain like a gearbox in a standard shift car. There is a continuous shifting between the layers of the brain, relative to the functions that are either sought or imposed.

To get a clearer idea of the "three-minds-in-one brain" imagine a three-layered, marble cake that is shaped like a ball. Each layer has its own color. In the center is a red core layer. Covering the core layer is a white layer. Surrounding the white layer is the third outer layer of blue. The frosting is the skull, which contains our three minds brain cake.

If you cut your imagined cake in half, you would see the inner core of red, covered by white, followed by a covering of blue.

The Red Layer – The "R-Complex" or the "Fight or Flight" Mind:

The red layer, also called the "R-Complex" (Reactionary Mind), is known as the "fight or flight" mind. It is active when you are protecting yourself against perceptions of "fear, threat, intimidation or put-downs." When you are in this mind, you feel the need to protect and defend yourself. It is the survival mind that acts, sometimes wrongly, to preserve privacy or territory. Arguing, defensiveness, negativity, cussing and cursing are the language tools of this mind. It builds rituals, routines and habits. Fetishes, fads the wearing of unique clothes, hoarding toys, and "mine" expressions come from this core mind. Bullying and picking on others to establish power and control also arise from this core part of the brain.

The "R-Complex" mind is sometimes called the "irrational" brain that just kicks and screams or pouts and whines to get its own way (to survive and protect itself). The "R-Complex" governs self-preservation and survival. It is responsible for individuality, territoriality, and privacy. Mating, nesting, and pecking order are all attributed to the function of the "R-Complex." It is in control during "down-shifting" and spurting chemicals, such as adrenalin, histamine and cortico-steriods.

The White Layer – The "Limbic System" or the "Feeling" Mind:

The next (white) layer of our cake that enfolds the red layer is called the "Limbic" mind or the "emotional" mind. It is responsible for emotions and is associated with the group, family and friends. This is the seat of love, caring, belonging, compassion, empathy and social awareness. The limbic mind governs kindness, gentleness, and appreciation. All perception first enters the limbic mind. If we detect fear, threat, intimation and put-downs, then we automatically activate our "fight or flight" mind and we "down-shift" into the survival mode.

On the other hand, if we experience love, joy, peace, kindness, gentleness or a positive feeling (along with no fear, threat, intimidation or put-downs), the limbic mind activates the "Neo-Cortex" or "thinking" mind represented by the blue layer of our imaginary cake. It is in the limbic system where memory is encoded for long-term recollection. All information that comes into the limbic system is coded with emotion, and the limbic system monitors our emotions, looking for fear, threat, put downs and intimidation.

The Blue Layer – The "Neo-Cortex" or the "Thinking" Mind:

The blue layer or outer layer is the "Neo-Cortex" ("neo" means new and "cortex" means layer). It has the function of reasoning, planning, speech and language, sensory discrimination, sight, hearing, projecting the future, creativity, inventiveness and making connections between the old and the new. Analyzing, spatial reasoning, figuring things out and imagination are all part of this neo-cortex. Most of the schoolwork our children do, along with reading, math, science, English and test taking, are part of what is sometimes called our "thinking cap" or "neo-cortex."

The neo-cortex is divided into two halves, often called the left brain and the right brain. This is the part of the brain about which most people know something. Even a popular country western tune will use this insight: "This ain't no left brain – right brain thing. This ain't no thinking thing. This is a heart thing," laments the singer. Although popular as an expression, few know the difference between the two hemispheres of the neo-cortex.

For example, the left side is responsible for verbal speech and language, along with detailed, logical and linear thinking. The left side processes communication in sequences and lists of details with step-by-step procedures and rules. *"One thing at a time"* is the slogan for the left side. This left side is *quantitative* and likes facts and details. Questions from the left side are: "Do I use a pencil or a pen?" "Will this be on the test?" and "What is the content and structure?"

The right half of the neo-cortex is visual-spatial and looks at the whole picture. It sees relationships. The right brain seeks patterns, and it processes spatial information and pictures, doodles and graphics. Boys are more visual and kinesthetic (body involvement) than auditory and enjoy exploring the territory around them, testing the boundaries and the make-up of things out there. The right side uses "imaginative thinking and enjoys music, color, and emotions connected to the white limbic layer. This right side is qualitative and likes stories and analogies that tie things together for whole meaning. Charts, maps, graphic organizers, doodles and drawing pictures, and "mind maps" tap this side of the brain. My fourth grade teacher, Ms. Flanders, often said to us boys, "What do I have to do, draw you a picture?" If she only knew! Questions from the right side are: "May I do this next week?" "How does this fit into the scheme of things?" "Why are we doing this anyway, because no one will care one hundred years from now?" and "What is the meaning and purpose in doing this?"

We become creative and make connections between what exists and what is new because of the neo-cortex. That flow of endorphins happens because of the neo-cortex, and it is in control during "whole brain activation," which is the brain state when all three of the layers of the brain are activated. That is to say, the limbic perceives no or little fear, threat or intimidation from the environment. There are positive sensations from color, light, sound, and expressions from people. The neo-cortex is activated and "whole brain activation" occurs with the potential for creativity and the "flow of endorphins."

Why the Three Layers Must Work Together

Regardless of gender or age, any anxiety, frustration, fear, threat, intimidation or put-down will cause a "down-shifting" into the "R-Complex" mind and shut down learning, memory and performance. This will disconnect the Thinking Mind and the positive Emotional Mind. This is what happens with "test anxiety" and, in some cases, what causes children to get sick and stay home from school. The positive, appreciative and loving emotions of the limbic mind need to be engaged to get optimal learning, success, and high self-esteem. Keep in mind that you have to do different things for different people, precisely because each one has different emotional needs and learns differently (see **Chapters Two and Five**). For example, if you are a parent you may have one child who needs you by her side to do things, and yet you may have another who wants to try things by herself.

You will be more successful if you identify your learning preferences, as well as identifying the styles of those around you, and create environments that are emotionally supportive and reduce fear and anxiety. Therefore, create the conditions for everyone to maximize praise and joy in learning. Tap strengths, but create experiences that develop weaknesses. For example, with children you might do multiplication facts by bouncing a basketball in the backyard to create a sound rhythm with the math facts. Also, draw pictures, graphics and diagrams of information you want to remember, even if it is simply for spelling or vocabulary. Do things that tap both sides of the brain in any task or learning requirement by using music, color, body movement and positive "can do" attitudes.

Remember that the best learning results when the whole brain is activated. This is when there is no fear, threat, intimidation, or put-downs, and when love, joy, appreciation and positive enthusiasm are present. Then, the Thinking Brain does better with creativity, innovation and memory, assisting in learning more in less time. Harvard psychologist Howard Gardner has a positive reminder for any parent or grandparent: "The most important moment in a child's education is the crystallizing experience when the child connects to something that engages curiosity and stimulates further exploration."

In so many cases, from Greek Stoicism to American Puritanism, emotions were thought to cloud reason and drain pure reason from the triune brain. Today we can understand why so many geniuses wrote about the passion of discovery and the joy of learning. We can appreciate also the agony of the high school dropouts who internalize "failure." Moreover, fear, vulnerability and stress cause withdrawal, flight, and a freeze on neocortical functioning. Separation of "thinking" from "feeling" and the polarization between conceptualization and emotion produces tension, stress and conflict in the operation of the brain. This leads to a kind of aloofness about learning as "unreal" and an uncontrollable emotional irrationality that yields frustration, anxiety and the desire to flee or fight.

A Learning Theory that incorporates a comfortable interplay between the intellectual and emotional functions of human beings structures the opportunity to provide a natural framework for optimal learning. When positive emotions and joy are brought into the rational process, downshifting to the R-Complex brain does not take place. The sullen, bored and anxious student who seeks to flee from school can be an obsolete experience in an enlightened school. If "down-shifting" has become a habit, it is still possible to regain access to Limbic and Neocortical functions through sufficient relaxation and joyful environments. In the medical and therapeutic environment, this is what Dr. Herbert Benson refers to as the "relaxation response" that has been responsible for the medical recovery in patients. So if you develop your control of the Three Minds in your brain, you, your family and those around you are sure to enjoy greater learning, health, and happiness.

 ACTION ITEMS:

1. If you are having difficulty or experiencing frustration with someone, go for a walk to get oxygen in your brain and realize that you and the other person must be in a state of positive emotion to have maximum learning success. Breathe through your nose and out your mouth at least five times to help you relax. Do not be judgmental and critical, as this will trigger the "R-Complex" mind. Your expression of enthusiasm, love, appreciation and positive attitude is the most effective model for all.

2. Make a list of what someone in your life does that aggravates you and puts you into your "fight or flight" mind. What do you or other family members do that triggers another's "fight or flight" mind? List what triggers your "R-Complex" or "fight or flight" mind. Make a list of three things you could do to avoid "down-shifting" in yourself. What could you do to avoid triggering someone else's "down-shifting"?

3.   Make a list of the things that someone you know does that causes her or him joy, gentleness, kindness and positive feelings when learning. Also, make a list of the things that this same person does that brings this positive, emotional mind out in you. What actions can you take that would create more "limbic" responses in your day-to-day routine? Jot them down.

The Split Brain Idea – Two Brains Working Together in Your Mind

Focusing specifically on the neo-cortex, the "Split Brain Theory" is popularly known as "left brain – right brain." This Model of the Brain won a Nobel Prize for a team of surgeons and scientists, including Joseph Bogden, who performed the surgery, and Dr. Roger Sperry, who studied the patients following surgery. Dr. Sperry summarized by stating, "The body plan of the mammal provides for two lungs, two kidneys, and paired organs such as eyes, ears and limbs. In a sense it also provides for a paired brain."[4] In attempting to solve the problem of chronic epilepsy, Dr. Sperry and his research team severed the connection between the two halves of the brain. His studies showed conclusively that each brain half functioned independently from the other after the operation. It was as if there were two people not communicating with one another inside one skull.

Consequently, the right side of the brain, which understands music, could not interpret language, and the left hemisphere, which understands verbal cues, could not comprehend spatial information. Having lost the interconnectedness, the two halves of the brain developed compensation strategies and different personalities. Through the use of experimental techniques that enabled him to communicate with each hemisphere, Dr. Sperry discovered the areas of both localization and specialty of each of the hemispheres.

He found that the left hemisphere is dominant in logic, sequencing, linearity, verbal language, quantitative reasoning and reductionism. (This means taking things apart and breaking them down into the smallest possible units of thought.) He identified the right hemisphere as responsible for imagination, visualization, spatial conceptualization, intuition, music and rhythm, creativity, globality and generalization. (This means pulling units or details together and creating a whole picture.) The left hemisphere operates in a process of breaking things down into a step-by-step fashion that acts on logic and language. The right hemisphere synthesizes information, creates maps of information for visual memory, and explores relationships in general concepts and archetypes. While relating emotions much more easily than the left hemisphere, the right hemisphere is also the seat of musical intelligence.

Split Brain and Gender Differences

Important gender differences make up the neo-cortex and affect learning and performance. Females are born with larger left brains, and males are born with larger right brains. Although the size becomes more equal in adolescence, the male and female brains function differently. Also, the bridge that connects the two halves (called the *corpus collosum*) is up to twenty percent larger and thicker in girls. This bridge allows the communication between the two halves to be more effective in girls in linking emotion and language and in thinking intuitively. Also in females, language functions in the center part of the left brain, while in males, speech and communication are processed in the front and rear of the left brain, making language use and reading more diffused and difficult to develop for boys in their early years

In American schools, 51% percent of the children are girls and 49% are boys. This means that students in special programs should be split in a ratio of 51:49 - girls to boys. Tragically, however, 90% of the children in special education programs are boys. According to Jane Healy, Ph.D. in her book ***Endangered Minds***, ninety-three percent of the prescriptions for the drug "Ritalin" are for boys. This has less to do with male inferiority and more to do with curriculum disability that ignores the research on gender differences and optimal brain function. Indeed, there are schools in this country where all children are on or above grade level, regardless of gender, but the professionals and parents in those communities have an enlightened view of instructional design and delivery.

My view is that our children are far less "learning disabled" and are more "curriculum disabled." For example, Leo Wood's chemistry classes rose from 52% passing with a C grade or better to 93% passing with a C grade or better by using the principles in this book. Moreover, his enrollment pattern shifted from 80% males to an enrollment of 50:50 of males and females. Another of several examples comes from a community in Idaho that adopted several principles in this book and implemented them among the faculty in the school system. In the year that we trained the faculty and staff, they experienced a two-thirds reduction in special education referrals.

Research shows that "traditional" reading approaches primarily rely on phonetic hearing or "auditory" brain processing. Girls have a finer auditory capability than boys and speak, read and write much earlier. They use language for interpersonal relationship building. That's why you likely can't keep a teen-age girl off the phone and can't get a teen-age boy to talk.

Researcher Dr. Anne Moir indicates in her co-authored book on gender differences (***Brain Sex***, 1991) that boys will out perform girls on tests that are visual and require identifying "S" shapes in a paragraph or story. However, when a list of words is read and the class is asked to pick those words that contain the letter "S," girls will do better. When taking a "whole-brain" approach to reading instruction, which combines the resources of the left and right hemisphere, Renee Fuller, Ph.D. taught reading and language acquisitions skills to both males and females with equal and staggering success. In addition to teaching the retarded in mental institutions how to read, Dr. Fuller routinely observed first grade boys and girls demonstrating competent reading at the third grade level or higher.

ACTION ITEM:
Have fun with the short quiz on the following pages to find out about yourself, your family members and others to determine Left-Analytic and Right-Global brain preference. This might help you in developing strategies to improve learning, rapport and increased self-esteem.

BRAIN DOMINANCE INVENTORY [19]

Some of the following choices may seem to be either both true or false.. Force yourself to choose the one sentence that is more accurate when you are learning new and difficult information. These questions will help you discover your personal thinking style in the way you do your work. If you neither require or prefer what is asked and if it depends on what you are learning that is new and difficult, then leave it blank.

Place a check mark by either A or B.

When Learning New And Difficult Information, I Require Or Prefer:
1.) Dim or low light in the environment   A. __
    Bright light in the environment   B. __

2.) Taking in food, chewing, drinking   A. __
    No intake of food, chewing or drink   B. __

3.) Music, sound in the environment   A. __
    Quiet and silence in the environment   B. __

4.) An informal room design with soft chairs   A. __
    A formal room design with formal chairs   B. __

5.) Many projects and many breaks   A. __
    One project at a time and persistence   B. __

Total the "A" and "B" responses you counted
TOTAL: A_____   or   B_____

If your score was in the following category, then circle the category

Category A
5 Strong Right hemisphere - Global orientation
3 Moderate Right hemisphere - Global orientation

Mixed
Less than three in A or B is Bilateral hemisphere or Mixed balance

Category B
3 Moderate Left hemisphere - Global orientation
5 Strong Left hemisphere - Global orientation

What does this mean? If you are bilateral, you tend to take things in stride and get the job done without too much consternation. If you are left brain oriented you have a tendency for detail, organization and specifics. A strong left orientation is quite uncomfortable with anything that does not have schedules, outlines and structure. Here, one wants to know, "Do I use pencil or pen?" Or "How many words are required to complete this essay." We say to left brained people, "Just the facts ma'am, just the facts!" On the other hand, the right orientation is more concerned with meaning and purpose and value. So, if you are right brain oriented, you will be uncomfortable unless you know the meaning or purpose of an assignment or activity. We often say to right brained people, "Do you get the picture?"

Questions from the right ask: "Why are we doing this, anyway? Or, "Who will care about this in a hundred years?" By the way, if you fall into one of these categories, you are most likely to be married to someone who falls into a different category. This is partly why you get into conflict with your spouse. And the child in your family who causes you the greatest stress will be in an opposing category than you.

After you have scored your inventory, consider the behaviors of the left brain orientation, as opposed to the right preference on the Chart that follows. In his Web Site - www.brainplace.com Daniel Amen, M.D. states the following as Left and Right brain functions and problems or misfires which can occur:

FUNCTIONS
Dominant Side (usually the left)

- understanding and processing language
- intermediate term memory
- long term memory
- auditory learning
- retrieval of words
- complex memories
- visual and auditory processing
- emotional stability

PROBLEMS
Dominant Temporal Lobe

- aggression, internally or externally driven
- dark or violent thoughts
- sensitivity to slights
- mild paranoia
- auditory learning
- word finding problems
- auditory processing problems
- reading difficulties
- emotional instability

Non-dominant Side (usually the right)

- recognizing facial expression
- decoding vocal intonation
- rhythm
- music
- visual learning

Non-dominant Side (usually the right)

- difficulty recognizing facial expression
- difficulty decoding vocal intonation
- implicated in social skill struggles

The Enriched Brain Grows – How To Grow Your Brain's Power and Strength

The biological psychologist Mark Rosenzweig and Neuroanatomist Marion C. Diamond (who conducted post mortem research on Einstein's brain tissue) have made significant contributions to the science of the brain. Although their work has been with rats, gerbils, squirrels and monkeys, the research holds unusual and exceptional promise for enhancing human mental performance. The results of the work of these two scientists has been so startling that their conclusions, repeated with scientific accuracy, have literally shocked the world of science. There are three stages to this discussion:

First, in working with rats, a biologist at the University of California in the 1920's noticed that some rats ran the mazes better than others. Consequently, he bred "maze bright" rats and "maze dull" rats. Forty years later, after generations and generations of rat experiments, Mark Rosenzweig and his team explored the relationship between brain chemistry and "intelligence." Their basic question was "If some rats run mazes better than others, is there a difference in brain chemistry?" In a broader context, they were interested in determining whether different learning environments and varying mental activity would constitute a change in brain chemistry. They hypothesized that learning memory and problem-solving activities would result in higher levels of the brain enzyme Acetylcholinesterase (AChE) in the cerebral cortex or "thinking cap."

They created standard environments (standard cage, three rats to a wire mesh cage with usual nourishment), impoverished environments (isolated rats in a cage with three opaque walls, little stimulation, no noise and dim light), and enriched environments (play groups of ten to twelve rats, large well lighted cage with swings, slides, ladders, bridges, toys, frequently changing stimuli in the environment).

They studied both "maze bright" rats in rich and poor environments and "maze dull" rats in rich and poor environments, as well as studying both groups in standard environments. The conclusion was emphatically that in all cases there were higher levels of AChE activity in the cerebral cortex of the brain in rats raised in the enriched environment as opposed to either of those raised in standard or impoverished cages. Regardless of genetic background, increases in AChE were significant. Since the cortex is the layer of outer material, the grey matter where problem solving and high order mental processing occurs, Rosenzweig concluded: "Rather than cortical AChE activity being a fixed individual characteristic, as we had supposed, it could apparently be altered by experience." [5]

The next step was an accident. They weighed the brain tissue. To the amazement of the team and other neuroscientists, not only had the AChE activity increased in the cortex of the rats in enriched environments, but also the brain weight and density increased. The stimulation of enriched environments had caused brains to grow. This was particularly startling in view of the traditional paradigm, which held that regardless of brain activity, brain weight and structure remain stable.

The third step involved the inclusion of a renowned Neuroanatomist, Marion C. Diamond, who became famous for her work in establishing that Einstein's brain was much heavier in glial cells than ordinary people and that the ratio of glial cells to neurons indicates superior mental capacity. She joined the University of California team to ward off the onslaught of skepticism about the increase of AChE activity and the increase in brain weight.

Dr. Diamond reported conclusively in her book *Enriching Heredity: The Impact of the Environment on the Anatomy of the Brain* that mammals in enriched environments revealed:[6]

1.   Increased thickness in the cerebral cortex.
2.   Fifteen percent increase in size of neurons in the cortex.
3.   Increases in protein in the brain corresponding to weight.
4.   Increases in the amount of dendritic branching.
5.   Increases in the number of dendrite spines per unit length.
6.   Increases in the number of synapses and size of synapse.
7.   Increase in the ratio of cortical size to the rest of brain.
8.   Fifteen percent increase in the number of glial cells in the cortex.

This also included those laboratory mammals that had been in an impoverished environment and had been genetically different and inferior in skill and performance in running through mazes. When put in an enriched environment, the "maze dull" mammals had significant gains in brain growth and maze performance. According to Dr. Diamond, "...it was Donald Hebb at McGill University who began experiments dealing with the effects of stimulating experiences on behavior. He showed that rats living in enriched conditions were better learners than those that had not benefited from such experience. The exciting results from his report led to the quantitative Berkley study of the chemistry of the brains from enriched and impoverished rats. The results of our studies indicated that either enriching or impoverishing the environmental complexity and training of rats caused measurable changes in brain chemistry and (cortical) brain weight."[7] These studies showed that previously impoverished mammals and previously enriched mammals had significant reversals when put in the opposite environment from which they were raised.

Not only was such substantial growth proven and documented, but Dr. Diamond also suggested that these sorts of results could be easily obtained in relatively short periods of time. And they can occur at any age, including the elders. When we consider the studies of Rosenzweig and Diamond in light of our understanding of the neo-cortex and our view of human intelligence, it becomes morally compelling to determine how increased varieties of mental stimulation, diversity of sensory experience and "enriched environments" with multi modal dimensions can be employed to enhance the brain functions and intelligence of people.

So what is an enriched environment? According to Diamond, "…an enriched environment contained many animals in a large cage with a variety of novel objects for the rats to explore, whereas the impoverished animals were caged singly and had neither the objects, nor the large living space, nor the companions. In essence, an enriched environment is one which introduces more stimulation to the body's surface receptors than does an impoverished one, whether it be for rats or human beings."[8]

Despite prior heredity, change to an enriched environment and you will change the chemistry and function of your brain to increase cortical brain structure, function, skill and performance. In humans, research shows that an enriched environment with love, joy, peace, goodness, patience, kindness, and behaviors associated with respect, dignity, and integrity dramatically increase cognitive performance, including creativity and inventions. An impoverished environment, notwithstanding malnourishment, includes the presence of overcrowding, fear, threat, intimidation, isolation, alienation and the lack of novelty and multiple stimulations to the body's surface receptors (Chapter Six also reveals the conditions of an enriched and impoverished environment).

The Chemical Brain-Body – How You "Feel" Determines How You Think

Pioneer neuroscientist, Candace Pert, Ph.D., is famous for discovering the "opiate receptor" on the human cell in 1972. Very few modern pharmacy drugs would exist today if it were not for her discoveries. Her research addresses the age-old questions of body-mind and shows a basis, at the level of the molecule, to argue that the mind, emotions and body are all one interconnected system. The traditional distinction made by psychologists and educators about the "cognitive" (thinking) domain and the "affective" (feeling) domain is mistaken. Rather, these two dimensions to human growth and development are both parts of an underlying molecular structure. Her book, ***The Molecules of Emotion***, reveals that human brain and body is a soup, awash in a sea of chemicals that are commonly found throughout the cells of the body. Thus, chemicals, like AChE, present in the brain that can change the brain's structure, function and effectiveness, as shown by Drs. Diamond and Rosenzweig, may also show up in cells communicating in a network throughout the body, making the total being more receptive to learning and increased effectiveness.

Also, it might well be that learning in the context of an enriched environment with positive emotions increases the presence of those chemicals (AChE) that make you smarter. And there are chemicals that can make you shut down and increase fear, threat, and intimidation, while making you less functional and intelligent. Dr. Pert demonstrates "how the chemicals inside our bodies form a dynamic information network, linking mind and body, is not only provocative, it is revolutionary." By establishing the biomolecular basis for our emotions and explaining these new scientific developments in a clear and accessible way, Dr. Pert empowers us to understand ourselves, our feelings, and the connection between our minds and our bodies – or body-minds – in ways we could never possibly have imagined before.

She writes: "Think of the brain as a machine for not merely filtering and sorting this sensory input, but for associating it with other events or stimuli occurring simultaneously at any synapse or receptor along the way – that is, learning…. What this translates into in everyday experience is that positive emotional experiences are much more likely to be recalled when we're in an upbeat mood, while negative emotional experiences are recalled more easily when we're already in a bad mood. Not only is memory affected by the mood we're in, but so is actual performance. We're more likely to be helpful to others and perform in altruistic ways when we are experiencing a good mood. Conversely, hurt the ones you love enough times, and they will learn to feel threatened in your presence and remember to act accordingly. (*Many, many teachers and students call themselves "wounded learners." In what ways do our administrators, parents, teachers and fellow students "wound" each other in the effort to teach and learn?*) It doesn't take an expert in emotional theory to recognize that there is a very close intertwining of emotions and memory. For most of us, our earliest and oldest memory is an extremely emotion-laden one. One extremely important purpose of emotions from an evolutionary perspective is to help us decide what to remember and what to forget...." [9]

Ask any corporate manager whose employees have been away for a training seminar, or ask any teacher of any grade level whether their students or employees remember what they learned last week. The answer is usually, and sadly, "No, they don't remember!" One reason is that to increase the chemicals throughout the brain-body associated with increasing intelligence and learning, the learning experience must be positive, filled with multiple memory traces that can be recollected in a positive culture and climate for learning. Otherwise, forget it! (That's a joke).

Because you and I can choose how we relate to others and how we permit others to affect us at the emotional and molecular level, we must be aware of our actions, our words and our environments that can produce the emotional chemistry that can foster learning, intelligence, health, hardiness and happiness.

Brain Spurt Development – There is a Time for All Seasons and Brain Growth

If you look in any of your family albums, there might be some surprises. Do you recognize those baby pictures of you or your children? Do you have any photos of yourself when you were a toddler? What about the school pictures when you were in the fourth grade? And the high school senior class pictures? We all know that we go through stages and the pictures are there to prove it. We crawled, we toddled, we gurgled, we talked, we ran, we played sports and wrote poems. We graduated from high school (or took another path) and did something afterward.

Although there are definite stages in one sense of the term, did you know that there are specific, age related time periods when the brain grows in spurts and that these time periods closely correspond to the development of mental growth as defined by a French psychologist Dr. Jean Piaget? If your parents had measured the circumference of your head and kept the data, or if you had done the same with your children, you would have a record of physical brain growth that took place in approximately two-year segments. Also, if you had a brother or sister, the sibling of the opposite sex would have a chronological path of brain growth after age ten that showed a different picture than yours did. The growth of a female head is likely to be double that of a male during the "ten to twelve" brain spurt period, while during the fourteen to six-teen age period, the reverse is true for males. Dr. Epstein's theory of physical brain spurts corresponding to Piaget's mental growth periods is important for both parents and policy makers who determine how children are raised and taught.

Piaget's periods of cognitive, mental growth are summarized into four age categories, and they correspond to Epstein's research on the biological growth of the brain: (The following four categories are paraphrased from a chart in Kathleen Berger's book *The Developing Person Through the Life Span*):

1.) The *"sensorimotor"* period includes birth to two years old. Here the infant uses senses and physical motor abilities to explore and understand the world. There is no conceptual or reflective thought and an object is "known" in terms of what an infant can manipulate with it. The gains in cognitive growth in this period include the infant learning that an object still exists when it is out of sight, and the child begins to think through mental actions and strategies, as well as physical, motor actions.

2.) The *"pre-operational"* period of growth ranges from two to six years of age. In this period of development, the child begins to use symbolic language and thinking to comprehend the world and the experiences around him. Often the child is "self" oriented, with an egocentric perspective where "me, my and mine" characterize the perspective of the child's individual world. The mental faculty of "imagination" is excited and developed, with language becoming a useful form of expressing one's "self" and obtaining attention from others. Gradually during this period, the child becomes less "self" oriented or egocentric and becomes more sensitive to the presence of others' needs and wants and multiple perspectives. Here, the child begins to understand "yours" and "theirs."

3.) *"Concrete operational"* is the period that ranges from seven years to eleven years of age. During this period the child develops and understands and applies logical operations, inferential reasoning and principles to explain and interpret the world of experience through rational processes, rather that intuition. As a result of applying logical and rational abilities, children learn to understand the concepts of language, conversation, numerical reasoning and counting, classification and categorization, along with concepts such as cause and effect, sequencing and time ordering.

4.) *"Formal Operational"* covers the period from around twelve years through adulthood. The person in this period can think through abstractions and "if, then" hypothetical situations. Issues of "others" in relation to the self, such as "ethics," "politics," and "social issues," are of more interest and use as the adolescent takes a more pensive and theoretical approach to experience and understanding. (There is recent brain research that shows that the "frontal lobes" of the neo-cortex, which are responsible for empathy, consideration of others, planning and forecasting a future in relation to one's behavior, do not mature until the late teens and early twenties. This might explain why anything in learning that is immersed in positive emotions, with love, fun, joy and high active energy tends to have more success than the traditional drudgery of high school classrooms. How to accomplish success in this period is detailed throughout the remaining chapters of this book.)

Piaget's work has been corroborated around the world and shows these categories in growth, except for cultures that do not provide the cultural experience of periods three and four. One can easily imagine sub-groups in poverty of nutrition, finance and culture that restrict mental growth, with segments of society limited to being mentally arrested in period two or three. You can see how this can become a moral issue for any government whose Constitution requires the "equal protection" of people as does the Constitution of the United States. Georgia's Governor Zell Miller understood this and launched the funding and dissemination of an "infant kit" for all parents of newborns, which included classical music CDs and other resources designed to help parents develop their baby's emotional and mental growth during the first stages of life.

Imagine that both brain spurts and mental growth periods function much like traffic signals at a busy intersection. When the lights turn green in a certain lane, then traffic is permitted to flow. When it is red, traffic is halted. Think of traffic as potential mental growth during brain spurts at specific ages. Now, imagine a busy intersection on a four-lane street. This is an analogy to brain spurt theory. During the periods of growth (green lights) all sorts of traffic can occur, while under conditions of relaxed, no-growth (red lights), the brain is in a different functional state. When brain growth and expansion occur, so does mental growth and activity.

Epstein writes, "Given the body of facts sketched above, one can think of possible consequences for learning in general and for schooling in particular. One working hypothesis would be that intensive and novel intellectual inputs to children may be most effective during the brain growth stages. Anatomical data might be interpreted to lead to the inference that novel challenges to the child's mind at the wrong time might cause an active and potentially permanent turn-off of the ability to absorb some of those challenges at later and more appropriate ages. The question of what to do during the putative "fallow" periods will be answered definitively only by executing in schools (not in psychology laboratories!) some well-designed experiments aimed directly at that question."[10]

What Epstein is suggesting is that the conditions for enrichment, explored by Diamond and Rosenzweig, might well change from periods of growth to periods of "dormancy." Perhaps in the "dormant" periods, when the "red lights' are on, we need to focus on "emotional intelligence," character education, collaboration, citizenship and service to others, in juxtaposition to the academic growth (green light) focus.

The stages of growth of "brain spurts" and mental intelligence, according to Epstein's research (which excludes the work of Norman Geshwind's study of the "*in utero*" fetal brain), include:

1.) Three months to ten months following birth.
2.) Two years old to four years old. (It is interesting to note that there is ample evidence to show that hugging, cuddling and rocking an infant prior to two years of age is correlated to later academic performance in high school. There is also a relationship between early childhood abuse and incarceration.)
3.) Six years old to eight years old (generally first and second grade).
4.) Ten years old to twelve years old (fifth and sixth grade).
5.) Fourteen years to sixteen years old (ninth and tenth grade).

Epstein makes the critical point that: "It is important to emphasize that the brain growth stages are not a theoretical notion but a scientific fact...."[11] The implications for parents and educational policy makers is to realize that intense intellectual input and development "should be situated at the spurt ages."[12] "And further, that rigorous intellectual development (three R's) at the period of little or no brain and mind growth raises the possibility that attempts to inject novel intellectual competencies not only will fail if tried at certain age periods, but that such attempts may be counterproductive. Children exposed to intellectual pressures and inputs (*refer to all the individual state standardized tests that focus exclusively on intellectual, logical-mathematical and linguistic performance – I.Q.*) for which they have no proper receptive circuitry (*in the brain-body*) may learn to reject such inputs; such a rejection might even result in an inability to take in such inputs later when the circuitry has developed."[13]

We all have had experience with children "turning off " to the excitement of learning, especially when entering junior and senior high school. I remember my first job as a teacher was with junior high school seventh graders who were, according to "brain spurt" theory, in the cusp of brain dormancy. Rather than lecture to them, I took them outside and we built replicas of Onondaga Indian Long Houses and artifacts, with many, many field trips. This activity-oriented experience seemed to counter the dull interest in text material. Also, they were fascinated with music, art, culture and stories. On the other hand, the sophomores in high school could not seem to get enough of the intrigue of Hamlet and the horror of Gettysburg. They loved writing poems and collecting art to express their ideas. It seemed as if they emerged out of a cocoon of "I can't" and "Not for me to question 'why,' but for me to do or die."

As I wrote earlier, Epstein's "Brain Spurt" Theory parallels the long-standing work of Piaget, whose forty years of research spoke to the issue of "age appropriate" curriculum, learning strategies, and policy as it relates to intellectual and moral development. But this has all fallen on deaf ears. The contemporary American educational scene at the local, state and national level is focused on outcomes, standards for competencies, and standardized tests given all along the continuum of grade levels.

Virtually nothing is spoken to the issues of processes, whether appropriate to brain and mind growth or not. With respect to what to do and when to do it, there is an image of the three monkeys sitting together with one covering its ears, the other covering its eyes and the third covering its mouth.

Approximately one third of the children in the United States live below the poverty guidelines. We know there is a strong relationship between success in school and level of education of parents, as well as income level of the family. Low social and economic status is predictive of reading levels. And the fastest growing commercial construction industry is "prisons," whose industry leaders target fourth grade reading levels in communities, since the fourth grade reading level is predictive of incarceration.

Remember Albert Einstein's comment that the definition of insanity is that "If you always do what you've always done, you'll always get what you've always got." I would like to modify that and add: "If you always get what you always got, it is because you always 'think' what you've always thought."

If we are to be more successful with our children at home and those in our community, we must find the processes that produce the outcomes across the ages of development; and that requires that we both think and act differently in accordance with the guidance of research which validates processes which predict achievement at the academic, emotional, physical and spiritual levels.

The Story-Telling Brain – The Brain Organizes and Remembers in Stories

Renowned for her work in helping retarded children and adults learn to read, Dr. Renee Fuller discovered a process which enabled people with low IQ's to do what traditional tests and measures would say is impossible; namely, to read with comprehension. The crux of her success comes from the shift from feeding people "bits and pieces" of information to presenting "stories" as the basic unit of information and thinking. In her article *"The Brain-compatible Way of Teaching Humans,"* (available at www.ballstickbird.com). Dr. Fuller indicates that neither IQ nor aptitude tests adequately measure the true nature of intelligence. This includes all those tests used in both the state and national standards and test movement. Her contention, which is consistent with other cognitive psychologists I will introduce you to in the later chapters of this book, is that "our teaching and testing methods, instead of continuing their vain attempts to mimic successful computer programming, should be revised to fit the true nature of our intelligence."

What is the basic nature of human intelligence? As Dr. Fuller understands it, our capacity to organize bits and pieces of information, store them, combine and connect them for purposes of the creation of knowledge is the essence of "intelligence." This is consistent with my own definition of intelligence which is "what you do when you don't know what to do!" Amusing as this last definition might seem, on one level it tells the whole story of survival and "living to fight another day." However, the basic unit of intelligence is not "bits and pieces" of information, rather, it is the organizing mechanism which enables any person to put "bits and pieces" of information into meaningful and useful purposes. And that organizing mechanism, common to all humans is the "story."

According to Dr. Fuller, "I have called the basic unity of our human way of organizing information the *story-engram*. Around the age of one a child begins to learn the principles involved in building this basic unit as he/she attempts to understand (organize) the surrounding world and tries to communicate. Those first attempts begin with the naming of some important person or thing. English teachers would say the toddler has discovered nouns. By age two, the toddler has added verbs to his/her nouns. This noun-verb combination makes it possible to express a causal relationship."

Thus, equipped with just nouns and verbs, people of all ages can communicate meaning, which is the essence of the story structure. Whether elongated and protracted as in a novel or whether in the first stages of the mini or micro story, the noun-verb relationship organizes information for purposes of conveying meaning, comprehension and understanding.

Dr. Fuller continues beyond the noun-verb relation and says: "It doesn't take long before the toddler elaborates simple *story-engrams* with adjectives that describe the noun, and adverbs that describe the verb. With that accomplished, he/she experiments at attaching these elaborated *story-engrams* to each other with connectives and simple prepositions, thereby building an ever-bigger and sometimes complicated story. She/he is on the road to becoming expert in that peculiarly human way of structuring information; building with *story-engrams* complicated intellectual structures that make possible the understanding and communication of causal relationships and meanings. Our toddler has become a storyteller – something the computer cannot do. Contrary to those bits of information we humans tend to forget, the intellectual structures we build with *story-engrams* are easier for us to remember."

Therefore, not only is it easier to learn and remember in these basic units of stories, but more important, according to Dr. Fuller, *"story-engrams"* **function as our thinking units.** The more tools you have at your disposal to develop stories, the more capable you will be to think more effectively. Thus, in critiquing the traditional educational system and learning processes, Dr. Fuller writes that: "Bits of information cannot function as thinking units, that is unless we make *story-engrams* with them. Fundamental to human thinking is that we are story bound. Organizing the stimuli that surround us in story form is how we structure our world; how we make sense out of our environment; how we describe cause and effect relationships, and every other relationship."

We learned in **Chapter Two** that "Learning Style" is a frame of reference in which to receive information. So like any good author, one wants to know the audience, the reader or the listener in order to make the story relevant and interesting. And Learning Styles helps us with that customizing of information to make sure the learner "has it." As we proceed in **Chapters Four and Five**, you will discover alternative views of intelligence, which you will see provide a variety of ways of presenting information in a meaningful way or in a way which tells the story of information in several different ways. (You will find several important articles on human development, as well as the most comprehensive reading program at Dr. Fuller's web site - www.ballstickbird.com.

One of the most powerful ways of learning through the use of the story is with the assimilation of the Arts. Ivan Barzakov, Ph.D., remarkably survived a seven-mile, shark infested swim from Bulgaria to a refugee camp in 1979, where he taught until emigrating to the United States. In my last conversation with him, he was excited about the successful outcomes of learning when one surrounds oneself with art in an orchestrated and thematic way. Barzakov was quoted in an article by Hugh J. Delehanty of the San Francisco Focus Magazine as claiming that "In the West we are not trained to think globally or holistically. But the learning process does not consist of pieces of information or pieces of analysis. The learning process is a whole. Researchers have proved that memory doesn't exist in one specific part of the brain, or does it depend- as we thought before – on biofeedback or alpha states or special breathing. Memory depends on comprehension. Memory, analysis and comprehension are all one process." The ideal instructional process according to Barzakov, who was a protégé of Bulgaria's famous citizen Professor Georgi Lozonov, M.D., Ph.D. is a continuous flow of "messages that are both cognitive and artistic…and…the story flows into a song and the song flows into a game and the game flows into another story. And because everything is logical and interconnected, the overall effect is cumulative. Art is everywhere and learning is everywhere." Delehanty's complete article and other important articles are freely available from Dr. Barzakov at his web site- www.optimalearning.com.

My own experience in witnessing people of all ages learn more in less time with greater memory and creativity has been in the context of using storytelling, imagery, drama, skits, dialogues, poems, music, art, songs and raps. The key concepts and processes revealed in **Chapter Two** are available in a Rap video and audio instruction package with high school students singing and dancing the story line of "learning styles." (See www.intellilearn.org for more information on this and other learning products.) One extrapolation from the arts in the pursuit of learning and utilizing the brain and mind most effectively is in the use of storytelling and visual or guided imagery.

Dr. Anees Sheikh and I have collaborated on a few professional staff training projects to bring the use of the visioning, forecasting and imagination processes to improve learning among medical educators and medical personnel at all levels. He is the Chairman of the Psychology Department at Marquette University and is one of this nation's leading scholars of the Theory of Guided Imagery and "story-telling" and "story-recreation" as a vehicle for the enhancement of mental activity in education, medicine and therapy. In his book *Imagery in Education*, Dr. Sheikh assembles the thinking of several scholars who convey their research and beliefs about the importance of reviving and systematically renewing story-telling, visual and guided "imagery." Currently, guided imagery does not exist formally within teacher education curriculum, and usually the limited visualization that takes place is either on the playground or in the athletic program. "Pay attention!" and "Stop day-dreaming!" are symbolic of a thorough misunderstanding of the operation of the creative, story-telling brain.

That absence of knowledge and misunderstanding does not surface from maliciousness, but rather permeates our educational system as a cultural bias that has its roots in the Protestant Reformation. According to Dr. Sheikh, "The faculty of fantasy and imagination was held in high esteem in the West until the Renaissance. Then a dramatic re-evaluation took place and imagery was relegated to obscurity – where it remained until the 1960's, when a new and equally dramatic re-evaluation occurred."[14]

Only recently has the area of mental imagery and story telling been resurrected for scientific inquiry. It was buried in the Renaissance for many reasons. Protestant Reformationist Peter Ramus (1515-1572) can be credited with the demise of visual imagery from the process of communication and learning in Western Culture. As the age of reason emerged, Ramus developed a revolutionary system of education for the French schools that was tied to verbal memorization and linguistic performance. He shifted away from the Greek and Roman "pagan" strategies of oral traditions and myths with visual metaphor. Instead, he established a memory system that replaced mental images and was based on a hierarchical system of vocabulary that spread throughout Europe. The relatively new "printing press" provided a technological vehicle for the general diffusion of this "print" based linguistic strategy for memory and learning. From a neurological viewpoint, a shift occurred from right hemispheric visual memory to left hemispheric verbal memory.

Through Ramus' work, a major shift away from the scholastics occurred. The scholastics used imagery, metaphor and analogy as a part of prudence and the creative process. Imagery was also used in the teaching of a learning process about religious concepts and rituals. Jesus used the same parabolic teaching in His communication with the children, the general people, the Apostles, the rabbis and government leaders. (Under this view, gargoyles served as visual images of the existence of Satan and evil, as opposed to the more popular belief about their influence as relics of paganism and the occult.) Ramus swept away imagery as arbitrary, deceitful and capricious and replaced the process of teaching, remembering and learning with a linguistic dialectic-classification system of translating learning and retention to verbal processing.

That system evolved to its current status, which is exemplified in the standard I.Q. tests, Scholastic Achievement Examination, State Boards of Education Examinations and Standard Performance Examinations of all types throughout most of the professions.

A fresh approach has been gaining momentum in the past twenty-five years that challenges the wisdom of relying on a verbal mnemonic system for cognitive development. In part, this movement has been encouraged by the recent research in neuroscience in general and the "Split Brain Theory" in particular.

According to the late Professor Beverly-Colleene Galyean, "Influenced by advances in medical, biomedical, neurophysiological, and psychological research pointing to the desirable effects on physical, emotional and mental performance, some educators were quick to study and utilize adaptations of these techniques (Guided Imagery) in their respective education settings. A review of the literature related to affective/holistic education reveals that educators ordinarily use visualization and guided imagery activities in one or more of four ways:

1.   They employ it as a means of relaxing, centering and sharpening perception, thereby preparing individuals for the learning task at hand.

2.   They use it for teaching basic subject matter. This is referred to as "guided cognitive imagery."

3.   They see imagery as a vehicle for affective development, such as the increased awareness of inner senses and feelings and the expression of these wherever appropriate, expanded inner cognizance of personal images and symbols, introspective means to conflict resolution, culling feelings of self-love and appreciation, strengthening one's personal values schema and belief systems, and bonding with others. This is called "guided affective imagery."

4.   They utilize imagery as a means of recognizing and working with altered states of consciousness, experiencing energies beyond the normal field of awakened consciousness, probing the spiritual, mystical and transcendental aspects of life, experiencing concepts such as unity of being, oneness, wisdom, beauty, joy, love and self. This is labeled "guided transpersonal imagery."

These four types of imagery techniques often encompass health producing or health-maintaining activities, such as deep breathing, stress-reducing visualizations, sensory awareness, positive-thought producing and/or pleasureful memories, psychophysical visualizations and covert rehearsal strategies. These activities are being recommended by a growing number of health professionals in hopes that individuals will become increasingly more responsible for managing their own health care."[15]

Because of its association with right hemisphere performance, story telling, visualization and guided imagery become a conduit through which to achieve greater interaction, synchronicity or "wholeness" of brain performance. This has been attributed to combining the divergent right hemisphere (creativity) with the convergent left hemisphere (problem solving) in increasing health, well being, and hardiness.

The world of creativity, imagination, intuition and insight has been a necessary condition to all advances in human thought. Literature, history, anthropology and psychology are replete with accounts of "visions" that have given new paradigms and new models through which to understand human relations and the outer world. But in no area of human intellectual activity has the concept of "image" and "visual thinking" been more prominently expressed than in science by the scientific geniuses themselves.

When Albert Einstein reformed the electromagnetic theory, he began his famous Gedanken experiment in which he imagined himself traveling on a beam of light at nearly 200,000 miles per second. It was through that fantasy or imaginary perception of reality that a new concept of science was born. When Einstein spoke about his abilities, he said that he rarely thought in words, but rather in "visualizing...effects, consequences, and possibilities." (It is interesting to note that Albert Einstein did not talk until he was six years old.)

In J. C. Gowan's important article "The Production of Creativity Through the Right Hemisphere Imagery," he claims, "Right hemisphere (of the neo-cortex of the brain) is the vehicle through which incubation produces creativity. In his famous paradigm of the creative process, Graham Wallas (1926) identified four components: preparation, incubation, illumination, and verification. By incubation he meant any technique of relaxation of the conscious cognition (left hemisphere function) such as, but not confined to dreams, daydreams, fantasy hypnosis, meditation, diversion, play, etc., which allows subliminal processes (right hemisphere functions) to operate. He saw preparation (academic discipline), as the necessary and incubation (relaxation), as the sufficient condition for creative insights to emerge."[17]

What this means in pragmatic terms for both creativity and learning within education is suggested by Dr. Galyean in her summary of recent research on imagery, learning and behavior. She cites many research results where children's self-esteem rose, where they were more receptive to learning, where they thought more creatively, and where their communication skills increased, just to name a few. Although further research is needed in a variety of areas, the general consensus among theoreticians, such as Dr. Renee Fuller, and practitioners of reading, story-telling, visualization of goals and future states and Guided Imagery is that students who experience learning with visualization techniques are more attentive and less distracted, perform better on standard tests, are more involved in their work, learn more of the material taught, create more through their own imaginative talents, enjoy learning and school, do more original work, writing and organization, get along better with classmates and teachers, are more kind to one another and are more relaxed and confident.

As the Theory of Guided Imagery, story-telling and visualization evolve and as additional research shows the relationship and contribution to educational theory, as well as to improved personal performance and creativity, we might all come to a greater appreciation of Professor Ferguson's comments in *Science*, 1977: "Many features and qualities of the objects that a technologist thinks about cannot be reduced to unambiguous verbal descriptions; they are dealt with in his mind by a visual, nonverbal process. His mind's eye is a well developed organ that not only reviews the contents of his visual memory, but also forms such new or modified images as his thoughts require. It is nonverbal thinking, by and large, that has fixed the outlines and filled in the details of our material surroundings…Pyramids, cathedrals, and rockets exist not because of geometry, theory of structures or thermodynamics, but because they were first a picture – literally a vision – in the minds of those who built them."[18]

How much further can a child go if that process is neither stymied by a narrow focus of learning nor left to happenstance?

The "Q" Brain – The "four part" Quadra Brain that generates high performance

What we have learned about the brain so far is quite remarkable, don't you think? Indeed, the material discussed in this Chapter and its implication for learning, growth and happiness goes way beyond what is commonly known. Thus, what you have before you, in terms of the structure and function of the brain, can be used to empower your mind to operate more efficiently and effectively. However, there is another important consideration that is, perhaps, the most critical and recent perspective of the human brain and mind. I developed and implemented this Model of the Brain-Body-Mind when working with "closed head injured" and stroke patients in Syracuse, New York. What I did was to assimilate the Theory of the Triune Brain with the notion that the human "Heart" is the fourth component of the "brain-heart-mind-body" system. Not only is the heart geographically connected to the brain through nerve connections, but the functioning of the brain improves to a level of "whole brain activation," as a result of engaging the heart in conscious thinking and learning.

Recall Paul McLean's "three brains in one" which we reviewed and discussed? Well the mid-brain or the "limbic" system, which is responsible for many functions, including processing all information in terms of "fear, threat and intimidation," as well as converting experience into long-term memory, is connected directly to the heart. And that connection is made with nerve linkages, including the Vagus Nerve, which links the heart to the brain and the brain with the heart, with two pathways going from one to another. In the past, it was thought that the brain communicated with the heart and it was a one-way street – from brain to heart! Now we know that it works *both* ways and the heart does communicate and influence the brain.

What is more important for learning, health and happiness is that when the heart is engaged with love, joy, peace, respect, patience and dignity, (much like the "enriched" environment described by Marion Diamond in increasing brain growth and capacity) the brain increases its capability to learn, perform and remember. Some colleagues of mine who lead the Heart-Math Institute trained a Fortune 100 manufacturing division in processes which enable one to change heart rate variability and generate chemicals that are positive. This is one of the top 100 companies in the world and in this particular division, 26% of the employees suffered from high blood pressure. After using strategies for the heart, many of which are contained in this book, six months later, no one was on medication for high blood pressure. And, eighteen months after learning relaxation strategies and neuro-linguistic processes and "guided imagery," the division *doubled* the number of patents it submitted to the Federal Trade and Patent Office. This is a remarkable testimony to the power of the heart to influence the performance of the mind. Moreover, as we shall learn in the next Chapter, research is discussed that indicates that the human heart has its own brain, memory, thinking and communication system that can make the brain perform at unanticipated high levels of achievement.

Thus, a comprehensive view of the brain, compels us to acknowledge the physical and functional *"heart connection"* which is best described as the *"Q" Brain* or Quadra Brain, signifying the four components of the Heart-Brain System which function well together, when permitted to function together with proper training, habituation, disposition and environment. The "Q" Brain perspective is reinforced in the next Chapter, along with strategies, tactics and tools revealed throughout the remainder of this book to develop the optimal functioning of the "brain-mind-heart-body" system. Leave out the "heart connection" and you minimize and depreciate human cognition, consciousness and compassion.

The Third Secret Revealed

In the light of criticisms from neuroanatomists and other educational theorists who churn at the oversimplification of "Left Brain-Right Brain" research, it is useful to keep in mind that whether or not these theories can be taken literally, as models they provide valuable insights for understanding the educational process. Indeed, it is not as important to be concerned with lateralization or whether a specific function takes place in a particular part of the brain, as to understand that these functions do occur and there are possible ways of enhancing those functions in all of us. And it is toward that end that we explore, understand and apply the neuro-scientific research to enhance learning performance and achievement to realize the *miracle of learning.*

ACTION ITEMS:

1. Use the "Think and Listen" technique. This can be done with others by pairing up. It can be two adults, a child and an adult or two siblings. Pick a topic and one person speaks for two minutes without interruption or feedback. The listener simply gives loving attention and nods of appreciation. Then, the timer says switch and the listener speaks for two minutes, while the former speaker gives undivided attention. This activity can also be done in five, ten or thirty minute segments. The "think and listen" helps the visual, auditory and kinesthetic learner to listen and appreciate other people and develop creative ideas. Too often we complete each other's sentences and thoughts, without regard to the feelings of the "Limbic" mind. This strategy will help everyone listen through the heart. (See **Chapter Five**)

2. Remember how angels fly? They take themselves lightly! Laugh, tickle, enjoy and celebrate. Research shows that belly laughter increases health and hardiness. If scowling, criticizing and negativity are in your disposition, read and take self-help courses to develop your positive perspective. You can order any of the following from the public library and have a great learning experience at no cost. Read any of the books by physicians Larry Dossey, M.D. or Bernie Siegal, M.D., as well as Norman Vincent Peale's books, particularly *The Power of Positive Thinking*, Norman Cousin's, *The Anatomy of an Illness* and Scott Peck's *The Road Less Traveled and Beyond*.

Go on line to the Anthony Robbins Companies at webmaster@tonyrobbins.com to find the dates and locations of his seminars, and attend one of his seminars.

References

[1] MacLean, Paul, *Education and the Brain,* p. 308.
[2] Penfield, Wilder, *Epilepsy and the Functional Anatomy of the Human Brain*, Little Brown Medical Division, 1985.
[3] Pribram, Karl H., *Brain and Behavior*, Penguin.
[4] Sperry, Roger, *Education and the Brain*, NCCE, 1978, p. 40.
[5] Rosenweig, Mark, *Annual Review of Psychology*, 1975.

[6] Diamond, Marian, *Enriching Heredity: The Impact of the Environment on theAnatomy of the Brain*, New York: The Free Press, 1988.

[7] *ibid,* p. 54-55.

[8] *ibid*, p. 53.

[9] Pert, Candace, *The Molecules of Emotion: Why You Feel the Way You Feel*, Scribner, 1997.

[10] Epstein, Herman, *A Strategy for Education*, Oxford University Press, 1992, p. 344.

[11] *ibid,* p. 345.

[12] *ibid,* p. 362.

[13] *ibid,* p. 363.

[14] Sheikh, Anees, Dr., *Imagery in Education: Imagery in the Educational Process*, Baywood Publishing Co., 1995.

[15] Galyean, Beverly-Colleene, *Mind Sights*, Zephyr Press, 1984.

[17] Gowan, J.C., "The Production of Creativity through the Right Hemisphere Imagery"

[18] Ferguson, *Science*, 1997.

[19] This is based upon www.Learningstyles.net on the Dunn & Dunn Learning Styles Model

SECRET #4
Revealed.
Your Heart COMMUNICATES.

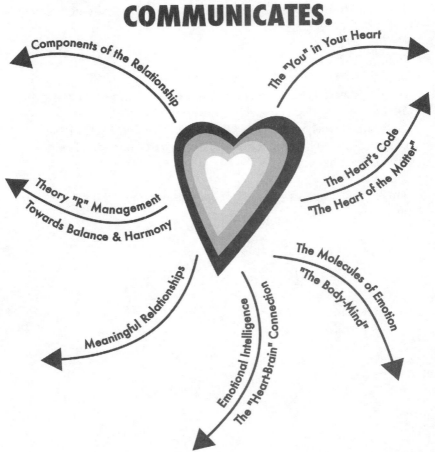

Components of the Relationship

The "You" in Your Heart

Theory "R" Management
Towards Balance & Harmony

The Heart's Code
"The Heart of the Matter"

Meaningful Relationships

The Molecules of Emotion
"The Body-Mind"

Emotional Intelligence
The "Heart-Brain" Connection

Chapter Four

Secret #4
Your Heart Communicates

Learn how your heart thinks, remembers, and energizes the mind for better learning and improved relationships.

D o you remember the song "If I give my heart to you, will you handle it with care?" Or have you ever heard the musical rendition, "Heart of my heart, how I love that melody; Heart of my heart, brings back fond memories!"? If these are not familiar, perhaps you can think of a popular song that includes the word "heart." It shouldn't be difficult. The world's songbooks are filled with themes about the human heart. Literature, drama and movies also reference the role of the heart in human happiness and disappointment, human comedy and tragedy.

Consider the children's book *The Wizard of Oz*, written by Frank L. Baum and popularized in the 1939 movie with Judy Garland. In her journey to return home, Dorothy met up with three friends who were in search of a missing part of their character. The scarecrow needed a "brain," while the lion needed "courage." And the tin man was incomplete because he didn't have a "heart." It turns out that they already had these elements, but *they* didn't realize they had them. The popular 1970's song portrays this by saying, "*Oz didn't give nothin' to the tin man that he didn't already have.*" The moral: You might not recognize that you have them, but as a human, you were created with "courage, brain and heart" or "determination, intelligence and love."

For centuries, the heart has been a symbol of love and kindness. I'd venture to guess that just about all of us associate the "heart" with love and emotions. Just think of Valentine's Day as an example of when we draw an image of the "heart" on all sorts of cards and gifts to express love to one another. We buy chocolates that are made in the shape of a heart, and we buy gift boxes that resemble hearts. The bottom line is that the heart in our culture is associated with love and empathy, with emotions and sympathy.

What would you think if I told you that the human heart has its own brain inside it, that it thinks and has memories? Indeed, there is a body of research proving that the human heart has its own brain and that it pumps thoughts and memories to all of the body's cells! Pretty startling, isn't it? Well it is true; the heart is not just a pump, but it is also a thinking brain that can make happiness possible in your life, because it determines the success of the "miracle of learning" in your life. Learning becomes more miraculous and ever present when the human heart is engaged. Without it, your life can be as miserable as "Scrooge" in the Dickens' story *The Christmas Carol*, or it can be as fulfilled as the life of "Tiny Tim," who always perceived the world from his heart.

The You in Your Heart

When you think about yourself, where is the *"you"* you think about? Are *"you"* in your head, like the "scarecrow," or in your heart, like the "tin man?" For centuries, philosophers, theologians and scientists have been debating the question about the location of the "self" or the human soul. In the past, the answer has been either in the brain or the heart, but not both. Today, the research is clear that there are many of "you" located in both the heart and brain, with different functions. For example, in the past, we thought that memory was only in the brain in the skull. Now, we know differently! It might be that memory is contained in all parts of the brain and body.

This idea comes, in part, from the Heart Transplant research. There are two thousand human heart transplants each year in the United States alone. Approximately two thirds of the heart transplant patients take on some memories, traits, characteristics or hobbies of the heart donor, long after the donor's death. In other words, the lady who never danced and who got the heart of a person who was a ballroom dancer started taking ballroom dancing lessons within three months after her operation. She does not know from whom or from where her new heart came. All she knows is that she is now passionate about her new hobby of ballroom dancing.

In this chapter, you will learn how we know that the human heart has its own brain. We will also find out how the heart influences how well or poorly the brain in our skull works. And we will examine how our *"heart-brain"* process can lead to our unfolding the "miracle of learning." Additionally, we will examine how the heart and brain work together to form an "intelligence" of its own, called the "emotional intelligence," as opposed to what our society values as "I.Q." We will then introduce a strategy for human growth, learning and happiness, based on developing and harvesting relationships.

The Heart's Code – "The Heart of the Matter"

Why does the brain grow and develop under a positive climate and deteriorate under a negative environment? Heart transplant researcher, Paul Pearsall, Ph.D., has an answer.

Dr. Paul Pearsall uncovered the medical and scientific research that proves "that the human heart, not the brain, holds the secrets that link body, mind and spirit." Pearsall acknowledges in his book *The Heart's Code*, published in 1998, what we all have experienced about the heart; namely, "You know that the heart loves and feels, but did you know that the heart also thinks, remembers, communicates with other hearts, helps regulate immunity, and contains stored information that continually pulses through your body?" In the new fields of energy cardiology and "cardio-psychology," new theories and scientific discoveries have emerged that lead to the conclusion that "The heart is not just a pump; it conducts the cellular symphony that is the very essence of our being."

What does this mean? It means at least two things for us in our daily lives. First, if you do not actively engage your heart in all of your life's activities, then your life will be less complete, less fulfilling, and less rewarding. This message is not new to you or to me. The ancient Scriptures constantly repeat this truth, as do modern psychologists like Leo Buscaglia and Dr. "Phil."

Second, it means that if the heart is disconnected from the "survival oriented" brain through fear, threat and intimidation and stress, the brain in your skull will suffer damage and parts of it might shrink. This causes "brain damage" and a poorer performing brain, and it increases the potential for disease and sickness. If, on the other hand, the brain is enriched by the connection with the heart, through the heart's code of positive emotions, with the flood of all the positive chemistry of endorphins that are present in acts of love, kindness, goodness, and gentleness, then the brain in the skull grows with increased neuronal connectivity. This leads to an enhanced brain, functioning with creativity, problem solving, and inventiveness through the heart's connection. Furthermore, it makes more probable a life of unfolding the "miracle of learning."

Is your heart thinking now about the meaning of these words? Probably. Your heart has a code that thinks and remembers independently from the brain. As such, your heart is the conductor of a symphony of your life's experiences.

But what are the musicians and instruments that the heart employs to influence your brain and create the "cellular symphony that is the very essence of life?" Dr. Pearsall answers this question from four sources of research:

1. Personal and professional clinical experience;
2. Indigenous cultures, such as the Hawaiian people;
3. Heart transplant recipients and their stories;
4. Theories and research from the new cardio-sciences.

"By combining aspects of all of the above…(*four*)… sources of support for the possibility of the existence of the heart's…*brain*…, you can make your own judgment as to whether further study of its existence is merited, and you can choose whether or not to be alert for what your heart has to say about the way you live, work, and love," Pearsall writes.[1](Italics are mine).

What would your heart say about the way you live, work and love? Do you start and end the day with joy in your heart, as "Tiny Tim" did. And if you lived your life with love and kindness, guided by your heart's code, what would the brain say about this?

Imagine for a moment that the brain could talk. Let's listen in to what it might say about the "heart" having its own brain and influence on the success in life. Pretend you are Ray Bolger who played the part of the *scarecrow* who was seeking a brain in the **Wizard of Oz.** Read the passage aloud as if you were the scarecrow who found the brain and now the brain is speaking:

"Well," says the brain, "I am remarkable and have developed over billions of years. I like to be aloof from the other systems of the body, especially the heart, and my entire goal is self-preservation. Some say I am exclusively designed to think, but that is not entirely true. The 'thinking' part of me is crumpled up above two other parts of me: my Limbic System (my location of emotions and long-term memory processing) and the R-Complex reptilian brain function (which controls my reactive, survival instincts, territoriality and pecking order.) I see others around me and the world at large as food for thought and a means to my personal and individual needs and wants. Some have named my three parts as 'id, ego and super-ego.' But 'id' best describes me! Without the influence of the heart, there would be no Ego or Super Ego. My concern for others is limited to the frontal portions of the neo-cortex and parts of the limbic system, which are directly connected to the heart through the vagus nerve. My mission, as a brain, is to keep myself alive with as much pleasure and avoidance of pain as possible. As far as connecting on an emotional level with caring and love, that is only my secondary function with the heart's effort to influence me."

For over two hundred years, we have built a society and institutions that reinforce the *brain-centric* focus. Any attention to "empathy, compassion, gentleness and love" has been relegated to a "second class" status of emotions and subjectivity or limited to the realm of churches, mosques and synagogues. Some argue that the separation of "church-state" mania among an alarmed few has pulled the heart and love out of the secular world altogether. Indeed, the separation of church & state mania has pulled the heart and love out of the secular domain. Recently in a conference, a school administrator said: "Yes, those are the feely-touchy things that get in the way of the bottom line results of learning."

If this sounds cynical, it is! According to Pearsall, "Once the brain has abused the heart with its clearly cynical code of self-preservation above all else, and driven the heart beyond its physiological limits, it can burn out its own life-support systems. The heart is the most powerful muscle in the human body, but even it can be strained and torn by the pressures applied by a stressed and stressful brain. In its potentially lethal covenant with its body, the brain never shuts up. It is designed to constantly be on some level of alert. Even as you dream, it tries to get your attention. It is in a state of perpetual readiness to react, defend, or attack when it or its body senses threats – real or not – to its self-enhancement. The brain is mortality phobic. Its greatest fear is its own end or any conscious state that seems to approximate the selflessness that the brain may experience as the end of its existence. ...The brain is self-protective and territorial. Its code is 'I'm, mine.' A natural pessimist, it evolved to expect and anticipate the worst as a form of self-defense left over from our primitive ancestors' necessary constant vigilance for outside threats."[2]

Consequently, the focus of the brain is "self centered" and "self–absorbed," making it almost impossible to function in a group with others without the presence of the heart. The research on serial killers shows the absence of early childhood hugging, rocking and parental loving relationships. In Canada, with David Lockett's initiative in reducing youth offender recidivism, a program that focuses on heartfelt feelings of the victim, families of the victim and families of the youth offender merge to re-frame the emotions and conscientiousness of the acts of aggression. The program has reduced recurrent offences from 42% recidivism to 0%.

"The energy that attracts and comes from the brain seems to be a darker, ready-to-fight, more negative energy than that of the heart," Pearsall concludes. Thus, a new "heart-brain" model for human learning is critical for personal growth and happiness. Dr. Larry Dossey is a surgeon who has written extensively about the role of negative thoughts and sickness. Writing about the role of unhappiness in health, Dossey points out that: "It is as if all our potential thoughts are a roulette wheel of possibilities, with only a single red, positive slot amid thousands of black, negative ones." But, if you engage the heart, you dramatically increase the number of red slots, increasing your chances of positive outcomes.

How, then, should we understand the *heart-brain* connection and its implication for learning, health and happiness. First of all, we must avoid the health hazards of a dominant brain that fosters stress and strain, utilizes energy for "selfish" purposes, disconnects us from others and distances us from "smelling the roses." You will never live a full and happy life if you live in accordance with the rules of the *"brain."* Rather than a popular "self-help" book written by the brain, the heart's book would be more like an "us help" book. The "us help" book would have four principles that I have paraphrased from Dr. Paul Pearsall and would provide four essential health advisories:

1.   Strengthen and enhance your heart by over-riding your brain's pre-occupation with "self survival" and its self-fulfilling demands that lead to continuous anxiety, stress and physical strain on the heart.

2.   Support and develop your heart by allowing it to be joyous and connected to the service of others in counter balance to your brain, which will expend its resources and energy for the "self" directed purposes.

3.   Engage and activate the heart's energy, intelligence and memory in the connection with others through love and kind-

ness and through service to others. This avoids your brain's natural tendency to push you away and disconnect you from the hearts of others, especially the ones you love (remember the popular song about "When we argue we often hurt the ones we love the most.")

4. Let the heart be in control some of the time, so you can "smell the roses," hold a baby in your arms, listen to the morning birds sing and just appreciate the beauty of creation in everything around you. Your brain is so preoccupied with staying alive and reacting to events that it often overlooks the purpose of life. We are so busy making a living that we often forget to enjoy our lives with appreciation and gratitude.

With these four heart advisories or "recommendations" in view, Pearsall concludes that the heart recognizes that human happiness and human success is a "...result of a more gentle, balance, caring, connected, and loving orientation to the world."[3] Indeed, ancient scriptures, such as the Bible, are filled with references to the heart and its role in human happiness. The New Testament, for example, defines the "Fruits of the Spirit" as energy from the heart: "Love, Joy, Peace, Goodness, Patience, Kindness," (Gal 5:22).

I want to emphasize that the miracle story of Michael told in Chapter One, and countless others who worked with me in our Head Injury Clinic, began the journey toward rehabilitation first and foremost through a positive connection to the heart. Building trust, confidence and affection with the patients was the crucial breakthrough that explained the remarkable advances in cognitive gains from the treatment. Although we did not have the scientific evidence to support our strategy, the tapping of the wellspring of the human heart had everything to do with the brain's recovery. Also at the level of social policy, the State of New York enacted legislation to enable disadvantaged youth to enter private colleges and universities – individuals who would otherwise be unable to attend such schools. Along with others at Syracuse University, I wrote a proposal with Tom Benzel and Tom Cummings to obtain grant money to establish the first, part-time college program for disadvantaged adults, most of whom were women of African American ancestry. The graduation rate was astounding and the research showed that it was the *supportive services* which included counseling, tutoring and special courses which made the difference between success and failure. In short, it was those strategies which built positive relationships and generated "heartfelt" optimism which enabled the kind of success which we and other programs across the state had.

This view is critical to the healthy development and full use of your brain and your heart. Its importance is not only psychological and social in your relationships with others, but it is also physical. Your physical health and hardiness depend on your learning how to engage the world around you in a more balanced and loving way. The physiology of your being depends on this, precisely because every emotion you permit yourself to express is made up of chemicals, some of which enhance you and your immune system, while others erode your health and make you sick. Fortunately, you can choose which is dominant in your life. If you choose the life-enhancing chemicals to flood your body, you will be choosing a "heart-brain" life, with reduced fear, threat, intimidation and putdowns. In short, it will be a life of "emotional intelligence" with love, joy, peace, kindness, goodness and patience.

The Molecules of Emotion – The Body-Mind

Taking the view of emotional intelligence and its influences even beyond the specific geography of either the brain or the heart to the cellular level, Dr. Candace Pert takes the subjectivity out of emotions and reveals good science in her brilliant book *The Molecules of Emotion*. Dr. Pert moves beyond separate components of the body-parts and introduces the notion of a "body-mind" *system* in which receptors at the cellular level throughout the body are in *constant communication* with thinking and memory existing at the level of the cell.

Pert writes, "Emotional states or moods are produced by the various neuro-peptide ligands (*chemical structures*), and what we experience as an emotion or a feeling is also a mechanism for activating a particular neuronal circuit (*at the level of the neuron cell*) – *simultaneously throughout the brain and body* (*including the heart*) – which generates a behavior involving the whole creature with all the necessary physiological changes that behavior would require. This fits nicely with Paul Ekman's elegant formulation that each emotion is experienced throughout the organism and not in just the head or the body, and has a corresponding facial expression. It's part of a constellation of bodily changes that occurs with each shift of subjective feeling."[4]

So, negativity, whether generated from others or from one's own negative energy field of "self-talk" generates chemical states and brain physiology that can shrink the brain and reduce mental capability and capacity. This state of negative emotion is as real in its physical damage as it is when having a head injury from an auto accident or a stroke from untreated high blood pressure.

On the other hand, positive emotions generated by the heart and heart energy flood the entire body-mind with chemicals called "neuro-peptides," which can enhance brain growth, improve brain-heart function and increase health, hardiness and happiness. Research on anger shows that when recalling an incident of being embittered or recalling an incident that makes you mad, the efficiency of the heart drops from five to seven percent in pumping capacity. This is a drop in blood flow considered dangerous by cardiologists. Remember this result of blood flow reduction was not in actually being angry and mad; it was from simply *recalling and recounting* the incident. Imagine the effect at the moment of anger. So, shall we bring on the anger management teams? [5]

How does this information feel to you? What could this mean to you and your loved ones? Have you got the picture? Do you like the sound of what you just read? How will you act in accordance with what you now know? Can you improve yourself to strengthen your heart-brain connection and the quality of your life? Will you accept the challenge to develop strategies to do the right thing at the right time with the right response with the right people?

ACTION ITEM:
Keep a log in your journal or daily planner and list all the negative things that happened to you on a given day. Then write how it made you feel and what your thoughts were. Also, keep a log on all the positive or good things that happened and how those made you think and feel. Go over what you wrote the next day and determine which is better for your health and hardiness, and practice responding to ALL events as if they were positive and that you can see something positive in them, even if it is negative at first reaction.

In his book *The Nicomachean Ethics*, the Greek Philosopher Aristotle wrote, "Anyone can become angry – that is easy. But to be angry with the right person, to the right degree, at the right time, for the right purpose, and in the right way – this is not easy." Making the right response was, for Aristotle, a definition of "justice."

To make the "just" response easier (that is to say what is good for you, right for you and just for you and others), we need to engage in the "miracle of learning" in order to create the "heart-brain," body-mind connection to make life enjoyable with balance, harmony and success.

Emotional Intelligence – The "Heart-Brain" Connection

A good brain, without a good heart, just doesn't seem to get people where they would like to go. They often end up ill, abandoned and alone as social outcasts. This does not mean that we abandon the brain's development. Rather, it means that you will not be as successful in fulfilling your purpose and dreams unless you develop both your brain and heart in tandem. When you develop your "heart-brain," you achieve wisdom, in addition to joy, happiness and abundance. You can also achieve efficiency and effectiveness. We find that increases in all kinds of measures of mental performance skyrocket when the heart is openly and actively engaged.

In my work with companies like Eastman Kodak, GulfStream Aerospace, and Sara Lee Knit Products, they experienced documented accelerated learning and increased retained revenues when they tapped into the heart-brain processes of the Model of Learning I designed. School districts all over the country from Harlem to the Apache Reservation witnessed unprecedented and unexpected increases in student learning outcomes by invoking the heart-brain strategies of the *IntelliLearn® Model* detailed later in **Chapter Seven**. Dorothy Joseph, one of the school principals who implemented the "heart-brain" model of *IntelliLearn®* in Brooklyn, New York under support of The Honorable Regent Adelaide Sanford and the New York State Black and Puerto Rican Legislative Caucus, published her successes in her award winning book, *A Tale of Two Systems*.

Unfortunately, despite what we currently know from the research of applying "heart-brain" models for learning, our society emphasizes the *brain* as the "king of the hill" when it comes to life and intelligence, while either disregarding "emotions" altogether or treating them as "feely-touchy." Our culture and other Western societies, along with Asian industrialized societies, value traditional academic intelligence tests as well as standardized achievement tests, virtually all of which are derived from the I.Q. Test, which is a paper pencil examination of your logical-mathematical and linguistic performance. The purpose of these tests is to predict people's futures by determining their intelligence and achievement levels, and to sort them and select them for life's chances, including placement in remedial programs and gifted and talented programs.

Just take a look at the newspaper headlines and read the accounts of state and national test scores for children. Every state except Iowa (which oddly enough has the highest standardized scores among the nation's children), has grade level standards and, constantly tests its children on academic, paper-pencil tests to determine achievement levels. I think this is going to backfire, as an increasing number of children think they are under a constant microscope that is forever determining their worthiness as humans.

Teachers in both Hawaii and North Carolina recently told me of the increasing numbers of students at all grade levels who simply put their names on the standard test and then doodle the bubble circles on the score sheet. So much for assessing achievement! Also, recently at a Chicago conference, the leader of a high school informed me that the school had been on probationary status for poor performance since the tests began in 1995. Seven years have passed with little or no improvement in the outcomes. Perhaps that is because they have done little to change the processes to improve the outcomes. And we know that the research is loud and clear: "If you want to improve the outcomes, you must focus on the processes that produce the outcomes you want." Thus, if you want to improve the outcomes of the brain, you must engage the processes of the heart.

In further support of this view of improving the quality of mental performance by connecting the heart in *"heart-brain"* processes, there have been many psychologists who have advanced the cause of *"emotions."* In his recent book ***Emotional Intelligence***, Daniel Goleman, Ph.D. pulls together research from neurosciences and cognitive psychology to support the notion that I.Q. (Intelligence Quotient) has an important counterpart called E.Q. (Emotional Quotient). Having academic achievement, without emotional achievement is not a winning formula. Research shows that heart-brain models of learning generate significant increases in learning performance, as in the case of the Dunn and Dunn award-winning Learning Styles Model (see **Chapter Two**). Research also shows that academic achievement has little to do with performance after formal school is over.

For example, Goleman documents the success of ninety-five Harvard graduates who were followed through middle age. He found that the "men with the highest test scores in college were not particularly successful compared to their lower-scoring peers in terms of salary, productivity, or status in their field. Nor did they have the greatest life satisfaction, nor the most happiness with friendships, family and romantic relationships."[6] In another study of four hundred and fifty sons of immigrants, IQ scores did not correlate to later life success. It was "...childhood abilities such as being able to handle frustrations, control emotions and get on with other people who made the greater difference."

What makes a difference for people in terms of health, hardiness and happiness is a balance of the emotional intelligence and the academic intelligence. Combining those activities and strategies that reinforce both the emotional climate and the academic culture of positive "heart-brain" processes provides the balance wheel for personal success.

Our culture is currently out of balance. Why are there so many school shootings, with countless assaults from young children talking about "getting revenge" on those who make them feel alone, unwanted and alienated? Being out of balance creates all sorts of dysfunction. Do you recall the two high school students from Texas who dated each other and were the top students in their schools? Both received "Commissions" to the National Academies, with one going to the Air Force and the other to the Coast Guard. Well, when they were still in high school, the girl found out that the boy had dated another girl. This created a jealous rage, and to prove his devotion, the boy and his jealous girlfriend led the other girl out into an unsuspecting car ride and killed her. The top academic students who had little moral fabric and no emotional control are now imprisoned for life.

Boston University professor Karen Arnold studied valedictorians and salutatorians from the class of 1981 in the mid-west. All had the highest grades in high school and went on to do well in college. However, as they arrived into their late twenties, they were achieving only average levels of success. "Ten years after graduating from high school, only one in four were at the highest level of young people of comparable age in their chosen profession, and many were doing much less well.

"I think we've discovered the 'dutiful' – people who know how to achieve in the system," notes Arnold. "But valedictorians struggle as surely as we all do. To know that a person is a valedictorian is to know only that he or she is exceedingly good at achievement as measured by grades. It tells you nothing about how they react to the vicissitudes of life." [7]

And it tells us nothing about their stress levels or their capacity to emotionally transcend life's challenges. In one major longitudinal study of medical students at Johns Hopkins University, it was found that two variables or items on the entrance psychological evaluation strongly correlated with the students' relatively early death after they were physicians. A poor relationship with their parents and an emotional temperament that did not explode and get angry, but rather, "took it, and took it, and took it, until they imploded." These physicians went on to die of cancer or heart disease.

However, had they learned to balance the "heart-brain" functions, they might have gone on to have happy and lengthy careers of service to patients. By learning "heart-brain" strategies of those "relaxation responses" developed by Herbert Benson, M.D. at Harvard, "Guided Imagery" processes developed by Psychologist Anees Sheik, Ph.D. at Marquette University, or "musical affirmation tapes" invented by psychologist John Ortiz, Ph.D., these physicians might have flourished, rather than have suffered the pain and agony of uncontrolled stress and anxiety.

"Much evidence testifies that people who are emotionally adept – *who know and manage their own feelings well* and who read and deal effectively with other people's feelings – are at an advantage in any domain of life…. People with well developed emotional skills are also more likely to be content and effective in their lives, mastering the habits of mind that foster their own productivity; people who *cannot* marshal some control over their emotional life *fight inner battles that sabotage their ability* for focused work and clear thought," says Goleman.[8]

Building *your* personal "*heart-brain*" relationship, which determines physiology and your chemical make-up, including facial expressions and body language, is the first business of learning and should be the curriculum for a life of continuous growth, improvement and service. However, we all know that our selfish selves cannot live in a vacuum. We must grow and develop in the context of our relationships with others. And if you simply view "others" as an extension of yourself, then you will want a healthy and balanced interaction and relationship with those in your world. This balance and effort toward character development will even guide your feelings and attitudes toward others, including strangers and perceived foes. Might this be expressed in the ancient, but not often followed, wisdom of "love your enemies?"

Toward that end, we want to turn to the process of "relationship" building. It is in our capacity and capability to build "heart-felt" relationships that moves us one step further in the evolution of shifting from a *brain-based system* to a *heart-brain system* with the flow of endorphins as a chemical wash of love, health, happiness, abundance and peace.

Toward Meaningful Relationships

Since my early days at Syracuse University, with funding from a variety of sources, including the National Institute of Education and The Fund for the Improvement of Postsecondary Education, my work has concentrated on the "human" side of cognitive development and educational policy. This means that the emphasis was on those factors that build the best in people and allow people to achieve their potential in both personal learning and achievement in areas of work, family life and community relationships. The key to success in individual and organizational learning and performance is in developing relationship processes to help people achieve "process" ways of perceiving and engaging in the world with others. The success stories and case studies throughout this book and in Appendix A are evidence of the commitment to developing the "heart-brain" processes. These four "heart-brain" processes are:

1. Learning to learn;
2. Learning to choose;
3. Learning to relate;
4. Learning to create.

I felt that all four of these "process ways" were critical to any learning system or organization that would empower people, young and old, to function as independent thinkers and decision makers, whose emotional balance is constantly challenged in a rapidly changing society that requires learning and creative problem solving.

Supporting this view of personal growth and development in the context of relationship building is another author whose book, co-authored with his daughter, is exemplary and mirrors my own research. It sets the framework for employing the research on the *"heart-brain"* system outlined above, along with cultivating E.Q. or emotional intelligence. The book, *Theory "R" Management*, written by Wayne T. Alderson and Nancy Alderson McDonnell, is profound in its focus, consistency and application to personal and organizational achievement, in the context of managing *"relationships."* Published in 1994, the book anticipates the later research depicted and discussed in this book that supports Theory "R" Management in the emphasis on people loving one another, while constantly building relationships of trust and integrity. Although arguably rare in business, education and public policy, a focus on "relationships" is the bottom line of any successful family, organization, corporation or democratic nation.

Theory "R" Management – Toward Balance and Harmony

As I mentioned earlier in this chapter, when Aristotle, who has influenced the entire history of Western thought, wrote about acting toward another individual, as in the case of "anger" above, he wrote of "justice" as "doing the right thing (whether it was being angry or any other action), at the right time, with the right person, under the right circumstances. In other words, Aristotle defined the "just" relationship as the "appropriate" relationship, in accordance with first principles of ethics.

This requires both knowledge and thinking along the lines presented in the remaining chapters of this book. One must learn to learn, learn to choose, learn to relate and learn to create. These four process goals elevate us to a level of consciousness about our relationships and interaction with others. There is no "one size fits all" formula for relationship building, although there are first principles. What the Aldersons have contributed is a guidebook for the identification and application of those first principles to personal and organizational development and operation. The content and skills in their book features "relationships" as the foundation to human conduct, performance and success. The Alderson writes that:

> "Every person has a need for relationships. Relationships encompass a give-and-take with other people. They include communication, care, shared experiences, and a feeling of commonality. A person's need for relationship doesn't stop at the factory gate or cease to exist the minute the person steps off the elevator into the department. Relationships make any enterprise meaningful and fulfilling.

> "Furthermore the strength of a relationship always has a definite impact on the human being's ability and desire to do relationship related tasks (such as carrying out roles and responsibilities of teaching and learning, husband and wife, parenting and leadership at all levels).

> "Leave the workplace and think about a marriage for a moment. The spouse who is in a great relationship with the partner in marriage may not like taking out the trash or doing the laundry, but the person is a lot more willing to do the tasks that are related to the relationship if the relationship itself is a good

one – marked by mutually and shared commitment – than if the relationship is sour.

"Within the workplace, the same dynamic is evident. Employees who enjoy working with their colleagues, bosses, and subordinates and who have an ongoing healthy relationship with them are a lot more willing to work, even at tasks they may not find pleasurable.

"All the money, all the benefits, and all the added features of the workplace can't create relationships. Small groups (*quality circles in business or cooperative learning in schools*) may provide a means of putting people together, but even they do not in and of themselves create relationships.

"People create relationships. And *create* is the operative word. Those that have been engineered usually turn out to be big disasters. Relationships are built by people who find ways and means of sharing things, experiences, ideas, feelings, and processes that are mutually meaningful to all parties involved.

"Relationships are also fragile. They take work to make them strong. They require time and effort. They don't emerge full-blown and strong overnight. And even the most solid relationship can be shattered by uncaring actions or hurtful words. (*One of the great lies perpetuated in our culture is that "sticks and stones may break my bones but names or words will never hurt me." Names and words can destroy a person or a relationship for a lifetime. That may have been the trigger and underlying basis of the Columbine, Colorado school disaster*).
"Above all, relationships are valuable. They are the true stuff that makes life meaningful."[9] (Italics are mine)

What keeps a relationship from being developed and what seeps in when a relationship is faltering is the negative emotion "fear." In his book, ***Human Brain; Human Learning***, Leslie Hart called this experience of fear "downshifting" in referring to Paul MacLean's model of the triune brain and my extension of that into the "Q" Brain, which includes the Heart as a component. The "Q" Brain Model shows us that the neo-cortex functions best when the limbic system is engaged with positive emotions. Also, the R-Complex was satisfied with no fear, threat, intimidation or putdowns. So positive emotions are proven to be a key to learning and long-term memory. That shift from to the "R-Complex" is accompanied with the surge of chemicals in the body-mind, which prepares a person for "fight or flight." The presence of "fear, threat, intimidation and putdowns" (including negative humor that feeds off sabotaging other people by laughing *AT* them, rather than uplifting humor, which laughs *WITH* them), destroys the conditions for problem identification, problem solving and creativity. When fearful, people of all ages shut down into a level of "survival mode."

Living in fear, threat, intimidation, anxiety and stress not only makes you "feel" bad, but that state of emotion is filled with chemicals (including the stress hormone: gluco-corticoid hydrocortisone) which, on a long term basis, can erode the body's systems and actually shrink the brain and cause memory impairment. According to Stanford University Professor of Biological Sciences Robert Sapolsky, people with long-term stress from traumatic events suffer a shrinkage of up to fifteen percent in the "hippocampus," which is the part of the limbic system that controls a variety of learning processes and memory. Although conducting his research from Palo Alto, California, Sapolsky studied four university groups from around the country. The research showed that the elevated levels of stress hormones shrank the brain because it killed the brain's communication cells and branches, called "neurons and neuronal dendrites."

As detailed in **Chapter Three** in this book, leading brain scientists Marion Diamond and Karl Rosenzweig corroborated this recent research by showing that restricted, overcrowded and depressive environments with no enrichment reduce the brain weight of laboratory animals. And they proved, to the surprise of the scientific world, that the opposite, (enriched environment) increased neuronal brain growth through the expansion of neuronal dendrites and their interconnection throughout the brain.

President Roosevelt once said, "We have nothing to fear, but fear itself!" Nevertheless, many families, organizations, schools, corporations and governments are organized around principles of fear. Can you think of a situation you are in that contains the manipulation of people through *fear*? Consider the following theories of management that are taught in every first year college business course.

ACTION ITEM:
Try to identify a situation or environment you are in that fits each of these categories below. Perhaps you can imagine an environment that has all of these characteristics or shifts from one to another depending on the circumstances.

1. Theory X is built on the view that humans are selfish, lazy and irresponsible. To get any work from them, including learning with school children, the supervisor must ride them with a heavy hand, rules and procedures to control people.

2. Theory Y arises from those who hold that people were basically neutral or good and held positive motives to achieve. Create an environment that is supportive and provide leadership direction and human beings will accomplish and achieve. Here, the guidance is in the goal and direction and controlling outcomes, not in the controlling of people.

3. Theory Z emerges from the idea of involving people from all levels within the organization in both planning and decision-making. Theory Z is expressed in the "Total Quality Leadership" movement. The principle here is that people achieve far more if they are involved in the processes. In business we hear of "Quality Circles" and in education there is an increasing movement toward "shared governance" and "site based" management. Democracy, at some level, operates here with the notion of shared decision-making and participation. The control focus is on the processes of involving people.

In my consulting work with Fortune 100 Corporations, Federal Agencies, State Legislatures, Education Departments and local schools, I have witnessed each of these Models of Management operating at different levels of intensity and degree: from tyrants to peace makers. But in all cases, there is one thing in common with these long standing and accepted theories of organization and people management – they each employ "adversity, negativity and confrontation" as a basis of human performance.

"All of these theories – X, Y and Z – are rooted in confrontation as opposed to reconciliation. Theory X openly advocates confrontation….", according to the Aldersons.[10] If the supervisor (parent, teacher, administrator or boss) is not riding the backs of people, nothing will get done. We have a modern version of this with the "Standards and Testing" movement in the United States where students and teachers are being measured constantly about student outcomes, with results published with stigmas. Yet, "Theory Y is no less confrontational – the confrontational style is simply wearing kid gloves. Cajoling replaces confrontation…," state the Aldersons. "Speak softly and carry a big stick" is the motto of Theory Y.

Finally, as you continue to examine Theory Z more closely, you will see evidence of heavy-handedness in the "rules of engagement." You either participate in accordance with the rules or you are out of a job or out of school as a "drop out." This "bait and switch" happened to a close friend who *did* play by the rules, as evidenced by his winning a prestigious award. But a new CEO changed the game and bounced the "quality" leadership out with sixty days to find a new job within the company. Before walking out of the Vice President's office, my friend tossed his acclaimed award on the desk of the Human Resources Head and said, "What does *this* and thirty years of loyalty get me and my family now?" (He was so well regarded that he got snapped up by another division, but that is not the case with many of the others who were wiped out with a stroke of "we don't care about relationships" attitude that often accompanies "red ink."

People play their cards quite "close to the vest" in Theory Z. And if things don't go the way management wants, then the deck is shuffled into different groups with different players getting different assignments, as in the case of my friend. Also, according to the Aldersons, sometimes new players are brought in from the outside to shake things up, whether in the form of different consultants or new employees. I have run into this all the time from elementary schools to the Department of Defense to major corporations. In such instances the people closest to the work and responsibilities, people such as school teachers and corporate employees, call this bringing in the "flavor of the month" or the "program of the year." If this sounds sarcastic, it is, because it often is intended to be so!

On the other hand, Theory R Management challenges these other theories at the very level of the assumptions about human beings. Theory R Management is guided by solid empirical research in the fields of organizational management, as well as the more recent research from what I call the new "Science of Learning," including but not limited to neurosciences, neuro-cardiology and intelligence theory. You can read a full expansion of this in **Chapter Seven**, which builds the framework for the new "Science of Learning" combined with the view of "Learning as a Performing Art."

The authors of *Theory " R " Management* did not know the scientific research that shows that fear, threat, intimidation and putdowns create "downshifting" and minimal "heart-brain" performance. Neither did the famous organizational theorist Edwards Deming when he called for an abolishment of "fear" from the workplace and learning place *(and, I presume, the family place)*. But, the Aldersons' values, experience and intuition are right on the mark when they claim that: "Most people want to contribute unconditionally to the environment in which they live and work. They want to be wholly a part of something. There are pleasure and fulfillment in feeling needed, wanted, useful and connected. Each person has a basic need to serve because a life that encompasses nothing beyond oneself becomes barren." [11]

I chose to include "Theory R Management," not only because it parallels my own *"Building a Learning Community Leadership Model"* of *"Learnership"* discussed in **Chapter Seven**, but also precisely because it takes us to the level of building "heart-brain" processes in the context of organizations, whether family or company. It expresses the maximum synergy between the Heart and the Brain in human interaction with others. It creates a framework for personal and collaborative conduct, whose value is in perpetuating optimal brain performance and creative thinking with positive heart involvement and activated emotional intelligence. The best expression of that state of consciousness is in the positive "relationships" that we establish and nourish. And we have personally experienced and seen throughout the pages of this book that positive interactions lead to positive emotions, which lead to a bath of positive chemicals in the "body-mind" that generates health, hardiness and happiness.

Components of the Relationship

To paraphrase Theory R Management, the five components of the relationship that we want to develop and sustain "heart brain" processes are:

1.   Do what is right – follow Aristotle's guideline for "Justice" published about 2500 years ago.

2.   Build relationships through a mutual recognition of another's worth. The underlying motive here is "Love, joy, peace, dignity, integrity and honesty."

3.   Engage in only that activity that builds relationships and leads toward reconciliation, as opposed to leading to confrontation, condemnation or judgment.

4. Take personal responsibility for personal actions toward others, while avoiding blaming others or side-stepping your role, responsibility or accountability.

5. Focus on positive results. ("As you ramble on through life, whatever may be your goal, keep your eye upon the donut, and not upon the hole.") Be grateful for what you have, as opposed to worrying about what you do not have. As the contemporary song has it: "Learn to love what you have, rather than have to have what you love."

The last of the philosophical idealists in the United States was Josiah Royce, who wrote that the first principle of human community was "loyalty to loyalty." What he may have missed in his formula is that loyalty is a function of love, trust, communication and service. When we act out of an internal sense of love toward others, our trust increases at the very same time that we open our communication to others. Under these conditions, our capability and capacity to serve others increase. And "service to others" generates positive feedback that elevates self-esteem and increases motivation to continuously improve and achieve.

Ancient in its origin but also contemporary in its application is both steadfast love and unconditional love. When Mother Theresa walked into the streets of Calcutta with a wheelbarrow, her goal was to lift the dying into her cart and take them back to the makeshift sanctuary to let them die with dignity. When she was asked how she could do such a repulsive thing as to carry off the near dead day in and day out, she replied: "I see God in the spirit of each person I lift up and I know that I am looking into the face of Christ in each person." Steadfast and unconditional love strengthened Mother Theresa in her work with the dying.

To what degree do you think that steadfast and unconditional love can improve the quality of *your* life and the lives of those with whom you interact? In any regard, you must first love yourself. Know yourself, continue to grow and improve yourself and affirm yourself, as well as those around you. Perhaps the worst influence in our lives is the perpetual negative self-talk that we give ourselves, not to mention the barrage of criticism we have for everyone else we fear, mistrust and to whom we pledge no loyalty.

Read Norman Vincent Peale's book, *The Power of Positive Thinking* or Dale Carnegie's famous book, *How to Win Friends and Influence People*, along with any of Leo Buscaglia's books on Love. Also, you can find the children's story, *The Velveteen Rabbit*, in any children's bookstore. Look for a copy of Bernie Siegel's, *Peace, Love and Healing*. Finally, read the amazing book of scientific research on prayer and healing by surgeon, Larry Dossey, M.D., entitled, *Healing Beyond the Body*.

What did you do to learn to ride your bicycle? Most likely, you practiced every day until you "got it!" So practice the art of love in your life. You can begin through helpful affirmations. Listed below are some affirmations the Aldersons offer. Feel free to add to the list so that they apply to particular individuals in your family, at school or at work. Practice using these affirmations every day and every night, just the way you practiced anything you learned to do well.

When we repeat phrases that support us in our behavior or behavior change, we call them "mantras." Here are some mantras for your affirmation of love to others. Remember that they represent different ways of acknowledging your love for the other person (don't fake it or say it if you don't mean it, because the other person will pick up fraudulent language and gestures and body language before you open your mouth):

"I'm for you." (Since this is a "heart" statement, repeat this a couple of times to orient your stingy, self-centered brain that wants to say, "I'm for me; what the heck are you talking about?")

"I believe in you."

"I support you."

"I'm working for your best."

"I desire to see you win."

"I value you."

"I hope for your highest level of achievement."

"I appreciate you."

"I hope for your best possible performance."

"I admire you and your efforts."

"I feel good about you."

"I'm your fan."

" I enjoy telling others about you and the things you do."

"When we affirm others in these ways, we encourage them. Affirmation (of ourselves and others) is always a building up process. To build up people is to affirm their positive traits and to encourage them to continue to pursue excellence. Affirmation does not deny that people have weaknesses; rather, it puts the emphasis on their ability to overcome weaknesses or to transform them into strengths," note the Aldersons.

As you conclude reading this chapter, consider the old adage:

"Nature forms us
Education informs us
Transgression deforms us
Prisons reform us
The Path of Love
Transforms us."

-Anonymous

And from the New Testament on the importance of "Love":

"Though I speak with the tongues of men and of angels, and have not Love; I have become as a sounding brass or a tinkling cymbal;

And though I have the gift of prophecy, and understand all mysteries, and all knowledge, and though I have all faith, so that I could remove mountains, and have not Love; I am nothing;

And though I bestow all my goods to feed the poor, and though I give my body to be burned, and have not Love; it profits me nothing;

Love *is patient and* Love *is kind;* Love is not envious, Love *is not self-serving and* Love *is not prideful and arrogant;*

Love *is not unseemly, and* Love *does not covet others*; Love *is not easily provoked and thinks of good - not of evil;*

Love *does not rejoice in gossip or lies;* Love *rejoices in Truth;*

Love *bears all things, has faith in all things, hopes for all things and endures all things;*

And now, live your life in these three: faith, hope and Love, *but the greatest of these is* LOVE. "

(1 Corinthians: 13: 1-13, King James Version)

The Fourth Secret Revealed

While your heart has its own brain and memory and is critical to your learning success, it is important to point out here that in the previous chapter of this book, we reviewed several models of the brain's structure, organization and function. All of the Brain Models reviewed and discussed in **Chapter Three** and in the remainder of this book reinforce each other, leading to the view that a *"heart connection,"* with an enriched environment of love, kindness, joy, novelty and peace, without stress, stimulates brain growth at the level of the human cell and inspires us all at the level of the human spirit. Moreover, it is the *human heart* that has its own brain, thinks, stores memories and communicates with other hearts. The heart drives and inspires the desire for human interaction, connection and comfort.

The journey of life is a process of continuous learning where our capacity is elevated with new knowledge and new skills. And a portion of this new knowledge which will assist us on our journey toward "enlightenment" and the miracle of learning is contained in the next chapter, revealing Secret #5, the Theory of Multiple Intelligences.

References

[1] Pearsall, Paul, *The Heart's Code*, Broadway Books, 2000.

[2] *ibid.*

[3] *ibid.*

[4] Pert, Candace, *The Molecules of Emotion: Why You Feel the Way You Feel*, Scribner, 1997.

[5] Goleman, Daniel, *Emotional Intelligences*, New York: Bantam Books, 1995, p. 169.

[6] *ibid,* p. 35.

[7] *ibid,* p. 36.

[8] *ibid,* p. 36.

[9] Alderson, Wayne T. & Nancy Alderson McDonnell, *Theory "R" Management*, p. 24. Books may be ordered from Value of Person Consultants, 246 Washington Road, Mt. Lebanon; Pittsburgh, PA 15126. phone: 412-341-9070; email: info@valueoftheperson.com.

[10] *ibid,* p. 27.

[11] *ibid,* p. 28.

SECRET #5
Revealed.

Prescription:
Bold Stroke

New View
of
Intelligences

Multiple
Gateways

Emotion
MUSICAL
Unifies All

ETHICAL
Moral

Useful and Powerful
Strategies & Exercises
to Improve
Your Intelligences

SPIRITUAL
Meaning

AESTHETIC
Beauty

VISUAL
Spatial

LINGUISTIC
Reading & Writing

LOGICAL -
Mathematical

INTERPERSONAL
Partners/Group Activity

Story
INTRAPERSONAL
Self

KINESTHETIC
Body Movements

Chapter Five

Secret #5
Power
Up!

Are you running on only two cylinders instead of the ten that you have?

For years, legislators, public educators and the academic community have measured people's intelligence through the use of standardized IQ tests, which judge a person's reasoning ability or language comprehension. Now we know that those judgments are based on a narrow view of intelligence, limiting the assessment to just *two* intelligences. In addition to being incomplete and inadequate, most of these tests are biased toward one group or another. Using such tests, educators labeled some kids "learning disabled" so they could secure additional resources for the school, such as federal and state funds. Harvard University psychologists claim that each of us has at least seven intelligences, not two. Indeed, additional research, including my own, reveals three more intelligences for a total of at least ten intelligences which can be utilized in the learning process, instead of the traditional two which are valued in terms of instruction and national testing; namely, the "Linguistic and Logical-Mathematical Intelligences." It must be pointed out that virtually all views of "learning disability" and "attention deficits" are determined in terms of performance on these two intelligences, leaving the others out of the equation altogether.

For many educational reformers, this narrow view of intelligence and its implication for teaching and learning is outrageous at best and morally repugnant at worst. For example, in her book, *Endangered Minds*, Jane Healy discusses the myth of "Attention Deficit Disorder Syndrome." "How do you get a kid to sit still while the teacher is droning on endlessly?" asks Dr. Healy. The answer most often is:

"Medicate him!" However, many "learning disabled" children are actually what I call "curriculum disabled"– they are not given an opportunity to learn in their best way with their favored intelligences.

For well over a century, those in control of education have shielded us from the consequences of a narrow view of intelligence and learning, primarily because those views adequately served the contemporary workplace. The Industrial Revolution's focus on manufacturing, production lines, uniformity, centralization, hierarchical management, as well as the national defense need for military infantry personnel created limited demand for creativity, problem solving and group skills. In the workplace and national defense of the 21st century, however, creativity, problem identification and problem solving, along with team skills are precisely the type of skills that are most in demand and least cultivated by contemporary educational methods. They are in demand to equip people with productivity skills to support the culture. Therefore, we need nothing less than a major shift in our entire national *approach* to the processes of learning that would respond to corporate organizational leader Peter Drucker's call for the "knowledge worker" and what the author of the Constitution of the United States, James Madison, envisioned as the "knowledgeable citizen."

Some apologists for traditional methods argue that the real failures stem from an unmotivated and undisciplined student population. Certainly there is ample evidence that changing cultural values have intruded into the classroom; too many schools are being called upon to be surrogate parents, police, hospitals, welfare agencies and drug treatment centers. Note the growth of programs across the United States like Communities in Schools, founded by Bill Millikan and Neil Shorthouse, which provide support services to fragile students. Even conceding this influence, however, the more fundamental defect is the out-dated and dysfunctional concept of how people learn that drives our entire educational establishment.

The American Educational System has long relied on a model of human intelligence that recognizes almost exclusively linguistic and logical/ mathematical capacities. Therefore, it is not surprising that educational philosophy, curriculum development and performance standards reflect this uniformity. Equally consistent is the teacher-centered, information transmission methodology and a preoccupation with standardized tests of dubious validity.

Prescription: Bold Stroke

The fairest criticism of these philosophical foundations is not that they were wrong, but rather that they were incomplete. A great deal of new research has opened vast horizons of insight into the nature of intelligence, the learning process, and the enormous diversity of learning strategies and methods, as described in previous chapters of this book. Among the most compelling is the work on multiple intelligences by Dr. Howard Gardner and a team of researchers at Harvard University. His book *Frames of Mind: The Theory of Multiple Intelligences* proposes seven "intelligences," each of which represents a learning resource for every student and, by extension, a diversity of learning styles. (See Figure 1: Multiple Gateways: Multiple Intelligences which follows). In addition to Gardner's Seven Intelligences, I build upon this perspective with extensive research and practical experience which reveals an additional three intelligences; the Spiritual, the Ethical and the Aesthetic. We shall discuss the last three following our examination of Gardner's Seven Intelligences, which are depicted in Figure 1.

Gardner's research, along with his co-director at Harvard's Project Zero Professor David Perkins, suggests there are at least seven different intelligences present in every human brain. They have identified seven and believe they may eventually be able to identify an additional one or more that are consistent with what I have detailed later in this chapter. For your convenience, I outline the seven intelligences and then follow those with an account of the additional three intelligences – all of which will give you a far greater perspective on learning possibilities than the current traditional views on either teaching and learning processes or intelligence theory. According to the Harvard group, we all possess seven multiple intelligences, but the relative strengths of these vary from person to person, partly because of the ways they have developed as a result of learning and teaching experiences. Following are some useful suggestions on the seven intelligences and how we might develop them to our personal advantage:

FIGURE 1: MULTIPLE GATEWAYS: MULTIPLE INTELLIGENCES
from the article "Multiple Gateways: Multiple Intelligences,"

Learner Type	Likes To	Is Good At	Learns Best By
Linguistic "The Word Player"	•read/write •use puns •tell stories	•Memorizing names, places, dates and trivia	•saying, hearing and seeing words and stories
Logical/ Mathematical "The Questioner"	•do experiments •figure things out •work with numbers •ask questions •explore patterns and relationships	•math •reasoning •logic •problem solving •quantitative analysis	•categorizing •classifying •working with abstract patterns and relationships •quantifying
Spatial "The Visualizer"	•draw, build, design and create things •daydream •look at pictures/slides •watch movies •play with machines	•Imagining things •sensing changes •mazes/puzzles •reading maps/charts •diagramming •charting	•visualizing •dreaming •using the mind's eye •working with colors and/ or pictures •outlining
Musical "The Music Lover"	•sing, hum •listen to music •play an instrument •respond to music	•picking up sounds •remembering melodies •noticing pitches/rhythms •keeping time	•rhythm •melody •music •sound •drumming •listening
Bodily/Kinesthetic "The Mover"	•move around •touch and talk •use body language •engage in activity •interact physically •experiment	•physical activities (sports/dance/acting) •crafts •making things •mapping •body models of concepts	•touching •moving •interacting with space •processing knowledge through bodily sensations
Interpersonal "The Socializer"	•having lots of friends •talk to people •join groups •interest •network •personalize	•understanding people •leading others •organizing •communicating •manipulating •mediating conflicts	•sharing •comparing •relating •cooperating •interviewing •leading •interacting •listening
Intrapersonal "The Individual"	•work alone •pursue own interests •reflect •observe	•understanding self •focusing inward on feeling/dreams •following instincts •pursuing interests •being intuitive	•reflection •individualized projects •self-paced instruction •having own space •intuition

by General (ret.) Pete Todd &. Dr. Laurence Martel

The first two intelligences, Linguistic and Logical/Mathematical, are those that traditional education values. These two are also the basis of the standard I.Q. test with all of its derivative tests, such as state and national examinations. The others, equally valuable in successful learning, have generally been at best relegated to a peripheral role or at worst ignored altogether. Each intelligence plays a role, such as music, art, drama and social clubs, in learning. Everyone has a distinct pattern of more and less dominant intelligences that can be tapped to optimize learning, performance and productivity in a learner-centered environment. The other five include:

- √ **Spatial:** Capacity for keen observation, visual thinking, mental images, and a sense of gestalt.
- √ **Musical:** Sensitivity to pitch, rhythm, and timbre; the emotional power and complex organization of music.
- √ **Body/Kinesthetic:** Control of one's body and of objects, timing, and trained responses that function like reflexes.
- √ **Interpersonal:** Sensitivity to others, ability to read the intentions and desires of others and potentially to influence them.
- √ **Intrapersonal:** Self-knowledge, sensitivity to one's own values, purpose, and feelings; a developed sense of self.

I have found that training parents, teachers, administrators, managers and leaders in all sorts of public and private organizations to utilize all "seven intelligences" as an instructional strategy provides increases in observable and measurable learning achievement and outcomes. For instance, shortly after Dr. Gardner published his book ***Frames of Mind, Theory of Multiple Intelligences***, we trained the entire faculty at the Guggenheim Elementary School in Southside Chicago at 71st and Morgan Streets. The school had just hired a new principal, Mike Alexander, to lead the children and faculty forward, as they were on the bottom in District Test scores, ranked 18 out of 18. Mike came with a business background, but perhaps more important, he was a good tennis player. As a tennis player, he had read a book entitled ***The Inner Game of Tennis***, which features skills in the power of positive thinking, along with strategies to accomplish high expectations.

I introduced Mike to the concept of Multiple Intelligences, which fit into his format of coaching the faculty in high performance strategies. The faculty had been exposed to some key principles of "mental focusing" and positive climate building by P. Kline. They were then provided with the critical success factor that led to the kind of consistent instructional outcomes, for which they won numerous awards; namely, an instructional format of "Accelerated Learning," initially developed by G. Lozonov in Bulgaria, but designed for application to schools by   Dr. John Grassi, Vice President of Cambridge College in Massachusetts. That Model is called "ALPS" (*Accelerated Learning Process in Schools – Whole Brain Learning and Teaching Techniques for Teachers and Trainers*). Applying from pre-kindergarten to graduate school and corporate training, Dr. Grassi originated his system for bilingual teachers in the City of Boston in 1981. Grassi's ALPS Model employs strategies to activate each of Gardner's seven intelligences.

The good news for Guggenheim faculty and students was that Dr. Grassi provided scores of curriculum units prepared by his former graduate students and by him as prototypes for Guggenheim to shape and fashion for their own teaching objectives. Nothing was left out, from math to science and from reading to language development at all K-8 grade levels. Two years after Dr. Grassi's curriculum and instructional process was introduced, with faculty re-writing their teaching plans and processes, the Guggenheim School rose in performance from 18 out of 18 to number 2 out of 18 on the district-wide Iowa Tests. At the time of the training, there was only one club, a cheerleading club for seventh and eighth grade girls. Four years after the initial training, followed by on going training in a variety of strategies to develop the seven intelligences in the context of Grassi's Model, and with financial support from the Joyce Foundation, the school's new science club won two city-wide first prizes in science; two second prizes and a third prize.

Later in New York when I was presenting the results to the New York State Board of Education, people were surprised at the results, but cautious about another "flavor of the month." They said that *"seeing is believing!"* So, I asked them if they would be willing to travel to Chicago to visit the *"beacon of light"* in the Southside of Chicago. Taking up my offer, they said they would go if I paid for the trip. Well, I did not have the funds in my budget at Syracuse University, but we did have commitment, tenacity and creativity. In the end, twenty leaders from New York City, including representatives from the City Board and the New York State Education Department, traveled to Guggenheim Elementary School.

This trip was only possible because of the generosity of a friend and fellow Trustee at Green Mountain College in Vermont, Mr. Hicks Waldron, who was then Chairman of Avon Corporation and provided some funds through the Avon Foundation. Northwest Airlines partially matched Avon with deep discounts in fares, and the Chicago Sheraton made rooms available at scholarship rates. One of those present was Dorothy Joseph, Principal of P.S. 27. She recently wrote about her experience and her school's dramatic improvement as a result of our training her faculty in her 2002 award winning book, *A Tale of Two Systems*.

I recall people leaving the school with tears in their eyes at the accomplishment of the students and the obvious climate of love and kindness. After viewing the special education room, headed by long time teacher Nancy Ellis, several of the visitors thought they had been in the "Gifted and Talented" room.

To my knowledge, Guggenheim Elementary School, which went on to be adopted by IBM as a TLC school of excellence, was the first school to adopt the Multiple Intelligence Theory as an instructional strategy, where all of the "intelligences" were incorporated into daily lessons at all K-8 grade levels. The faculty and staff development process began in 1984. Ironically, Mike Alexander left for graduate school at Harvard in Cambridge where both Multiple Intelligences Theory and ALPS sprang forward into the marketplace of educational ideas. Nancy Ellis, who had initially been skeptical and who later coined the phrase to describe as herself and others, such as Dr. Rober Kelly, Superintendent of Schools as *"born-again educators,"* stepped in as principal to carry on the tradition, while also going on to complete her Doctorate, retiring in 2000.

The spin-off for New York was remarkable in its initiation of successful school reform, with Regent Adelaide Sanford, currently Deputy Chancellor of the Board of Regents for the State of New York, and the New York Legislative Black and Puerto Rican Caucus providing funds to launch a replication of Guggenheim. Following the initial successes with measurable test score gains, Senator James Donovan stepped up and provided legislation to support the replication of what is now called *IntelliLearn*® across the state. Now, children around the world have benefited from the Model depicted in **Chapter Seven**.

When I first personally met Howard Gardner at a college-sponsored symposium in Central New York, he said to me, "Who has ever heard of an 'intelligence' theory being used as an 'instructional design' strategy?" Intelligence tests are used to sort and select people, but the Theory of Multiple Intelligences provides a framework for people to shift from "the one best way" of doing things to focusing on multiple pathways and strategies to foster a variety of input to the central nervous system, to allow for informational incubation in the brain and nervous system of the learner. and finally, to witness higher levels of memory and performance output on standardized exams than previously experienced.

Multiple Intelligence Theory is an educational opportunity that helps students of any age not only learn better, but also learn *how* to learn better. By treating diversity as a learning resource rather than as a deviation to be suppressed, and by exploiting the potential of multiple intelligences to serve as gateways to the learner's mind, we can potentially revolutionize both formal education and business training. (The *IntelliLearn*® Model for learning success unfolds throughout this book and is summarized in **Chapter Seven**.)

The New View of Intelligence

When we recognize and acknowledge that people learn in many different ways with several varied intelligences, we can teach and learn so all (or at least several) of the intelligences are stimulated. When we recognize differences between people and how they learn, we can better adjust our communication with them so we're likely to be understood. Mr. Rick Butler, principal at Springfield, Ohio's urban "South High School" believed this. In the year in which his faculty learned the strategies, tactics and tools of *IntelliLearn*®, of which The Theory of Multiple Intelligences is a component, 1600 students enjoyed an increase in overall grade performance by 10%, while a 17% decline in discipline referrals occurred.

I specifically remember one math teacher who told me: "I am not going to use music and sing songs in my class. It makes me uncomfortable!" I encouraged her to employ the new strategies she had learned and to "go easy" on the use of music. Four months later, when I returned with our team to continue to train the administrators, faculty and parents, this same math teacher came running across the seminar room chanting, "Wait till you hear them; wait till you hear them!" She stopped in front of me, somewhat breathless, but joyful.

I asked: "What can't you wait for me to hear?"

She said, "Why I have doubled our enrollment in Calculus and the passing rate with C's or better has sky-rocketed; and *you should hear the songs we sing in Calculus!*"

"But I thought you were not going to sing songs," I said gently.

She exclaimed, "Oh, I don't sing songs, but the students do and love it."

My friends, this was a courageous teacher who realized that many of her students learned best in ways that she did not. Indeed, this led me to believe that the popular notion, "teachers teach the way they were taught," is false. Rather, "teachers teach the way they *learn best*, often imposing what is comfortable to them on others, resulting in some students being uncomfortable in the ways the teacher learns." We must find other ways to teach, valuing the way our learners perceive and process information and bypassing the imposition of "our" way. The expression "my way or the highway" has no place in the learning enterprise.

Common sense tells us that we only need to look around at the people we know to see that each one has a special talent, whether it is singing, swimming, solving puzzles, or drawing. Why is it that some of these talents are considered to be indications of intelligence, while others are not? Highly publicized studies in brain research clearly show that there are indeed intelligences that standardized tests do not currently measure. Both Daniel Goleman's book *Emotional Intelligence* and Robert Sternberg's *Successful Intelligence* document this view of diversity of intelligences, which make up the complexity of human performance. These researchers also support Gardner's call for a broader view of intelligence, rather that the limiting, narrow view currently directing educational policy, practice and testing. There is an old view in the history of science that says, "Reality is what you measure." Under this framework, your tools of measurement limit your view of reality. This is a little like Maslow's comment that if the only tool you have is a "hammer," you tend to go around treating everything as if it were a nail. So, if your tools of measurement are limiting, paper-pencil intelligence tests based on two intelligences, your world view of human performance, achievement, capacity and capability will be as narrow as your tools.

A more enlightened view, according to Gardner, Goleman and Sternberg is a view that embraces a more comprehensive "diversity theorist" perspective, rather that the current "uniformist" mis-perception. Everyone has all seven of these intelligences, so it's not a question of us using some instead of others. However, no two people develop any of their intelligences in exactly the same way. For example, you or your child probably hasn't developed the musical intelligence of Mozart or Michael Jackson. Your child might even have difficulty carrying a tune. But if certain rhythmic patters are helpful to your child in remembering things, that may suggest cultivating his musical intelligence.

Or you (or your spouse or your child) may always have had trouble in staff meetings or English class, and get uncomfortable whenever you have to put words together. Yet, the thought of hearing an interesting story might appeal to you or others in your family life. If that is so, developing your linguistic intelligence may occur as a result of hearing and responding to a good story.

Traditionally, schools emphasize Logical-Mathematical and Linguistic Intelligence with little or no attention to the other five, except as "frills" like gym, art, music, and social events. Because each of the Multiple Intelligences is dominant for large numbers of people, it's easy to understand why so many students have difficulty in the present educational system. Those who possess strong Logical-Mathematical and Linguistic abilities have the best chance of success, while many others struggle with an environment that may seem so hostile that they eventually give up.

If you've ever wanted to say to someone, "What do you want me to do, draw you a picture?" you may be giving yourself good advice. And if you've caught yourself saying, "Stop fidgeting while I'm talking to you," you may be in conversation with a Bodily-Kinesthetic learner who needs to feel the meanings inside his or her body. Checking out the seven intelligences not only makes it more likely that all people will learn better, but helps everyone strengthen underused abilities and intelligences as well.

The more you or your children form the habit of using all the intelligences in relationship to each other when they're trying to learn something new, the easier they'll find it becomes to learn new things. Let's say your child is very strong in one of the intelligences, but not in the others. She'll find that if she practices doing things with the one she's not so good at, she'll learn to make even better use of her strongest ones. That's because whenever you consider anything that's understood in one of your intelligences from the point of view of a different intelligence, you automatically have to think about it in a new way – this tends to deepen your understanding and flexibility in learning that particular way.

It's hard to get the best out of any resource if you use only a small part of it, and the human brain is no exception. If we have been measuring only two forms of human intelligence and have largely ignored the other five, we are a society that has not been performing or learning as efficiently as we can.

Here are some useful tools to cultivate the Multiple Intelligences, levels of intelligence and modes of learning for you and your family members.

Useful and Powerful Strategies and Exercises to Improve Your Intelligences

#1. THE LINGUISTIC INTELLIGENCE – You have a sensitivity to the meaning and order of words, with a capability of using spoken or written language to express yourself to others.

Increase Your Linguistic and Intrapersonal Intelligences

Have your spouse or your child keep a diary or journal of the things that happen in his life. He should state his goals, wishes, and dreams on paper, and record events and what they mean for him. Using written language more and more will increase his ability to communicate verbally and on paper. Or, do this for yourself. Also, play games like "scrabble" and "boggle," as well as complete crossword puzzles, regardless of how simple they are for you. Buy a Thesaurus and a Dictionary and make a game by picking a word every day to use in different ways by yourself, or with others in the family. Be "mellifluous" in your use of language. (By the way, my wife, Mary, taught me that word, and it means, "flowing with sweetness." Go ahead and look it up for yourself!)

ACTION ITEM & APPLICATION:
Storytelling, Guided Imagery and Its Relation to Achieving your Goals

Everyone loves a good story! And here is why. In the world of brain sciences and heart sciences, many researchers think that what permits memory to be glued together is the "story." Indeed, Dr Renee Fuller taught people in mental institutions with IQ's as low as 30 to read with comprehension, based on a reading series she wrote that presupposes the "story" as the basic element of memory. Much like the atom is the basic element of all matter, Dr Fuller put forward the notion that the building blocks of reading and cognitive development follow the structure of the story – subjects, then verbs in a world of high interest, modified by adjectives and adverbs. Dr. Fuller coined the term "*story engram*" to describe this basic unit of *thinking* (see **Chapter Three's** section on the "storytelling brain" and go to www.ballstickbird.com for a wealth of articles on this and other issues related to cognitive development and easy success in teaching reading). Notice that when anything is embellished with a story, no matter how dry the sermon or the lecture, our interest peaks. The history of humanity is a history of people telling their stories, and for many, living out the personal scripts they make for themselves through positive or negative self-talk. Whenever we meet for an educational training, business meeting or personal visit in Hawaii, it is a longstanding tradition to first, "talk story."

And yet, from the time we are very young, we are told not to "tell stories." The meaning here is "not to tell lies." But the translation of this statement often comes across to people in a way that reduces or eliminates the imagination and the skill of fabricating stories as visions, myths, anecdotes or helpful scripts for life's journey.

Management and Discipline with Stories

David Armstrong's little book entitled **Managing by Storying Around** is about a major corporation that shelved the rules and regulations and replaced them with a book of the best stories about how someone followed the procedures or implemented a particular rule and the huge benefit that resulted. The book is filled with employee and customer stories on how to act, behave and conduct business toward one another in such a way as to build a procedure manual out of actual stories. Creating a corporate culture, or a family filled with myths and legends that tap the imagination, can have far reaching consequences on both behavior and loyalty.

With respect to discipline, my granddaughter, Spencer Virginia, was about seven years old when she was visiting. She was just coming out of a hot bath when I saw her running on some slick tile in our foyer. Towel strapped around her, she had the speed of an Olympic champion. I was tempted to yell out to her to stop her running. But the idea of barking out "Stop Running!" did not appeal to me, since I knew that when you say "stop" anything, the person with whom you are trying to communicate focuses on the word after the word "stop." I did not want her to focus on running.

Instead I said, "Spencer Virginia, did I ever tell you the story about Princess Heidi?"

She stopped in her tracks and said to me: "Grampa, I don't think so!"

So, I told her the story of little Princess Heidi who had taken a bath in the castle that was tiled, just like ours. The little Princess got out of the golden tub, ran down the hallway, and then slipped and fell, hurting her knees and hitting her head on the hard tile. The little Princess Heidi could not move. Everyone came quickly to help the hurt Princess, but she couldn't move. Finally, her mother and father came and picked her up and held her. They washed the blood from her head as the pain started to go away. The little Princess then looked up at her parents and said, "I will never run on this tile again, because it is easy to slip and fall and hurt yourself." The mother and father smiled, kissing the little Princess.

Well, with wide eyes and a look of empathy in her face, Spencer Virginia said she, too, would not run on the tile, especially with wet feet. She announced that she wanted to tell Grandmother the story and slowly walked away on the tile. At least she walked slowly, until she reached the carpet, then she resumed rocket speed. From that moment onward, when I feel she will endanger herself by running in a delicate situation, I simply say, "Spencer Virginia, do you remember the story of Princess Heidi?" and she slows her pace to slow motion. On one occasion when she was much older and baby-sitting her younger sister, Mary Piper, I overheard Spencer Virginia telling the story of Princess Heidi to prevent Mary Piper from running on the tile. We can accomplish so much more with stories than with screaming and floggings at all age levels. Of course this requires using your existing creativity and imagination. Myron Radio and Rod Johnson have written a book entitled, ***Inside Out-Using Classic Children's Stories for Personal and Professional Growth***, which uses stories to teach about life's core principles and values for people at all age levels and in all walks of life.

You don't have to be a child or young person to enjoy stories. Indeed, stories play a big part in our lives, all the way from rumors to news reports about the latest events in the neighborhood, nation or world. In fact, they are called "news stories." Lately, the news networks know the attraction of morbid and "juicy" stories to attract viewers. Bill O'Reilly's program on Fox News Cable has a basic theme that people tune into each night, which is the story of good triumphing over evil. Bill couches his entire program around the human need for security in pointing out the extremes that can hurt or harm you. His stories always have the main characters, antagonists or villains (usually guests or representatives) against the protagonists who are "the folks" – the good and decent Americans who want the best for themselves and their families. O'Reilly is the "Story Teller."

Einstein once wrote that "Imagination is greater than knowledge." In just that one statement, he was calling for a greater use of the imagination for creativity, invention and fresh new perspectives. The fastest road to new ideas is through the creation of stories and guided images that forecast a future different than today. Now that future might include a new widget or other invention, or it might include your own personal future. If you do not imagine the future to be different than it is today, you erase the conditions for hope, optimism and imagination to create new opportunities.

ACTION ITEM: Please complete the two exercises below.

What is your Future State Story?

Write a vision or imagery of what you see yourself doing a year from now, *the way you would like it to be that is different from today*. Who is there and what are you doing in your ideal state a year from now? What does it smell like? What do the colors look like in the environment? What are the sounds? How does it feel? Notice what you started doing a year ago that put you on this path toward your desired state. What steps did you take? What new decisions did you make that allowed you to change and get to this position a year from now? Write them down.

Make a list of the necessary steps and decisions you need to take to get you where you want to be. Write this down in a vision statement that expresses who you are and what it feels like in this "achieved state." Read it every day and log your progress.

What was your Scrooge Story?

Imagine that you are attending a funeral. You look around and see all your friends and relatives, along with business associates and former teachers, classmates and co-workers. You look in the casket and, to your surprise, it is you and this is your funeral. Several people come to the podium, one at a time. Each gives a speech about you, much like Scrooge when he saw Christmas past and present. Imagine each of these people and what they would say. What do they say about you and your life? Now, imagine that they say what you *WANT* them to say! What would you want them to say about you and imagine how they say it. What are their expressions? How do they look? Imagine how you want it to be and then live your life each day in a way that will enable others to speak of you in this way you imagine. Like Scrooge you can have your Christmas future.

Keep a journal or a diary. Famous people do and that is how biographies are often written. Each day write about what you did toward meeting your vision, as well as reflecting on the steps you are taking or the obstacles that emerged and how you handled them. Keep a record, for your life is worth the story you write each day.

#2. THE LOGICAL-MATHEMATICAL INTELLIGENCE

You're good at conceptualizing and strong in math and science and in dealing with complex logical systems.

Increase Your Logical- Mathematical Intelligence

Find some common items around the house and determine several categories into which you or your family members can sort them. Are some objects glass, or metal, or shaped round or square? Into how many classifications can the item fit? This sorting game will help challenge you to think in terms of order and organization. Do this yourself or have your child borrow a book of math or logic puzzles from the library and challenge your family and friends to a puzzle solving session. Books of "brain teasers" are great for this exercise.

ACTION ITEM & APPLICATION:

1) Keep a journal of "If, then" statements in which you observe and also forecast. You might write: "If so and so happens, then such and such has occurred in the past (and will occur)." Make a list of these and begin to notice the logical relationship between specific behaviors and other behaviors. For instance, "If I don't do my homework, then (make a list), e.g., mom will yell at me; I will fail; I'll have to go to summer school; my friends won't think it's cool, etc."

2) Now, make a list of the things in life that you want to happen and create the "If, then" statements required to either make them happen or to cause them not to happen. This is a kind of logical forecasting, which research shows can help you achieve your goals. If you don't write down goals, then chances are you will be without direction. Virtually every successful person keeps a journal and writes (and revises) goals. So when you state your goal, state it in an "If, then" statement. For example, "If I want to graduate from high school, then I must pass my courses. If I want to pass my courses, I must do my homework everyday. If I do my homework everyday, I must plan and schedule regular time every day to complete my homework."

Get the idea? This is a planning and thinking process that can help you develop logical thinking.

3) Practice putting things in an order or in a sequence! (You can start with a Mind Map, if you want to – then use it to make a list. See the next section on visual-spatial intelligence.) This means "first things first, then second and third and so on. When you have to do something, write out the steps and sequence of the steps to get it done. This applies to extremely simple tasks and to complicated jobs, from cleaning your room or house to straightening your desk or office, to planning your day or scheduling your time. Write out the sequence in detail. For example, when seeing someone for the first time during the day, what kind of greeting will you want to give and in what way and why? If you want to have a positive day, then you will want to greet people with a cheery smile of optimism and joyfulness. What you give to others comes back tenfold. That includes both happiness, as well as grief. Apply this thinking to your work by breaking tasks down into simple sequence steps. If you want to, you can put a time estimate on how long the task will take. People who have trouble learning and with school don't do any of these things; rather, they tend to "wing" it and simply experience "what's happening."

4) Draw a large "T" in the middle of the paper. On the top left side, write the word "Pro" or "for," and on the top right side, write the word, "con" or "against." Now pick a topic from home, work or school. Then list all the reasons "Pro or for" that you can think of for doing the thing you think you want to do or buying the item you want. After you have made that list, make a list of the reasons "con or against" your idea, action, behavior or thing you think you want to do. List all the "pros and cons" and state them out loud to yourself as you contemplate your topic or action. Then make a decision based on the benefits to you and avoiding the possible dis-benefits to you. I have known many high school students who used this tool to make college selection decisions, as well as employees in planning steps forward.

5) I know some of you will struggle with this idea and some of you will say "I do that now!" In either case, go out and buy a friendly "day-planner" and practice using it every day and every night. No one accomplishes much without practice. Michael Jordan shot 900 baskets a day while in high school, just to practice to become the top basketball player in the world. Do not feel guilty if you have a planner and it is still in last year's Christmas wrapping in the bottom drawer of your dresser. And forget that procrastination excuse you keep using. As the Nike commercial says, "Just do it!" Becoming organized requires planning and planning requires some assistance. The daily planner can assist you as a guide, not as a harness. Enter the things you know you have to do. Then add to those things. For example, you do have to get up, so write that down with the time and sequence of events. This routine will help you achieve far more in less time with maximum use of you valuable time.

#3.   THE VISUAL-SPATIAL INTELLIGENCE– You have the ability to perceive the visual world accurately, or to re-create or alter it on paper, in the mind, or in direction and distances. Non-sighted people also have a strong spatial sense, which helps them think about moving around in the world without the benefit of sight.

Increase Your Visual-Spatial Intelligence

Play a game with your friends or family in which you try to communicate words through pictures. One person chooses a word (or is assigned one by a non-participant or member of a different team). The player then draws pictures or symbols (or both) of the word until it is correctly guessed or a time limit is reached. If this game is played in competitive teams, the team that is best able to guess and decipher one another's drawings wins. The game Pictionary®, available in toy stores, is a good family drawing game.

Make your family visually adept. Try drawing maps instead of writing verbal directions. Record achievements on graphs; for example, time spent to skills learned. Write recipes or plans as flow charts.

Mind Map on Mind-Mapping

Use of Mind Map
(create your own drawings)
Color
Images
Doodles
Cartoons
Geometric Shapes
Three Dimensions as well as Two

Structure: Tree Trunk & Branches
(Trunk) Main Concept, Topic, Theme
(Branches) Subtopic or Ideas
(Secondary Branches) Related Points and Keywords

Brain Storming
Inquiry Questions?
New Information...
Facts!

Mind Map on Mind Mapping

Classroom Use
Note Taking
Organize Thoughts
Study Guides
Review
Tests
Lectures/Books & TV Programs
Outline Textbook Information your own way
Prepare Presentations
Creative Writing
poems, stories, songs
use as a check list
lessons, discussions

Personal Use
Your Ideas
Plan for Day/Week
Plan for an Activity
Feelings
Self Autobiography/Diary
Record an Event, Ball Game, Dance, Date, Phone Conversation

ACTION ITEM & APPLICATION:
Mind Maps or a Magical Mystery Tour of Your Thought Processes

You can use a Mind Map to arrange much information in a way that is easy to understand and remember. One of the reasons we often have trouble handling large amounts of information is that we don't see how the different parts of the information relate to one another. Mind Mapping allows you to get the big picture, see the whole system, and keep the details in their proper perspective.

Unlike a list or an outline, the Mind Map illustrates connections among the various parts of a subject. This visual representation allows us to think about a subject more globally (as a whole) rather than if the outline were written step by step. And when you think globally, you increase your ability to understand both meaning and implications.

Use it to Create, Organize, Get New Ideas and Plan Your Thinking

Mind Mapping is highly effective for organizing and remembering things that come from outside you – information or ideas from books or other people. But it is also a terrific tool for getting thoughts and ideas out of your head and onto paper where you can look at them, play with them, and develop them in new ways.

Suppose you want to plan a report or a project, or suppose you've just had a stimulating *Think & Listen Exercise* (See page 177), when all sorts of new ideas came to mind that you wanted to explore and organize. If you are like most people, it's often hard to know where to begin. Sometimes you're not even sure you're clear in your own mind about what you're trying to do. How do you start when you don't know where you're going?

That's where Mind Mapping can help. It's not like an outline where you have to know how every idea is related to every other idea before you can write down the number "1." And it's not like a school assignment where you might be asked for a beginning, a middle, and a conclusion. Most of us don't think about things that way – though we might want to express our ideas that way once we've thought them through.

The Right Tool for Your Way of Thinking

The beauty of Mind Mapping is that it is flexible; it can be made up and constantly revised as you go along, and there are many ways to modify the basic structure with the topic in the middle and the branches flowing from the middle outward as do branches from a tree trunk. Then, from those branches, you might have several sub-branches until you reach the twig level. That is your choice. In fact, you can adapt it to the way you actually think. Mind Mapping is something like thinking out loud except that it has the extra advantage that you can structure what you've thought into a pattern that helps you make the connection between and across ideas. When you're finished with Mind Mapping (unlike thinking out loud) you have a record of what you've thought, which can be altered as you think of new things later on or as you change your purpose and use for the Mind Map you created.

Equipped with your new skill in making Mind Maps, you can now easily create, plan and organize your ideas for any particular purpose – whether it is for preparing a shopping list (as I do), a talk or something you're planning to write or design.

How To Do It

You can get a good idea of how a Mind Map is created by looking at the one shown earlier or those at the beginning of each chapter. This one contains both words and drawings. If you draw Mind Maps with both, the words will help you organize the ideas and the drawings will help you remember the words.

Basically, all you need to begin Mind Mapping is a few sheets of blank paper, something to write with, and perhaps some colored pencils or markers. Draw a circle in the center of your paper, and put in it the main idea. Pretending it's the hub of a wheel, draw spokes out from it with supporting ideas. Each of these spokes can have different colored lines that branch off and lead to other ideas. Thus, you can begin to group ideas by color so they reveal their relationships to each other.

Your Mind Map shows your artistic rendition of your feelings, thoughts and sounds about a topic. This, then, is your mirror of *your* understanding, not someone else's, and therefore it may not look like anyone else's Mind Map. Give it the stamp of your own personality any way you like. However, remember to make sure you draw key branches from all 360 degrees of the circle or symbol in the middle. Do not simply draw straight lines out from one side of the center.

When you have your first draft, or upon final completion, then you can order or organize your main branches into a sequence of numbers corresponding to the traditional Harvard outlining method. Thus, you can have it both ways – a global overview and a detailed outline. But making your Mind Map in the first place is what's important, because you're creating a new way of getting information into your brain, organizing creativity, keeping a visual record of your thinking and providing a way to present your thinking in a solid, creative and logical structure.

When making a Mind Map, it's not necessary to put everything into it. You want to confine yourself to the most important words in an idea. Keep it by your bedside, however, because you'll likely wake up in the middle of the night with a great new idea to include. Mind Maps are "organic," rather than static, since they can always grow as you get new thoughts. As you work with Mind Maps, you may find that color-coding is useful in exploring the relationships among ideas.

Developing a Positive Outlook

Getting the overview of a subject is an empowering experience. That's because people naturally feel less stress when they understand the relationships they're working with. The mastery of Mind Mapping allows you to understand relationships and see connections among things. Moreover, you begin to appreciate the parts and wholes of things more quickly. If you are more left brain and dwell in the parts, this tool serves to also develop your sense of the "whole picture." On the other hand, if you are more right brain, you'll quickly get the "picture" and develop your capacity to get into the detail more easily.

Increasing Your Brain Power – From Road Map to Mind Map

It might surprise you, but what we're talking about here is how your mind works. According to the research of Nobel Prize neurologist Roger Sperry, the right side of the brain likes to see the big picture, or the global overview. The left side prefers to analyze and sort out details into their appropriate linear sequence. One of the best ways to understand, organize, and recall information on a particular subject is to develop a Mind Map that explores the subject in a way that appeals to the right side of the brain.

And because Mind Maps translate ideas (the left brain Logical Intelligence) into pictures (the right brain Spatial Intelligence), you can use them to get these two parts of your brain to talk to each other (cross-crawl).

The Mind Map will help you develop your Interpersonal Intelligence if you use it to keep records of discussions or to explore your relationships with other people. And it will help you understand yourself better (intrapersonal Intelligence) if you use it to explore some things or ideas you think are important.

#4. THE BODILY-KINESTHETIC INTELLIGENCE – This is your capacity for muscles and movement to be studied and utilized for hands-on, body movement learning. It's the ability to use your body skillfully for self-expression or toward a goal – like dancers, actors, and athletes. Some of the world's greatest thinkers have had to feel their ideas in their bodies to think effectively.

Increase Your Kinesthetic Intelligence

Play charades with your family. One player communicates a topic (book title, movie, song, or idea) through body movement and gestures alone. The rest of the group guesses what is being acted out.

Experiment with kinesthetic movement the next time you're working on a problem or thinking something through. Determine if movement helps or hinders concentration. Try performing a mechanical task, like drying dishes or digging a hole, when you're thinking. You may be the kind of person who can get two things done at once and improve your thinking while you do it.

ACTION ITEM & APPLICATION:
Brain Gym

Many people call the heart a pump because one of its functions is to pump blood throughout the body. But did you know that there is no pump for the endocrine system or for the respiration system? The only way that toxic trash leaves the body cells is through body movement. Also, movement enables the lungs to draw in oxygen and to exhale the body's pollution from the lungs. Additionally, when you move, as in active walking, your heart moves faster, providing more oxygen to both the brain and all parts of the body. The Ancient Chinese knew this when they designed the exercise program called Tai Chi thousands of years ago. It is growing in popularity here in the United States, along with relaxation strategies, such as yoga.

"Brain gym" and the more formal word, "kinesiology," refer to the study and use of muscles and movement. When you use "brain gym" movements or exercises you improve your perception, coordination and mental functioning. Dr. George Goodheart (What a wonderful name for a physician, don't you agree?) first used the term "applied kinesiology" to refer to his discovery. He found that the presence of stimuli, such as positive nutrients, would strengthen indicator muscles, while negative influences, like artificial sweeteners such as "aspartame" would cause the muscles to weaken. A person stands looking forward and holds an arm parallel to the ground. Then a second person stands behind and attempts to pull the arm down in a firm and gentle manner. If the muscle goes weak, the arm goes down. If the muscle is strong you cannot pull the arm down. And one need only hold the positive or negative substance to conduct a "muscle test." That is, you do not need to take and digest the product, only hold it next to the breast plate and the muscles will respond to someone's pressing your arm down, regardless of ethnicity, gender or geographic location.

Dr. Paul Dennison took this further in his work in the late 70's and expanded the field into "behavioral kinesiology." He is a pioneer in educational kinesiology and has documented the relationship of emotional and intellectual stimuli to muscle strength through muscle testing. He also demonstrated the relationship between body movement and brain balancing to learning performance. One of his students is Dr. Carla Hannaford, who wrote a useful book entitled *Smart Moves*. In her book, Dr. Hannaford outlines in detail why learning is not all in your "head" and that learning occurs throughout the body. As a result, body movement can enhance the learning that we traditionally think of as "book" learning or learning in your head. Try these four brain gym exercises by yourself or with family members.

1. *The Cross Crawl*

In this exercise, which you can do standing up or in a seated position, the idea is to tap one hand to a body part on the opposite side of your body. Using upbeat music with no words, such as popular theme songs from movies, is helpful to use with these exercises. So, start with your left hand and touch your right knee, then quickly switch and tap the left knee with your right hand. Do this back and forth in a marching fashion for about two minutes. Then touch your right hand to your left heel (swing your left leg behind you); then switch and touch your left hand to your right heel (swing your right leg behind you). Do this for a minute. Then touch your left hand to your right elbow; and then do the opposite – your right hand to your left elbow.

How does that feel? You should be more alert for test taking, reading or anything that requires you to be alert mentally, but relaxed physically.

2. *Unfolding Your Ears*

Have you ever had acupuncture or acupressure? I remember the first experience I had with acupuncture at a Chiropractor's office after I severely strained my back. I went into the doctor's office and on the wall was a large poster of a human ear. Pictured on this ear, all around the inner and outer structure, were the key pressure points related to the major body systems, as well as symptoms. Did you know that all the major body systems have critical nerves that come out and appear on the ear? Headaches, nausea, allergies, stomach pain, back pain – take your pick. Acupuncture or acupressure often relieves many of these ailments. Well, "unfolding your ears" is a mild substitute for acupressure. The result is increased alertness, concentration, focus and relaxation, among other benefits.

This is something you do to yourself, or you can do it to another, as in the case of your hyperactive child who, just like your pets at home, will love to have their ears rubbed. Start at the top of your ears, where your ear connects to your head. Hold your index finger (your first finger) opposite your thumb and squeeze them together, pinching your ear at the top. Repeat the process, making certain that you have pinched the entire ear as you progress downward to the ear lobe. Now, as you pinch, pull the ear out and back toward the head, permitting the ear to slide through your tight grasp. This might be sensitive and I assure you that your ear will return to its natural shape. But you will experience a warming and reddening of the entire ear due to increased blood flow to the area. You have then stimulated all of the acupressure points. Do this three to five times.

3. *The Lazy Eight*

In a standing or seated position, imagine looking straight ahead and seeing a large outline of a figure eight on its side laying parallel in front of you. It is a big eight, whose intersection is right in front of your head, and whose round parts extend out just beyond your shoulders. Now, hold your dominant hand out in front of you with your thumb upright, as if you were sighting an object in the distance. Keep your head still and allow your eyes to follow your thumb as it traces the imaginary eight in front of you. Begin at the intersection in front of you and make sure you start with an upward motion with your thumb as you trace the complete outline of the figure eight. Repeat this motion at least five times and then do the same thing with your non-dominant thumb (for 95% of the population that is the left thumb). Remember to start the motion with an upward sweep then go around the complete figure. Again, do this at least five times. Then, hold both hands together, with both thumbs up and repeat the process.

If you have difficulty doing this, you may have some coordination challenges. I have witnessed people who draw a figure in front of them that is only about two inches apart, rather than the recommended large figure that extends at least a foot beyond each shoulder. Keep at it until you get it and witness the improvements in a variety of your tasks requiring concentration, focus and attention.

4. *Breathing Exercises*

Whether you are on the couch or on a treadmill, here is a simple breathing technique for you, commonly used in Tai Chi and Yoga. The idea is to breathe in through your nose, hold your breath, and then exhale slowly through your mouth. Now there is a counting process to all of this. The ratio is "one to four to two." So if you breathe in through your nose for a count of four, you would hold your breath for a count of four times that number, or sixteen in this example, and then exhale for a count two times the original count, which is eight in this case. So try it.

A helpful way to keep count is to lift each finger on the left hand and then the right hand as you count. For "one," you lift one finger; for "two," lift two fingers; and so forth. (I know you only have ten fingers, so when you get to eleven, start with the first hand again.) Start by using the 4:16:8 count. Breathe in your nose for a count of 4; hold your breath for a count of 16; exhale for a count of 8. Repeat this process five times, three times a day and monitor the difference in your mental performance. (This activity also appears in **Chapter Six** in the section Air Quality.)

Brain Gym and Educational Kinesiology is an important area for you to explore and you can do so in a variety of different ways, including buying the book *Smart Moves* by Carla Hannaford, Ph.D., or Dr. Paul Dennison's *Brain Gym, Teacher Edition,* or John Diamond's *Your Body Doesn't Lie*, or David Hawkins, MD, Ph.D. *Power vs Force in Medicine & Spirituality.*

#5. THE MUSICAL INTELLIGENCE – Even if you're tone deaf and can't carry a tune in a bucket, you have some ability to understand or create music (or both).

Increase Your Musical Intelligence

Listen to a piece of classical music in a relaxed atmosphere. While you are listening, keep a pad of paper next to you and write down the names of the instruments you hear. Listen for themes in the music that repeat. Tap out what you feel is the music's rhythm; decide whether you feel the music is happy or sad, strong or weak, quiet or loud, and think about what the composer may be trying to say to you. Beethoven expressed a variety of moods and emotions in his music.

Increase Your Musical and Visual Intelligence

While you are listening to music, freely draw pictures that express the mood, story, feeling, or theme of the music. You can make your pictures realistic, abstract, or whatever you please. Remember someone saying, "What have I got to do, draw you a picture?" Well, many people don't process new information very well unless they get it in a picture. So when you draw while you are listening to music, you might get your ideas across better than if you did not have music to guide you. Below in the next section, you will learn which music best suits this sort of task.

Increase Your Musical Awareness

When we refer to "musical intelligence" it is not just music on the radio or your favorite tune you have. We are referring to all rhythmic intonations in the environment, including your voice, the cadence of your speaking, the tone and modulation and evocative power. Do you remember a teacher who drove you nearly batty because of his or her droning voice that bored you to tears? Everyone who talks to another person or teaches should be aware of how the voice can affect the outcomes of learning. Just listen to the differences in the way nurses talk to babies versus senior citizens in a nursing home. Be aware of the "teacher voice" in you as well. It is important for you to recognize that your voice is the carrier of your message, and if you have a battering voice, go out and get some voice lessons, especially if you are a teacher spending 75 percent of your time talking to people.

How Music Can Heal and Communicate

Music and singing taps different parts of the heart-brain system than does talking or speaking. For example, when corporate employees, teachers and parents are trained in the processes of using music to communicate, performance rates increase. For example, at Sara Lee Knit Products, after a training we conducted, managers and line workers went home and wrote a few songs to represent the quality process. After producing these "songs," employees around the plants said they enjoyed learning the material through the words of these "singing learning commercials." In high school chemistry, Leo Wood's students went from 52 % passing with a C grade to 93 % passing, partly by learning material through thirty-five songs they had written. (These songs are available on tape with workbooks from www.intellilearn.org.)

The following story from a music teacher at our family church speaks volumes to the power of music and singing:

" Dear Dr. Martel,

As we discussed at church on Sunday, here's my story about the effects of music on our ill son, along with sister, Ameila, father, Keith and me. Our three-week-old son, Stewart, was in Pediatric Intensive Care at the Medical University of South Carolina with a severe case of bacterial meningitis. The attending physician told us they would do all they could for him, but that the infection was so pervasive that they were not confident he could be saved. Our minister came to baptize the baby there in the hospital.

Since the exact germ was uncertain during the first hours, he was in an isolation ward. As parents, we felt so helpless – we couldn't even touch him because of the IVs and other equipment. Amid the sounds of beeping monitors and whooshing ventilator, I did the only thing for him that I could – I sang a lullaby that had been a favorite of our older child and that he had heard many times:

'…If I could, I would give you wings, to carry you out of the storm.

They'd take you higher than the wind, and you'd be safe and warm.

Sing, little wings, wings in the wink of an eye.

Soon your little wings will be big enough to fly…'

As the last notes of the song faded, the monitor showed that his racing heartbeat had slowed significantly. The nurse said, 'He can hear you.' Technology and skilled staff all contributed to his eventual recovery, but the effects of a calming song when he needed it most also played a part.

Jane"

Beyond the intuition of a loving mother, Children's Hospital Medical Center of Akron has evidence that providing soothing music helps premature babies leave the hospital earlier, as they are bigger and stronger. Although the general trend is that babies who hear lullabies and classical music with an embedded heart beat leave the hospital before those who don't get such music, a new study is being conducted among 300 premature babies. Dr. Anand Kantak is studying 300 infants over the next two years in Children's Hospital and three other Cleveland Hospitals. The infants will be divided into two groups. All will have the music devices, but only half will have the actual music piped into the sleeping bed. It is predicted that those with music will get healthier faster and depart sooner.

With respect to other patients, music has been shown to have a positive impact on recovery. For example, Paul Pearsall wrote in *The Heart's Code* about the role of music in his own therapy with cancer recovery. Indeed, the Ireland Cancer Center in Cleveland uses music therapy for cancer patients and has been for nearly twenty years. Deforia Lane is the director of music therapy for the center and claims that they combine patient's favorite music with classical, relaxation music. However, all "music" is not helpful. Even for those who like it, "heavy metal" doesn't help much with reduced heart rate, blood pressure, respiration or improved relaxation.

Dr. John Ortiz, a clinical psychologist, agrees with the position that the therapeutic value of music often begins with a person's personal choice of favorite selections, BUT, then gradually shifts to the music structures which have been *proven* to enhance learning, memory, relaxation, health and hardiness. You can benefit greatly by reading his book which I mention below - *The Tao of Music.*

For as long as recorded history, we have seen evidence that music has played a vital role in the culture and vitality of life. Whether the purpose is to heighten the spirits of military soldiers going off to combat or to soothe the infant's sleepy body, music has been an internationally recognized part of every civilization. Despite its many purposes to influence the body, mind and soul of people, it was Dr. Georgi Lozanov, M.D., Ph.D. who discovered the relationship between certain structures of music and their impact on cognitive performance and memory. His protégé and former trainer in Bulgaria, Ivan Barzakov, Ph.D., has taken the theory and applied it to recent brain research, leading to the production of musical tapes which enhance mental and emotional performance. These tapes or CD's are known by their trademark name as OptimaLearning® Classics and are available with instructions for your use. According to my recent conversations with Dr. Barzakov, he wanted you to know that "OptimaLearning® Classics contain music for optimal brain stimulation and receptivity for either concentration and performance or relaxation. Two carefully crafted techniques are offered the listener: Reading with Music™ (RWM) and Music for Optimal Receptivity and Concentration ™ (MORC). The OptimaLearning® Classic CDs and cassettes provide uniquely sequenced excerpts of great classical music compositions – sequenced by tempo, key, pitch, instrumentation and themes – to stimulate your brain in specific ways. Essential in OptimaLearning® Classics is the **CONTRAST AND COMPLEMENTATION™** of movements – **SLOW** and **FAST**- which both Dr. Lozanov and Dr. Barzakov found, after 30 years of research, to produce maximum effect.

Using the "Music for Optimal Receptivity and Concentration (MORC) technique with these specialized music backgrounds, you simply listen before or during your study, work or in daily life; in relaxation or healing. The Reading with Music™ (RWM) technique provides a more advanced process for accelerating memory and recall. All OptimaLearning® albums combine beautiful music with written instructions about how and when to use each selection most effectively. These OptimaLearning® techniques combine specially sequenced music with focused methods of use to yield optimal receptivity and concentration. *The integrity of music remains intact. There are absolutely no subliminal suggestions nor instructions, and no change of frequencies. It is the same music created by the genius of Bach, Vivaldi, Corelli, Berlioz, Debussy and many others.*

Through these OptimaLearning® techniques, the inherent harmonies and structures within the music (rhythm, melody, dynamics, etc.) are being synchronized with specific neurophysiological mechanisms of the brain to release dormant energy and optimally stimulate the brain and mind. The end result is significantly enhanced learning or teaching, thinking and creativity, as well as work performance, relaxation and well-being.

The written text gives the listener concise information about the impact of these techniques on the mind of listeners. Music selections and their particular sequence augment the effect of the music itself. You will experience how the conscious mind (cognitive perception) empowers the "non-conscious" (direct musical perception). You will also feel how the beauty of great music unites with the neurophysiological stimulation of the newly created sequences for optimal enjoyment and multiple benefits."

The OptimaLearning® Classics Library consists of four types of albums:

Baroque Music for Learning & Relaxation (3 albums)

Music for Optimal Performance (2 albums)
Music for Imagination & Creativity (2 albums)
Mozart and Baroque Music (1 album)

With respect to the value of these special music tape series, according to Barzakov, Marilyn Hughes, a teacher in Tulsa, Oklahoma used it to overcome what she called "terminal" writer's block. Michael Dwarkin, a research assistant in British Columbia, broke through his lifelong fear of abstract mathematics. And Art Titus, an engineer in Los Gatos, amassed enough knowledge in three months to land a job in a field he knew nothing about – semi-conductors. I have seen teachers, administrators, parents and corporate employees at all levels have transformative effects in personal and organizational performance with the use of music after attending one of our **IntelliLearn®** seminars.

Dr. Barzakov designed a system of *"accelerated and harmonious development* that activates several levels of the brain simultaneously and creates a strong interchange between the conscious and unconscious, making it easier for you to retrieve thoughts and memories that normally get buried in the dark recesses of the mind. This is how the brain was meant to work," he adds, "but few of us take advantage of it because of the fragmented, linear way we were taught to memorize in elementary school. Learning by rote may be effective for remembering telephone numbers and spelling-bee words, but it is inefficient in the long-run because it only addresses part of the brain – the cerebral cortex – and ignores the fundamental unity of the human mind."For more information please visit - www.optimalearning.com.

OptimaLearning's Language for Kids Series

Your whole family will love the original songs and lively conversations in these unique language courses. Although especially designed for ages 2 to 12, these programs are fun and easy for all ages. No previous language experience is required of the parent/caregiver to use this highly motivational program. The new language is spoken and sung by native speakers in both adult and children's voices. The vocabulary of the songs and lively conversations will be learned quickly and soon become a special part of your family's daily routines. Based entirely on the proven OptimaLearning® method, these language courses increase total learning capacities for success in today's global economy. Excellent for home schooled, early childhood and primary children. Available in French, Spanish and English. For more information please visit-www.optimalearning.com.

ACTION ITEM & APPLICATION:
"Use of Music in the Classroom, at Home, in the Office, at Work" by Cinda Fisher and Leo Wood

NOTE: The following action item and application was written by Cinda Fisher, who was elected "teacher of the year" in Arizona, and by Leo Wood, who is one of the world's leading chemistry teachers. Because I wished to honor their work in their endless pursuit of educational opportunity and excellence through the use and application of music, they gave me permission to include this section. Since both Cinda and Leo studied with Dr. Barzakov, they draw heavily on his ideas and strategies, along with those of Professor Georgi Lozanov, M.D., Ph.D. in Bulgaria, and Pamela Rand Barzakov. Cinda's vitality for children of special needs kept her on a quest for innovations in learning that could tap the giftedness in all children. Since she has passed on, her work will live with you here as a tribute to her vision that, "I touch the future, I teach." An accomplished musician with a Masters Degree in "Musicology," Mr. Wood coordinates the Science, Math and Reading initiatives of the National Academy of Integrative Learning, Inc., as well as providing international training in instruction and curriculum design.

They write: "In our busy and hectic pace of daily life in our society, there is a great need for relaxation. Why is relaxation necessary? Relaxation is needed as a therapeutic support system. Relaxation is also needed to eliminate and reduce accumulated stress. There are all types of physical activities and stress-reduction programs on the market that are designed to reduce stress, but there is one very simple and effective way to reduce stress and obtain relaxation. One can begin right away. And you know what? This simple and effective way is not only relaxing, but it increases mental receptivity. It not only is relaxing and increases receptivity, but also increases motivation. Relaxation, receptivity, and motivation are all affected by the "use of music."

Music is the art of organizing tones in a coherent sequence so as to produce a unified and continuous composition. Music involves vocal or instrumental sounds possessing rhythm, melody, and harmony. Music is an esthetically pleasing or harmonious sound or combination of sounds. This is according to the definitions of music found in the dictionary.

The use of music was readily discovered by merchants and advertisers as they began to market their products. It has been discovered that music's relaxation effects stimulate the mind and increase long-term memory. Advertisement commercials use music very effectively in impressing upon the minds of the public the need for the use of their products. The movie industry uses music very effectively. Can you imagine watching a movie with no music? As you walk through department stores, grocery stores, or sit in a doctor's office or a dentist's office, contemplate the reasons why music is playing through their intercom systems.

Research has shown that music is very effective in stimulating emotions. And according to recent brain research studies, it has been shown that emotions are used to code information as it is stored into memory in the brain. Music is a very powerful learning tool that, if used properly, can greatly enhance learning and memory retention in the brains of our students as well as in that of the teacher.

History of Music

Music historians have classified music into eras or periods. Three of the main eras or periods of music become important as we discuss how music is effectively used. The Baroque Era is a period of music that occurred between 1600-1750. The end of the Baroque Era is usually associated with the death of Handel and Bach. The Classical Era usually denotes the music period of Haydn, Mozart, Beethoven, and Schubert. The period of music covers a time scale of 1750-1830. The Romantic Era is designated between 1830-1900 and is associated with famous composers such as Debussy, Wagner, Borodin, and Berlioz.

The Baroque Era (1600-1750) is the era of Ecstasy and Exuberance. The word Baroque means "pearl of irregular form." It is characterized by a "thorough bass" or a walking bass with an expressive melody. Themes are introduced and weave about with great mastery on the part of the composer. The walking bass establishes a soft easy rhythm pattern that easily coordinates with the rhythm of the brain and the body as they are found in a relaxed condition. Baroque music, according to Warren Scharf (unpublished notes – 1989), establishes a multiplicity of pulses. Once these pulses begin, they continue to the end of the composition. One needs to feel this pulse and go with it. The rhythm of the music establishes a pulse. The heartbeat is a pulse. This pulse is in all forms of life. It is found in learning, teaching, feeling, and work experience. The two contours of the music, the melody and the bass, are usually accompanied by improvised harmony. The music experiences dynamic tension and sweeping gestures that causes one's being to become relaxed and peaceful. This era of music affects the center of the long-term memory systems of the brain (limbic system) and allows them to be activated and opens them up to information that comes along with the music. Representative composers of this era are: Bach, Vivaldi, Corelli, Pachelbel, and Handel.

The Classical Era (1750-1830) is the era of stability, clarity, balance, and structure. The forms and style of this period of music evolved in a very complex development that started around 1740 and included composers from Germany, Vienna, Italy and Bohemia. The sonata form, Symphony and the Quartet became popular forms. The music is very objective, giving an impression of self-reliance. The Classical period of music is characteristic of traditionalism. Because of the stability and clarity of structure, this music is excellent for keeping the mind active while doing uninteresting chores or activities where the mind is not very active. Such chores or activities include dish washing, gardening, working on the car, etc. Representative composers of this era are: Mozart, Rossini, Haydn, Schubert, etc.

The Romantic Era (1830-1900) resulted from an incessant shift from the Classical Period. The Romantic period of music adopted the meaning of unrest, exaggeration, experimentation, ostentation, diffusion and subjectivism. This music is highly emotional. It has changes of mood. Because of the emotional and mood changing characteristics, music from the Romantic period is excellent for creative activities like creative writing, art work, and lesson planning, etc. Representative composers are: Wagner, Grieg, Ravel, Debussy, Borodin, etc.

Knowledge of the historical "Eras" or "Periods" of music is essential to be able to more intelligently select the proper type of music for the proper type of activity. Once a selection of music has been made, one should study and listen to it thoroughly before it is used. Many times emphasis can be effectively made when one knows the composition well. Historical information about the composition and the composer can sometimes add to the impact and beauty of the activity using the selected composition.

You can purchase CD's or tapes with specific instructions on what to use, when and how from the Barzak Educational Institute; 885 Olive Avenue, Suite A; Novato, California, 94945. Phone: 1-800-672-1717. Their email is barzak@optimalearning.com.

Principles While Selecting Music

Two principles must be kept in mind while selecting music. The first principle is Contrast & Complementation. To keep the mind fresh and alert, this principle is essential. The mind will dull with the same type of music playing for a period of time. By using a contrast of selections one can make the learning environment more attractive for the brain. Carefully selecting compositions that compliment each other during a music listening activity will also be perceived by the brain as an attractive learning environment.

The second principle from Ivan Barzakov research is V-E-B (variety-economy-balance). The brain thrives on a variety of music being played. Music should be used economically – not all the time. Sometimes you do want to play music. The brain also loves silence as a contrast. Always use a balance of activities – something different each day. Always have a good mix of activities with music being one of the activities used. This helps to keep the expectation level of the mind high – not knowing what is going to happen next, but knowing that something exciting is going to happen. Always try to have a surprise in store for the mind to thrive on. You can tell a good activity using music as a surprise activity when learners say: "Wow! – that was neat." By using the principles of variety-economy-balance (V-E-B), one can become an effective user of music for oneself and/or in the classroom for the students as well as in the home, office, or work place.

Use of Music in the Classroom

√   **Music Playing** as students are coming into the classroom.

√   **Song Singing** to invest information into long-term memory (in place of memorization).

√   **Theme Song** that resonates with the theme of the class lesson - can have lyrics – play often. (You can have a theme song at home for doing dishes or getting ready for bed.)

√   **Activity Sheets, Creative Writing, Story Writing and Journal Writing** - Use instrumental classical music only – no vocal lyrics – Baroque and Romantic music would be ideal.

√ **Demonstrations** with music – special emotional moments – instrumental music only.

√ **During Lab** – fewer accidents – less glass breakage – Discussions are more about lab work – no loud and boisterous talking or giggling – improved lab write-ups – the Classical Era music is recommended – like Mozart and Vivaldi's "Four Seasons," etc.

√ **Exam Taking** – Covers up body noises, sneezes and stomach noises, etc. – also covers up background noises – buzzing lights – outside traffic and other disruptions, etc.

√ **"Reading with Music," Story Telling with Music, Review Sessions with Music, Investing Information into Long-term-memory.** The voice becomes the solo instrument and the music becomes the accompaniment. The music becomes the wave of the ocean and the voice is like the surfer riding the wave. The information slips right into long-term-memory with the music. Baroque Era Music is the most effective music to use for "Reading with Music" technique. Use instrumental music only. No vocal lyrics – the words of songs interfere with the thoughts of the mind.

√ **Special Effects** – special music for special purposes.

Use of Music in Personal Life

√ **Enjoyment and Fun**!

√ **Relaxation/Meditation/Pondering** – Baroque Era and Romantic Era music is most effective. Use instrumental music only – no vocal lyrics or words.

√ **"Read with Music" – Story with Music – Reading Scriptures with Music** – use to invest information into long-term-memory (instead of rote memorization). Baroque Era music works the best. Use instrumental music only – no vocal lyrics.

√ **Lesson Planning – Studying Notes – Reading Textbook – Reorganization of Information.**

√ **Special Moments – Journal Writing** – recall special moments or experiences in real life – mental visits to favorite landscapes or special events or special places that have occurred in your life. Use instrumental music only – no vocal lyrics or words.

√ **Create a Mood – Change a Mood – Build Self-Esteem – Resolve Conflicts – Create Harmony** – Romantic Era Music works very well.

√ **Household Chores** – Classical Era Music works very well. – lawn work - car repair – washing.

√ **Driving** – especially long distances and rush hour traffic – Classical Era Music works well.

√ **Dining** – having that real special dinner – especially a candle light dinner – Classical Era Music, especially Mozart's piano sonatas and concertos and Vivaldi's "Four Seasons."

√ **Exercise, Training, Workout Sessions** – use Classical Era Music – avoid Rock Music and especially heavy metal – the goal is to harmonize (*not disrupt*) the body systems.

√ **Theme Songs** – for special events in your life – have your own theme song for yourself – theme song for each day as you get ready and in moments to help uplift yourself – theme song for each family member – theme song for that special date or special event, etc.

√ **Health Improvement** – getting well from an illness or injury – surgery and dental recovery – hospital stay – child bearing – stress release and recovery- mental preparation, etc. (Remember that, as Dr. Ortiz suggests, you can make your own tape.)

√ **Mental Preparation** – for special events – performances, like a musical performance, a ball game, drama, dance – a date (1st time) a speech or class presentation – an interview.

Your Sound Environment

When you are concentrating on a task, experiment with different kinds of music and sound to determine which kind of sound best aids your concentration. Feel free to contact Barzak Educational Institute at barzak@optimalearning.com. Another outstanding reference for personal music use is a book written by Dr John Ortiz called *The Tao of Music*, which assists the reader in building one's own special affirmation music therapy and achievement tapes to help direct your life in the direction you seek and choose. Another book of value was written by Don Campbell entitled *The Mozart Effect*. Additionally, you might wish to contact the Lind Institute, founded by a friend of all learners, Charles Schmid. Chuck did some outstanding projects with us, teaching teachers the process of using music in the classroom and corporate trainers in how to use music in the workplace. He also conducted a major project for us in the country of Brunei, just before he passed on. You can obtain a catalog at The Lind Institute at www.RelaxWithTheClassics.com. You can also purchase Ole Andersen and Dr. Arthur Harvey and Marcy Marsh's book, *Learn with The Classics*. Telephone 1-800-462-3766.

#6. THE INTERPERSONAL INTELLIGENCE - You have a good perception and understanding of other individuals: their moods, desires, and willingness to interact with you.

Increase your Interpersonal Intelligence

Encourage your family members to talk to each other and contribute something that happened that day. Introduce something from history so your family gets the idea of their connection to the past and how they benefit from the work of our forebears. Also, help them participate in study groups, book review groups, or interest groups, such as religious study groups, in which everyone can discuss topics of mutual interest. You can learn a lot of new ideas and information from other people in a fun and social way.

ACTION ITEM & APPLICATION:
Think and Listen
(or How To Grow Your Brain Power to Extra Large)

Perhaps the biggest problem with thinking in our society is that most people barely get a chance to even spurt and sputter at it, and seldom have an opportunity to take a thought all the way from start to finish. This is, in part, because listening in America is simply waiting to speak! Many of us complete the sentences of other people. Are there people in your family who don't get a chance to finish a sentence without interruption? Well, this interruption can block a person's thinking.

"Thinking out loud" is one of the most useful ways to develop fresh new ideas and perspectives. Even if you rarely get the chance to talk out loud without interruption with another person listening, you probably know how much thinking out loud can help you focus and clarify your own ideas. Nevertheless, to create and develop your thoughts fully, you have to be heard by another person without interruption. The problem is that most people don't get listened to long enough to be able to hear, feel or see where their thinking leads, particularly when they're feeling their way through it and aren't quite certain yet where it's going. When someone stammers and falters, most of us will try to help, supplying words and completing sentences for the person. Yet this is precisely what keeps the thinker from following through with the "thought process," which is different for visual learners, auditory learners and kinesthetic learners.

Thinking, talking and expressing oneself becomes more difficult and is often shut down as a result of interruptions, other people's opinions, time limitations, and other barriers to the creative process. When a person is shut down because of interruptions (sometimes called "feedback") ideas of real power and originality simply may be dropped, never to be heard again.

I recall an Air Force Lieutenant Colonel returning for the second day of our training. The night before we had finished the day with the "Think & Listen" as a tool to overcome this problem of talking and listening. He told us he had gone home with this in his mind. And then he told everyone about his experience with his fifteen-year-old son. He said he used the "think & listen" technique, only to be amazed that he had never heard his son completely through a thought, as he continually finished his sentences for him. He said, "Last night I heard my son for the first time, and he went on talking for a half hour."

Most of us are so addicted to conversational give and take that our interruptions, contradictions, and opinions actually keep the thinker from completing a thought. This is why some individuals never get to finish the delicate job of thinking, and therefore remain locked up inside themselves, because no one has ever really listened to them.

The Think & Listen – A Five-Minute Miracle

There's a wonderful exercise called the Think & Listen that can help you learn to think effectively, efficiently and excellently, and it's fun to use. As you get more comfortable with the process of thinking, you will enjoy a bountiful harvest of creativity and new ideas.

Let's explore how the Think & Listen can help. Creativity stems from the free flow of ideas arising at random and then being connected together in ways that are meaningful and exciting – at first for the thinker, and later for those who can enjoy and profit from the thinker's good ideas.

Why Have a Listener?

You might wonder why it's so important to be telling your thoughts to someone else instead of just talking to yourself or into a tape recorder.

It's true that you could derive some value from either talking to yourself or using the recorder, because any exercise in exploring your thoughts is valuable. However, there's something about the awareness of another mind and heart that helps us focus our thoughts better. Trying to formulate thinking so that another person can really understand the ideas demands a more complete and probing development of thoughts. You don't actually know what your listener is thinking, but it's important to you that he or she is. You can tell by body language and facial expressions whether or not your idea is getting across. Later, if it's appropriate, you can get a reaction from the other person.

How To Do It – Getting Started

Now that you understand the purpose, pair off with one other person and agree to an amount of time each of you will have to talk on any subject you or your partner might choose. Five minutes is a good start, but you can make the time shorter or longer. One of you can begin talking while the other listens without interruption or feedback for the agreed-upon time. The listener simply listens. The topic can be one of free choice, or one agreed to in advance.

When the talker's time is up, that person becomes the listener and the listener becomes the talker. The rules are the same, and it is important to keep track of time. Don't be alarmed by pauses or if the talker's eyes wander while speaking. These are signs of natural brain function.

After each has had a turn to talk, you may want to offer feedback to one another about what was said. Feedback should be offered respectfully and constructively.

Learning to Live with the Think & Listen

It is interesting to hear what people have to say about this process once they have completed it. Some say, "I can't believe how hard it is to talk for five minutes! I had to search for things to say!" Others say, "I wanted to interrupt and put in my thoughts. It was so hard to be quiet for five minutes!" These attitudes tend to crop up the first few times you attempt a Think & Listen, but once you're used to it, you'll be able to keep going more easily, whether you're the thinker or the listener.

Positive Benefits

The Think & Listen is inherently a positive experience, because it is a way of being treated with respect by another person. There's nothing more rewarding than having someone appreciate your own good thinking.

Even if you don't appreciate your own thinking much at first, by repeatedly doing the Think & Listen you will soon find that it improves, and that there are many good ideas inside you never before allowed to be expressed. This can only make you feel better about yourself and your ability to do the things you want to with your life.

This increase will also help you become more articulate. In time, you'll get over any fears of public speaking. Just imagine what it would be like if you could really enjoy collecting your thoughts in front of a large audience, entertaining them with your wit, and being generally admired for your excellent point of view and fine use of language. The practice you'll gain with the Think & Listen can help you get closer to realizing such a dream.

And you'll find the Think & Listen helps you reveal things you haven't been paying attention to and give them the attention they need. Soon you'll be clearing up many problems you've been living with and feeling better about yourself as a result.

 # 7. THE INTRAPERSONAL INTELLIGENCE – You understand yourself, how you think and feel, and you know what you want out of life.

Increase Intrapersonal Intelligence –
This is Hamlet's world of "to be or not to be."

Identify how you feel about what you are doing or what you are simply experiencing. Write a poem about that feeling and imagine the colors, the sounds, and the shapes associated with the feeling. Ask where you fit in and what your duties are in this situation. Focus on "I am" and determine where you belong in the circumstance. Draw a picture of this experience if you wish.

ACTION ITEM & APPLICATION:
The Heart Map

Several years ago in the Springfield, Ohio City School District, I was introducing some concepts from this book to the District's administrative staff. Jean Leonardi, formerly with Xerox, was presenting the processes of "Quality Leadership" with me. She had completed training with the Heart-Math Institute and was certified to deliver a variety of strategies that helped people relax and reduce stress, much like the strategies of the personal self-help process known as neuro-linguistic programming (NLP).

In one session, she showed participants how to shift from anxiety and stress to a state of "heartfelt" appreciation. Later in the day, each administrator completed a "mind map," much like the ones you have been reading about. After completing their Mind Maps, I suggested that they take another piece of paper and, with the topic of the mind map, complete a "heart map."

"What's a heart map?" said one principal.

I responded, rather spontaneously since I was inventing it on the spot, to go to their hearts through the process taught by Jean and then draw a map with ideas that emerge from your heart. Everyone found that the Heart Map had new and different, yet very important, ideas that *did not* appear on the earlier mind map. Then I said, "Add the components of your Heart Map to your Mind Map." People were awestruck at the complete portrait of their thinking that seemed to be balanced between reason and emotional content – between left and right brain perspectives with the heart connection.

So, for yourself, select an issue or topic of concern to you. Maybe it is a problem at work or a speech you must deliver. Perhaps it is a talk you need to give to a child or a problem you are trying to solve. Place the topic in the middle of the page with a heart around it, as opposed to a circle or symbol in the earlier "mind map" process. Now concentrate on your heart and do a Heart Map. Remember, listen to your heart as you write or draw your map. After it is complete, reflect on the fresh new perspective you now have. This is a good tool to develop your Intrapersonal Intelligence, as well as to strengthen the other intelligences.

The Good & New

Using the process of Good & New provides an excellent opportunity to set a tone of positive thinking for the rest of the day. It is something you can do by yourself in quiet reflection at the beginning and ending of each day. Or you can do it with others. This enhances your opportunity for productive experiences. Emphasizing the good in our lives reduces stress and allows our energy to focus on finding solutions to problems or completing tasks. The Good & New may be seen as a therapeutic cleansing or stabilizing strategy. It provides an avenue to give oneself recognition for having provided something positive for oneself and for others. The idea of expressing something that has happened to you may start out as a simple act, but when you are talking about it to someone else, it can take on a more meaningful aspect. The fact of going home and having dinner with your family can seem more important as a result. In short, this exercise is a good stimulus to shape a positive self-image.

Each person takes a turn to mention something good that's happened in the last twenty-four hours. This can be as simple as appreciating the morning sunshine, or it can be an elaborate account of something that went well and makes the person proud.

Specifically, you want to form the habit of identifying particular events or experiences that you feel good about. Answer the question: "What good things have happened in my life recently?" The answer that comes is your Good & New.

The power of the Good & New activity is in its simplicity. If you form the habit of starting regular meetings, classes, or family get-togethers with a Good & New, you'll see immediate improvement in what you can accomplish with a group, as well as improving your own outlook on life. A lot of people don't see much good or new in their lives. If another person can't think of something good and new, ask what could be good or new if it were to happen.

Over time, members of a group develop a deeper appreciation for each other and look forward to learning from one another. They find they're sharing their lives with each other in a new way and developing a tendency to listen to each other as full human beings, instead of just fellow workers or associates.

Soon, they become amazed at the kinds of interests and talents reflected in the group. Some topics for consideration:

What's good and new in your life?

What's good and new in your work?

What's good and new in this meeting?

What's good and new about this lesson or topic we are studying?

Thus, a team-building experience occurs. Because the Good & New is shared without any judgment or criticism of what people are saying, members of the group will begin to enjoy a feeling of increased safety within the group. In addition, they'll approach the experience with a more positive attitude, because they'll have learned to look automatically on the bright side of life as they enter the group.

With small or larger groups, passing around a soft item like a beanbag or "Koosh®" ball helps keep order by clarifying which speaker has the floor at a time. It's only fair that everyone has a chance to speak at least once so no one monopolizes the privilege. The ball is passed around until everyone has had a turn giving a Good & New, although anyone is allowed to "pass" and not say anything. It's not a good idea to force this exercise on people, although most will want to participate when they see others enjoying this activity.

Communication Styles

What makes you comfortable when you are communicating with another person or just listening to a lecture or speech? Do you get "vibes?" Well, Stefan Neilson has developed a process that helps you identify your comfort zone when communicating with others. Based partly on the work of Psychologist Carl Jung and Communications Theorist Marshall McLuhan, Stefan Neilson developed "Winning Colors" – a communications strategy for intra and inter personal skills to reduce conflict and anxiety, as well as to increase achievement and happiness.

On the next page is a list of colors and their meanings. With which list are you most comfortable? Recognizing that we all use the words on each list, and that each list describes some aspects of us, which describes you in the work you do, regardless of whether you are being a parent, an employee, or a student? Remember that all the words do apply in some way to each of us, but *as a group* of words which list *best* describes how you approach your work and tasks. Then, sort the color categories in order of priority from "most like me" to "least like me." Avoid mixing the words between colors.

Also, there is a color associated with each list of words. Imagine the color as you read the list and decide which color list describes you best and which depicts you least. This list comes from Stefan Neilson's recent book **Conflict Resolution**.[1]

> **1. Brown**: Control, power, results, tradition, be prepared, duty, responsible, accountable, rules, dependable, decisive, orderly, productive, achieving.
> **2. Green**: Imagination, thinking, inventing, creative, mystery, being one's best, knowing more, perfection, dreaming, changing, improving, reasonable, better ways.
> **3. Blue**: Feelings, emotions, touch, friendly, love, romantic, warm heart, affection, giving, adorable, being accepted, team member, harmony.
> **4. Red:** Action, excitement, playful, fun, joking, doing, challenge, risk, thrill, perform, quick, easy come – easy go.

Identify your preferences and the order of your list. Then, play a game with family members or office workers and have them order their preferences in the way they are comfortable with these categories of words in describing themselves. You will notice that within a family of four, you will most likely have each family member having a different color list as their first choice. And, if it is the workplace, the person who is most agitating to you will most often have a different color than you do. That is, if you choose blue, your wife will choose green or brown. If you choose brown, then your husband might choose red or blue. Make sure you don't tell each other or disclose the order of your color word list until all who are in the game have finished.

If you are Blue, you are a "relater," often suggesting that people share and develop harmony and participation. If you chose the Brown list, you are a "builder-leader," often duty bound and obedient, expecting others to be prepared, responsible and reliable, like you are. A Green choice puts you as a "planner" who often works alone, thinking, pursuing goals, questioning, making lists and logs in a daily planner. A Red choice means "adventurer," one who is spontaneous, action oriented, risk taking, humorous and on stage.

Browns want the "bottom line," while Blues want to be loved and cared about. Greens want to think and plan, while Reds are unhappy unless there is a lot of physical action and adventure.

Which did you think best describes you at work? Did you think,

"Well, sometimes, I am this and at other times I am that?" Most of us have a communication style and comfort zone that facilitates our ability to perceive and process information from the world at large and from the inner world of introspection. Knowing how you perceive and process information can be helpful in how you approach others in terms of the language you use and its effect on others. For example, if you have a boss who is Green, plan on endless meetings and lengthy memos with little action. However, a Brown wants the bottom line efficiency right now. The Blue boss is concerned about relationships and people caring about one another. And a Red boss is always shaking things up, with ever changing goals and directions.

Check out who in your life makes you miserable and use your imagination to plot that person's communication style by how they would see themselves on the color list. Then, even if it is your mother-in-law, you can make some adjustments in your attitude toward that person, using language more comfortable to her or him and increase the positive climate for communication.

As an example of written communication in the form of an agenda or purpose statement, consider the following, which includes all four colors and lists in its flow of logic. This is a sample purpose statement whose structure is designed to include everyone. Feel free to use it for your purposes by simply erasing out the content of **IntelliLearn**® and putting your own needs and wants right after the words that are underlined. In short, erase the content, leave the statements or expressions that are underlined, then add your own content. This is just an example of a communication strategy in the form of a purpose statement that pulls together all the communications styles and includes the multiple intelligences. See if you can identify the four colors in the following purpose statement.

A SAMPLE COMMUNICATIONS
TOOL USING ALL SEVEN INTELLIGENCES
A PURPOSE STATEMENT FOR THE *IntelliLearn*® WORKSHOP
*A Presentation to Learn More in Less Time and Increase
Memory and Creativity*

In this session you will experience how to successfully:

√   Present more information in less time
√   Increase the climate of your classes with positive tools of
    learning

√   Tap the diversity of learners with new strategies.
√   Improve learner performance in all courses
√   Increase memory and retention rates
√   Engage learners in active, creative and reflective learning
√   Drastically improve learner skills as "self-directed" learners
√   Increase communication, cooperation and reduce discipline problems.

The Purpose of this session is to invite participants to explore and experience and examine an innovative philosophy of learning and learning process called *IntelliLearn®*, which has been validated by the New York State Department of Education. This Model has been adopted by successful organizations nation-wide to achieve observable and measurable quality results and high performance:

In a way that participants learn and experience the values and benefits of the positive strategies, tactics and tools of *IntelliLearn®*. Active participation will relate these orchestrating and coaching processes to the classroom and to organizational management through a demonstration of specific whole-brain teaching techniques across various curriculum subject areas. Dynamic presentation techniques include: application of theory and neurosciences, role-playing, movement, dramatization, use of music and rhythmic activities, etc. This will be demonstrated by activating a variety of intelligences, learning modalities and communication styles.

So that participants develop new strategies, tactics and tools to create optimal and effective classrooms where the instructional climate and culture assures that all students learn more in less time with greater depth, breadth, retention and joy of learning.

And that participants explore how to reduce burnout through the increase of teaching performance, personal enthusiasm and positive outcomes. Educators have a full plate; this will strengthen their plates, rather than add more.

As measured by locally determined results as evidenced by gains on observable and measurable performance, standardized national, state and local instruments, as well as personal goals and results.

Involving: Whether you have attended a previous *IntelliLearn®* training, this session would be most appropriate for people at all levels of any organization with learning performance as a priority: school board members, administrators, teachers, parents, trainers, instructors, instructional designers and supervisors and staff who are interested in enhancing learning outcomes and processes.

Metaphors: "The New Science of Learning;" "Learning as a Performing Art;" Diversity as Capacity;" "Teacher as Orchestrator and Coach."

Musical Theme: "Reach out and Touch Someone."

Art Theme: "Three Musicians," by Picasso

Motto: "We become what we Think!"

Principles and Corecepts:

Message **received** is the **message sent**

You get **more** of what you **reinforce**

Any act of **learning** is an act of **creating**

Diversity as a **capacity**

Our **strength** is in our **connectedness**

Stupidity is a **learned** behavior

Everyone is born a **genius**

Requirements: High interest in increasing the effectiveness of instruction, as well as an interest in systems change, process improvement and high performance. Also required: **open minds, open hearts**.

For more information about the process of "communication styles," with the many books and materials for both children and adults, for education and conflict resolution, for interpreting Harry Potter and improving arbitration, contact Stefan Neilson at: Aeon Communications, Inc.; P.O. Box 7276; Seattle, WA 98133. 425-672-8222. e-mail: winningcolors@mindspring.com.

Put All the Seven Intelligences Together

Learning Modality Game

Discover the learning modalities of everyone in the room. Ask questions or use any other modality to find out how they feel about learning and how they prefer to receive new information. This will require some interesting and fun detective work. People are often not aware of their preferences if they haven't had a chance to think about them, so you may in fact get people to start thinking about how they learn, and what other new ways they can use to improve their learning.

Multiple Intelligence Charades

Play a game of charades with an added twist. In addition to picking a subject to charade, also assign a specific intelligence with which to communicate the topic. For example, Linguistic (you might use words to get the message across without referring directly to the title, plot, characters, or particulars of the story or idea); Logical-Mathematical (you could set up a logical or mathematical scenario or sequence that would lead to discovery of the topic); Musical (you could tap out a rhythm or hum a tune); Visual-Spatial (you could draw a picture or arrange spaces or items in a room; Kinesthetic (gesturing and acting out, much like the usual game of charades). Inter and Intra Personal (you could get another person to speak out or act out what you are thinking, so others must guess what you are thinking by observing the other person).

ACTION ITEM & APPLICATION:
When you select books from the perspective of "Seven Intelligences Theory," consider the following guideline:

Linguistic

- √ All books with words
- √ Books and read-along cassettes
- √ Computer chip books that teach you as you read
- √ Crossword puzzles

Spatial

- √ 3-D pop-up books
- √ Wordless all-picture books
- √ Lavishly illustrated books
- √ Comic books
- √ Puzzle books

Bodily-Kinesthetic

- √ Touch n' feel books
- √ Computer touch, listen and say books
- √ Pull and press books
- √ Practical activities books

Musical

- √ Computerized music books
- √ Books with sing-along cassettes
- √ Song books

Logical-Mathematical

√ Books on organization and time management
√ Puzzle books and word problems
√ Brain Teaser books
√ Computer software "books"
√ Science and math fun books

Intrapersonal

√ Personal skill books
√ Books on emotional themes(love, empathy, loss, anger, etc.)
√ Adventure books

Interpersonal

√ Interactive books
√ Mime books
√ Dramatic plays

Also, if you were teaching your child or an adult a language, such as English, consider how the initial consonant sounds might be taught using the "Multiple Intelligences."

Linguistic

√ Flip Chutes and Flash Cards
√ Worksheets
√ Thinking up similar sounding words

Spatial

√ Turning pictures into symbols (e.g. snake into "S")
√ Turning symbols into pictures
√ Drawing pictures with symbols
√ "Pictionary"

Bodily-Kinesthetic

√ Making symbol with the body
√ Tracing symbol with finger in the air
√ Tracing symbol on white salt poured on white cardboard

Musical

- √ Make up and sing songs with similar sounding words
- √ Write and perform songs with the vocabulary to be learned in the song
- √ Singing rhyme rhythmically with similar sounding words

Logical-Mathematical

- √ Explaining why symbols have sounds that correspond like "nicknames"
- √ Locating symbol as parts of words where they usually appear

Interpersonal

- √ Have one person teach sound to another
- √ Group people in teams and compete with each other's team to guess sound flashed up on a card for all to see.

Intrapersonal

- √ Ask people to choose whether they want to work alone, with pairs or in small groups and then let them select activities (read book, listen to tape, etc.)
- √ Have individuals write a poem about each consonant, showing how it looks, feels and sounds in the poem.

Reading Comprehension

Linguistic

- √ Read the passage
- √ Write questions/answers about passage

Spatial

- √ Do a mind map on the passage
- √ Conduct a guided imagery and imagine scene based on passage
- √ Do drawing or other art project based on passage

Bodily-Kinesthetic

- √ Pretend to be a character or item in the passage and act it out
- √ Mark key ideas in the passage with a pencil
- √ Draw how the passage made you feel

Logical-Mathematical

√   Make a list of the key ideas and thoughts
√   List the steps in the flow of the passage and what happened
√   Do a timeline in the sequence of action in the passage

Musical

√   Play background music while studying passage
√   Sing key sentences in passage

Interpersonal

√   Turn to neighbor and do a "think and listen" about passage
√   Pick a small study team to go over passage

Intrapersonal

√   Ask people to "reflect" on what the passage means to them
√   Write a poem or sentence on how the passage made them feel

Thus far, we have reviewed and explored how the seven intelligences can be used to increase the effectiveness of learning. At one time, Howard Gardner told me he did not believe that the intelligences crossed over, influencing one another. My experience and research, however, contradicts that view. Anybody can be taught the mathematical principles of geometry (mathematical intelligence) by using a pool table and demonstrating the angles and directions of the balls (kinesthetic intelligence), along with reinforcement from the textual material (linguistic intelligence.) Jeannie Panka's New York Regent's Biology classes increased in test scores from 74 % to 96 % by using strategies in this book that employed all the intelligences to introduce, process and demonstrate knowledge of new and difficult information, while activating individual learning styles.

8, #9, and #10 THE ADDITIONAL THREE INTELLIGENCES COMMON TO HUMANITY: SPIRITUAL, MORAL AND AESTHETIC

Whereas the seven intelligences identified by the Harvard Project Zero Researchers are specific to particular functions and structures of the brain, the following three synthesize all components of the human mental and physical being and can be understood as holistic, permeating the fiber of consciousness. One sees the spiritual, ethical and aesthetic woven within and across the other seven as they are manifest in daily behavior. Let's look at these critical and pervasive intelligences. For personal growth and development in each of these three areas, as well as to establish a guideline for yourself in the use and application of all intelligences, I suggest you read and explore the basic arts and science literature available in all libraries, as well as in condensed versions such as "The Great Books Series." Further, I will suggest some titles in each of the intelligence categories below.

#8 - The Spiritual Intelligence

No culture exists or has ever existed that anthropologists know of which does not express a sense of "awe" for "the greater than which there is no other." This is the expression of purpose, meaning, value and wonder in all of creation. Creation stories abound in all cultures about a Greater Being, the Creator of all. Even in atheistic cultures, there is a God whose existence is denied. People seek meaning, value and purpose in their lives. And they feel abandoned, alone and alienated in the absence and pursuit of a connection greater than themselves. This "spiritual" intelligence creates the conditions for people to respond to others with love and appreciation; kindness and empathy; much like the nearly universal response to the 9/11 disasters in New York, Washington and Pennsylvania. Denying the essence of Being reduces meaning, value and purpose to a mechanistic world-view of existence, whose shadow casts a doom and gloom perspective. In the dramatic arts, this alienating view is expressed in John Cage's "theatre of the absurd." In acknowledging and elevating the spiritual intelligence of people, we create the condition through which people feel honor, humility, wonder, amazement, joy and purpose. Read the *New Testament* as well as *The Psalms & Proverbs* for an insight into the spiritual intelligence.

#9 - The Moral Intelligence

All cultures abide by values, norms, and mores which are understood as distinguishing between "Good and Evil." In the modern world of "moral relativity," where the intellectual position and the popular culture speaks of "anything goes," there is the appearance that morals, values and mores are like magazines; namely something one either subscribes to or doesn't. In truth, what does change is one's subscription to things that are good, versus those things that are evil, as opposed to the idea that "good and evil" change depending on the culture. And regardless of the fact that there are irrefutable truths about good and evil, the fact is that every culture subscribes to some notion of some good and evil and establishes the human condition that has a moral code. For instance, matricide, cannibalism, theft, rape and murder are historically and universally held to be acts of evil, even though some cultures practice these things routinely. The acts of 9/11 in the United States were judged throughout the world as horrific acts of evil, as were the genocide ovens of the Nazis and prison camps in Japan, as well as the "Slaughter of the Innocents" by Herod of Jerusalem.

Collectively and personally, each of us seeks to know good versus evil in order to have predictability and stability in our lives. When immoral acts of outrage occur, such as the Columbine Massacre, the scales are tipped and the normal conditions of civilization and mental health are undermined, removing the predictable validity of rational conduct. All of us seek to understand those things that enhance the condition of human quality and to resist those debasing conditions which dehumanize people. Without such stability in predicting the behavior of human decency and dignity, the human regresses into a state of brain "downshifting" or "fight or flight," as well as a state that psychiatrists call "Post-traumatic Syndrome." This goes beyond simple dysfunction to a level of physical illness. For an important reference on this issue of good and evil, read clinical psychologist Dr. Renee Fuller's article on "Good and Evil" freely available at her website: www.ballstickbird.com Read Aristotle's *Nicomachean Ethics* and William Bennett's set of readings in *The Moral Compass*.

#10 - The Aesthetic Intelligence

The need for beauty, balance and harmony is a human cultural and psychological need expressed in all cultures at all times and in all places. One might say that "beauty is in the eye of the beholder," but we cannot say that people do not seek beauty. The evidence of the history of art and the history of cultures is filled with the personal attempt to capture, express and honor beauty, harmony and balance in nature. The ancient Chinese, in an effort to provide for "harmony" for the spirits of deceased loved ones, developed a process for balance of burial. This later evolved into the current practice and art of Feng Shui (see **Chapter Six**) which considers the forces of nature in the placement and construction of buildings, as well as location of furniture, doors and energy flow. Similarly, the West has been guided in its art and architecture by the balancing forces in nature, ranging from the geometric balance of the Pyramids to the symmetry of Gothic arches, taken from the intersecting bows of live oak trees. In classic architecture, as Jonathan Hale argues in his book, *The Old Way of Seeing*, there is balance, harmony and beauty. If you build a house with two columns on the left of the door, harmony demands that you have two columns on the right side of the door. Part of this sense of balance and beauty, comes from the human perspective of brain physiology. Ned Hermann, who wrote *The Creative Brain*, served with me as one of the keynote trainers for Xerox the year following their winning the Baldridge Award. Ned has developed a process to determine one's brain dominance index, as well as one's sense of beauty and balance. He has linked the Neo Cortex with the Limbic Brain to provide an individual portrait of perspective on logic and linearity, as well as balance, beauty and harmony. "Where do you stand on this continuum?" of reason and emotion; of logic and beauty is the question Ned's Brain Dominance Indicator answers for you. In an experiment by missionaries in South America, Mozart's "Magic Flute" was played for the natives. They smiled and danced for joy to the beauty of the structure of the music. Shortly after, "Heavy Metal" music was played and the natives ran and hid in the jungle. We know from scientific research that certain harmonies (the golden harmonies) and structures, like those of Mozart, actually excite and enhance living tissue in plants and animals. Similarly, we know that discordance in music like "heavy metal" kills plant and animal tissue. The intelligence that recognized beauty, as in the seven wonders of the world, supports and enhances the quality of life, whereas, that intelligence also recognizes discordance, disharmony and decadence which inhibits and stifles life at the cellular level. If this intelligence is not developed, the result can be self-inflicted chaos.

In summation of the Spiritual, Ethical and Aesthetic Intelligences, let me say that they must be developed, just like the other seven. Left to themselves, without proper interaction, nourishment and environment, they can go fallow and atrophy on a personal, as well as cultural basis. I am reminded of the popular cliché, "Use it or Lose it!" I should also point out the inter-linkage and inter-connection among and across the intelligences. While one is developing the "inter-personal" intelligence, one is also likely to engage the "ethical" intelligence, as well. I recall the Dean of the Harvard Medical School who was fired a few years ago for plagiarism (a form of cheating by claiming that you wrote something which was actually the idea or writing of another). Skilled as a physician and advanced as a medical researcher, most would credit this man with many well-developed intelligences, except the ethical intelligence, whose lack in this man caused him and his family disgrace, dishonor and dismissal. There is a movement, sparked by some of Hollywood's movies and video games for young people to explore, even worship, the "dark" side as expressed in the popular "goth" appearance. On the rise is demonology, devil worship, and dehumanizing cults.

The Fifth Secret Revealed

If you are like most people, you began this chapter with two intelligences that our culture values. Those two intelligences constitute what we call I.Q. or Intelligence Quotient, which is a general score on your ability to perform logical-mathematical operations and linguistic performance. That's it. Your life is sorted and selected in schools, and your income and life's chances are largely associated with your capacity to achieve in these two areas of mental performance. Indeed, to become a member of the Mensa Society, one must obtain a specific score on the I.Q Examination.

Well, now we know that you and I have at least *TEN INTELLIGENCES, NOT* two! What greater value is that? In the few pages of this chapter, you progressed from two intelligences to ten. How does it feel to have this knowledge that can change the way you look at yourself and change how you regard others and the world? This view gives us a fresh new look at what is called "learning disabilities." Perhaps our young people and adults are *LESS* learning disabled and *MORE Curriculum Disabled*! If our schools and corporations teach and train to the two intelligences and use only those two intelligences in communication, perhaps people who are strong in the other eight intelligences are mislabeled.

By using *ALL TEN INTELLIGENCES* in learning input, learning processing and learning outcomes, we can expect everyone to learn more in less time with far greater memory and enthusiasm for learning. Armed with this new knowledge from The Fifth Secret, you can go forward in a spirit of compassion and empathy for the diverse ways in which people perceive and process information, as well as how they look at the world around them and the inner universe within.

In the next chapter, we'll unveil the cloak surrounding the intense impact your environment can have on your capacity to learn and retain knowledge and skills in the pursuit of the "miracle of learning."

References

[1] Neilson, Stefan, *Conflict Resolution Through Winning Colors Vol. I: A Workable Process for Resolving Personal Differences (Hostility, Anger, Miscommunication, Agendas)*, Aeon Hierophant, 1999.

SECRET #6
Revealed.

IRLEN SYNDROME:
You Might Need
"Rose Colored" Glasses.

ADHD:
Learning Disabilities,
Food Allergies, and
Environmental Illness.

LIGHT:
What You See
is What You Get?

SOUND:
Can You Hear
Me Now?

WATER HYDRATION:
The One Drink that
Lets You Think.

ELEMENTS IN THE ERGONOMICS OF LEARNING

Can Lead You to

Success or

Failure

NUTRITION:
Food for Thought...

EMF:
Electro-Magnetic
Force Fields
Can Hurt You!

TEMPERATURE:
Some Like it Hot,
Some Like it Cold!

AIR QUALITY:
It Can Influence
Your Thinking!

**INSTRUCTIONAL
DESIGN:**
The Fun, Joy and
Excitement
of Learning!

FACT:
90% of our Day
is Spent Indoors -
The Importance of
Sunshine!

FENG SHUI:
Bring Balance
and Harmony
in Life.

AROMA-THERAPY:
Smell a Rose by any
other Name!

COLOR:
Somewhere Over
the Rainbow...

PETS & PARASITES:
Your Pet May Not Be
Your Best Friend!

ROOM DESIGN:
Some Need a Bean Bag,
Others a Hard Chair.

Chapter Six

Secret #6
Environmental
Hazards

Watch out: What you know about environment can make or break you, leading you to success or failure.

W hat would a book about the secrets of learning be if it did not include at least one field trip? Do you remember the last field trip you took? Perhaps it was when you were in high school, or maybe it was with your child on an elementary school outing. Perhaps it was on a trip to visit another company or business. Wasn't it fun? Well, this chapter will take you on a field trip into the environment that can either make or break your learning experiences at home, at school or at work.

When I say "make or break," I mean that. Literally thousands of people are disconnected from learning because of a variety of environmental factors. Some of what you are about to read will startle you and might even alarm you. I do not wish to frighten you, but you should be aware of this important research on environmental influences on learning, health and achievement. In every section, I offer hope and suggest trails you can take on your own after you have finished with this particular field trip.

For example, if your child is not doing well in school, it might be because she can't hear the teacher, whose muffled voice is not clear. Up to twenty percent of the children in school would fail a normal hearing test on any given day. This would be random, so that if you and I passed today, we might fail next month. Or, the lighting might be oppressive, as it is in most work and school environments, not to mention the kitchens in our homes. The good news is that you can take steps to improve your environment that can make a difference in personal health, hardiness and learning achievement.

197

Sound and light are just a few of the environmental factors that we will explore on our field trip. And, as a bonus, I will give you directions to other locations you may wish to explore on a more in-depth basis on another day. Our goal on this journey is to increase your level of "awareness;" that is, to help you become aware of those factors that might retard or accelerate the function of your brain, restrain the capacity of your heart and restrict your happiness and personal success.

Let's call this field trip a journey to "ergonomics-land," where we will be examining those things in the external environment that have been shown to dramatically influence our capacity to learn. "Ergonomics" is a word that is often used to refer to the suitability of the environment, such as room design, furniture, lighting and other extensions of the human body that are most compatible with human functioning in work, at home or at school. Designers of automobiles are particularly tuned to "ergonomics" to build cars that operate easily in the space available and in accordance with the human body and grasp. Savvy manufacturers place radios, control knobs and seating adjustments for the consumers' ergonomics.

What kind of ergonomics is designed into learning at home, at work and at school? "Very little," is a shameful but appropriate answer. And, as a matter of fact, by making a few minor changes in the ergonomics of your home or your classroom, you could significantly improve learning performance (Review **Chapter Two** as a reminder of the impact of environment and learning styles).

So, strap on your hiking boots or tennis shoes and let's take the trek on our imaginary field trip.

Elements in the Ergonomics of Learning

What we must first know is that there is a wealth of research indicating that an environment's ergonomics significantly improves or retards individual and group learning performance. These elements include light, The Irlen Syndrome, sound enhancement, water hydration, ADHD, food and nutrition, electromagnetic fields, air quality, aroma, pets and parasites, color, room design, temperature, instructional design and "feng shui." What follows is a discussion of each element as a contributor to the enhancement of learning performance and achievement.

Light: What You See is What You Get
Malillumination vs. Posillumination

Since the first stop in our environment is "Light," take a look around you and evaluate the lighting. Do you see any incandescent lights? What about fluorescent lighting? Were you aware that many learning difficulties only occur under cool-white fluorescent lights? Are you bothered by bright light indoors? Does dim light make you perform better?

> *"Malillumination" is to* **"light"**
> *as "malnutrition" is to* **"food."**
> *"Posillumination" is to* **"health"**
> *as "nutrition" is to* **"life."**

"Exposure to environmental light has been recognized for its salutary effects on mood for hundreds of years. Aretaeus noted in the second century A.D. that 'Lethargics are to be laid in the light and exposed to the rays of the sun, for the disease is gloom.' The solarium was regarded as a valuable room in any place of healing, and sunlight, along with fresh air, was widely recommended as a panacea for a variety of ills," according to Norman E. Rosenthal, M.D., chief, Section on Environmental Psychiatry, National Institute of Mental Health,[1]

Pioneer light researcher Dr. John Ott coined the term "Malillumination" to describe sunlight deficiency and the negative, harmful effects of artificial pink or cool-white fluorescent lighting on behavior, learning, health, hardiness and longevity. On the other hand, "Posillumination" is the term I have chosen to refer to those artificial sunlight environments, about which an overwhelming body of research shows the positive impact of simulated sunlight (full spectrum lighting and color) on human behavior, learning, health, hardiness and longer life.

(For this section on 'Light," I draw from the brilliant and sensitive work of Dr. Jacob Liberman and encourage you to read his book *Light: Medicine of the Future* for an in-depth discussion and analysis of the research referenced in this overview on light.)

Homes, schools, classrooms and other work environments where people spend time learning and working under simulated sunlight (full spectrum lighting and color) experience less stress and anxiety, improved behavior and attitudes, improved health and attendance, and increased performance and academic achievement. Research in the use of light in schools has shown that cool-white fluorescent bulbs (which are used in virtually all classrooms) cause: *bodily stress, anxiety, hyper-*

activity, attention problems and other distress leading to poor learning performance. Are these issues in your life or the lives of people around you? As you will "see," the research is clear: we can do something about it.

For example, in 1999 William Titoff concluded, "There was a statistically significant difference between the students who worked under old-style fluorescent lights and those who worked under full-spectrum, visually-efficient lighting."This controlled study verified that depression was lowered among those students who experienced learning under full-spectrum lighting. Also, depression actually increased under standard fluorescent lights among the fourth graders. As an elementary school principal, Titoff conducted research for his Ph.D. dissertation and discovered that when the project was completed, "the teachers with the full-spectrum lighting refused to let me take it out and put back the old-style fluorescent bulbs."

The research into lighting has a history of several decades with a large volume and cross section of people. In 1938, Harmon found that over 4000 children developed observable deficiencies associated with Malillumination. In the late 1940's, conditions of the learning environment (lighting, seating and decor) were instituted in schools, resulting in the following student improvements: 65% reduction in visual difficulties, 47.8% decline in nutritional problems, 43.3% reduction in chronic infections, 25.6% reduction in postural problems and, finally, 55.6% decline in chronic fatigue. Despite this knowledge, legislators and policy makers still blame the "victim;" namely, the students and parents for not "working hard enough" to pass state standardized tests. Instead of such misdirected "blame," policy makers might also look at the negative influence of fluorescent lighting.

Beyond learning improvements, in 1960 Ott first discovered that other mammals (mice) lived twice as long and were hardier when they lived under natural, unfiltered daylight as opposed to under pink and daylight-white fluorescent lights. (Think about this result in terms of the rising tide of "learning disabilities and behavioral problems. If you want to close this book right now and replace the lights in your home or work area, go right ahead. But come back to our journey, for there is more insight into the ergonomics of learning. Source references are provided for further research and light bulb manufacturers-www.fullspectrumsolutions.com. By the way, you don't need to change the "fixture," but rather only replace the bulb.

Thirteen years later, in 1973, Ott studied four, first grade classes in Florida. Two classrooms had full-spectrum, radiation-shielded fluorescent light fixtures, while the other two classrooms remained with the traditional cool-white fluorescent bulbs. These are what you normally would see in fixtures in schools, public offices, hospitals and doctor's offices. In reporting the results of this study, Dr. Liberman stated that: "Concealed time-lapsed cameras took random sequences of students and teachers in the four classrooms. Although teachers were aware of the research program, neither they nor the students were aware of when they were being photographed.

"With cool-white fluorescent lighting, some students demonstrated hyperactivity, fatigue, irritability, and attention deficits. In the classrooms with full-spectrum lighting, however, behavior and classroom perfor-mance, as well as overall academic achievement, improved markedly within one month after the new lights were installed. Furthermore, *several learning-disabled children with extreme hyperactivity prob-lems miraculously calmed down and seemed to overcome some of their learning and reading problems while in classrooms with full-spectrum lighting.* This study additionally demonstrated that children in rooms with full-spectrum lighting developed one-third of the number of cavities in their teeth as children in the classrooms with the standard cool-white fluorescent lights." [2]

Notwithstanding the evidence from Ott's significant findings, in 1980 Hollwich discovered that cool-white fluorescent lighting produced in-creased levels of stress-producing hormones. Think of the increasing complaints of stress-related disorders in schools, at home and at work. Could the simple replacement of light bulbs make a tremendous differ-ence in not only learning outcomes, but also in the health of children and adults? The research says: **"YES!"** And yet, ask any educational policy maker in a State Education Department or the legislators on state edu-cation committees, local school board members, or corporate leaders about the negative impact of cool-white fluorescent lights on learning and human performance and the response you will likely receive is: "What?"

Further adding to the argument to "change the lights," according to Liberman, is the research of Wohlfarth and Sam, who in 1981 studied, "the combined impact of selected colors and full-spectrum lighting on the behavior and physiology of both blind children with severe behav-ioral disorders and sighted children with severe handicaps." *Under full-spectrum lighting, the children's blood pressure dropped signifi-cantly and their aggressive behavior reduced significantly.* How-ever, when the lights were replaced with standard *cool-white fluores-*

cent bulbs, their blood pressure increased and their aggressive and disorderly conduct increased. And the blind children were equally as affected as those with sight.

With this research and knowledge, Liberman cannot help but lament that "For years we have been labeling and re-labeling children who appear to have difficulties we do not understand. We test and tutor them continually, only to find out that they are usually very bright but that for some reason outside of our understanding they do not achieve in the expected manner within the traditional learning environment. Although the labels for these children have changed from dumb, stupid and lazy to dyslexic, minimally brain dysfunctional, and learning disabled, the labels nonetheless scar them for life...." [3]

Journalist Rhonda Stone, reported in her renowned, recent book, *The Light Barrier*, the results from a 1999 California energy study, conducted by a consulting firm. The study finds that "Fluorescent light is the type of light most commonly associated with fatigue, physical discomfort, and visual distortions. The Heschong Mahone Group, a well-known energy consulting team, evaluated the effects of natural light in elementary schools in three western United States communities. In Fort Collins, Colorado, it found 7% across-the-board improvement in both math and reading scores in locations where natural light was plentiful. In Seattle, Washington, the firm found an average improvement of 9% in math and 13% in reading in schools with an ample natural light source. In the Capistrano Unified School District in Orange County, California, it found that students on average performed 20% better in math and 26% better in reading when aided by natural light." Since full spectrum light mirrors natural light, there is absolutely no excuse to deprive our children, our workforce and our families of the optimal lighting conditions for learning. And it is a moral question for us to provide harmful lighting conditions when the research is so clear about the negative effects of artificial fluorescent lighting.

With funding from the Pride First Foundation Corporation, founded by Lloyd Campbell and administered by Gwen McEvilley, a school in Harlem was trained in the *IntelliLearn®* Model (see **Chapter Seven**). Three classrooms where equipped with "full spectrum" lighting and the reports from the teachers were outstanding in terms of increased grades and reduced discipline problems. One teacher told me she stopped experiencing headaches. Similarly, in Arco, Idaho, the year following the implementation of "full spectrum" lighting in the elementary school, the district reported a two-thirds reduction in special education referrals, with increased grades and reduced absenteeism.

When my personal physician was planning to build a new facility for holistic health, including an exercise and fitness training suite, along with a Sports Chiropractor, together with acupuncture and massage, I referred him to the lighting alternatives available to him. After the completion of the facility, I stopped in to see him and noticed the same old cool-white fluorescent lights. Two of the office staff were out sick with stress-related headaches, and the receptionist felt unwell and strained. I asked the physician what happened to the information I gave him on lights, and he said that, quite frankly, he had painted the walls the recommended mint green, but had forgotten about the lights with all of the other construction issues. I told him I had a half of a carton of light bulbs and would return shortly. He and I replaced the old bulbs with the new, full spectrum bulbs, and the receptionist remarked at how much better she felt. He ordered bulbs from Mike Nevins at Full Spectrum Solutions and transformed the entire facility. One of the other doctors told me that the entire staff was more upbeat and positive after the light change with no more headaches.

How many must suffer before we realize that stupidity is a learned behavior and that the giftedness in each individual can be tapped and developed under optimal learning ergonomics and strategies, including the strategic use of **"Posillumination"** and the elimination of **"Malillumination"**?

Using full-spectrum lighting has a positive impact on human behavior, learning, health, endurance and longevity. For information on replacing your lighting, go to www.fullspectrumsolutions.com where Mike Nevins is the President. (I also encourage you to read the book, ***Light: Medicine of the Future*** by Jacob Liberman.)

The Irlen Syndrome – You Might Need "Rose-Colored" Glasses!

No field trip is complete without someone starting a fire with a magnifying glass. Remember the first time you saw that happen? Like most people, you were probably amazed at the power of that lens. Well, this next stop in our trip has even more power, as it lights up the energy of learning for many who are disenfranchised and does so by changing the color of light that enters the eyes and travels to the mysterious visual cortex of the brain.

Helen Irlen is one of the most outstanding researchers and clinicians in the world. Although her work began in the United States, Irlen's discovery of the Scotopic Sensitivity Syndrome (also called the Irlen Syndrome) has been utilized for the "learning salvation" of countless people, young and old. What Irlen has accomplished through her loving sensitivity to people and her razor sharp clinical method is to discover that many people have a range of difficulties such as reading and physically coordinating their bodies without the medium of a colored lens for glasses or an acetate transparency as a reading aid (specific colors vary depending on the individual). This medium can include tinted, non-prescription glasses (like custom made sun glasses), prescription glasses or acetate colored, overhead transparencies. Her clinical work extends throughout the world.

In heralding Irlen's discovery, Dale Jordan, Ph.D. claims that: "Helen Irlen's contribution to the process of reading has made it possible for a special population to receive the gift of clear visual perception. My own work with Scotopic Sensitivity Syndrome (The Irlen Syndrome) has allowed me to witness the exploding joy that comes through suddenly being able to read the printed page. I have watched a generation of adults and youngsters weep with joy as the Irlen procedure has stopped moving print and cleared smudged lines to let strugglers perceive printed information clearly for the first time. This gift of clear visual perception through the Irlen procedure sets many strugglers free. Being able to read for sixty minutes instead of a few. Being able to stay with a prolonged reading task without a headache or painful stress is incredible. Acquiring stable depth perception and no longer being afraid of one's environment is blessed relief. Being comfortable under bright light without having to shade the page or squint the eyes allows relaxation instead of living with heavy dread and a build-up of anxiety."[4]

In a recent conversation with her, Dr. Irlen told me that from the general population, among those with learning problems, approximately 46% will find that the problems are related to light sensitivity resulting in difficulty with processing either words or numbers in high contrast, such as black letters and a white page. However, among those with behavioral problems, such as ADD, Anxiety Disorders, or ADHD, approximately 33% respond positively to the Irlen Method and do not need medication whatsoever.

Also, gifted students often get headaches or fatigue from reading and improve the quality of their lives through the Irlen Method and do even better. For other students who are always being told to "try harder" or "work harder" or practice more, the solution might be as simple as helping them keep their place on the page or be far more comfortable in reading. People with symptoms, in varying degrees of the Irlen Syndrome, can resolve them with little investment of time and energy and receive high results that include overcoming dyslexia and other reading disabilities. For a further discussion contact Helen Irlen at The Irlen Institute, International Headquarters, 5380 Village Road, Long Beach, CA 90808 – Phone: 562-496-2550 – www.Irlen.com.

Request the CBS Interviews and other available demonstration tapes so that you can personally see a nationally televised program showing people, young and old, whose lives have been transformed with a simple diagnostic assessment and treatment with a colored lens or acetate overlay. I would also love to show you the video of the head injured patient who, after months of rehabilitation, still had motor coordination problems. However, when she wore tinted glasses, colored to her specific needs, her motor coordination problems virtually disappeared. The lady took her glasses off to demonstrate to the video camera her pre and post glasses' behavior. After the demonstration, she remarked, "That is the last time I am going to take these glasses off."

For people with the Irlen Syndrome, schools have witlessly created the most aggravating environments, almost assuring failure. Bright fluorescent lights, black print on high gloss paper in books, white boards, overheads and computer screens are disabling for those with the Syndrome.

In her new book, *The Light Barrier*, author and mother Rhonda Stone reveals the personal journey her family traveled to discover the barriers to reading and learning for the children, Katie and Jacob. In a recent conversation, Rhonda shared with me how the book shares the pain and agony, along with the triumph of success of her family's uncovering the Irlen Syndrome and its miraculous solution to a problem that afflicts many, many struggling learners of all ages. This book is a must for teachers, administrators and parents, as well as legislators and career policy makers.

To capture some sense of the feelings and frustrations of the Irlen Syndrome, a college student wrote the following poem. For years he suffered from The Irlen Syndrome, as did Katie and Jacob Stone, with all the frustration and anxiety resulting from it. David Artuso wrote:
> "B's and d's look the same to me –
> And so do p's and q's.
> N's and u's I always confuse –
> And m's and w's.
> The page is bright. It hurts my eyes.

The words, they jump about.
Like little worms, they wiggle and squirm.
They make me want to shout.
The teachers tell me I must try.
I try! I try! I try!
It hurts my head. It hurts! It hurts!
And then I start to cry.
-David Artuso

We need to stop misdirecting the blame (blaming the student, learner or victim) and mistreating people by finding out what works (as the national treasure, Helen Irlen, did) and using it to the joyful benefit of our national family, with no child left behind (as was David). A lot less suffering can go a long way toward expanding education, employment and personal opportunities. As with many inventors, there are "copy-cats" and "pirates" of Dr. Irlen's diagnosis and treatment who have done more damage than good because of incomplete or wrong information. So be careful, and go to the original source for correct information.

Sound – Can You Hear Me Now?

The third stop on our journey is the important factor of sound, "sound amplification," and "audio enhancement." The audiology researchers shifted their focus from the "hearing impaired" to examining ordinary classrooms with children with normal hearing. They found that one in four (25%) of any given group of young people would fail a normal hearing examination on any given day. They conducted their test randomly, so that the children who failed today might pass in two months, while those who passed might fail in two months. This research includes the work of outstanding audiologists such as Dr. Carol Flexler at the University of Akron, Ohio and Dr. Carl Crandell at the University of Florida. In addition, researchers have found that the effect of the ubiquitous "walk-person" (walkman) has had a detrimental effect on hearing. In Arizona, one study reported that the hearing loss of the average high school junior was equal to that of a seventy (70) year old because of damage to the upper frequency range of hearing. Several professionals in the field of special education and learning disabilities have told me that the negative effects of CD and cassette players in damaging hearing is cascading downward to the elementary schools. (*Do you hear what I am saying?*)

Despite the importance of facial expressions and other body language, human efforts at communication are largely auditory-verbal. Classrooms are auditory-verbal environments with listening serving as the cornerstone of the educational system. According to researchers John Goodlad and Seymour Sarason of Yale University, 75% of the school day is spent with teachers talking and students listening. And 55% of that time is in telling rules, giving directions and disciplining students. This is consistent with my research and experience in corporate training, as well. Learners sit endlessly, while the trainer drones on with the "death ray" (overhead projector) ablaze.

I personally don't use or advocate much use of an overhead projector or computer projector, except as a minor support tool. Instead, we teach teachers and trainers to use sound enhancement equipment, with a wireless microphone in instructional design delivery that actively engages people in the teaching and learning process of diversity of experiences and feedback. Students engage in demonstration, role-playing and drama where they can "perform" in the theatrical sense and show others what they know as they learn any skill or process or content. One senior scientist at the Sandia National Laboratories said, after attending a weeklong seminar, that this was the first training he had attended in twenty-five years where he did not nod off or fall asleep. Not only was he engaged, but also he could hear.

In today's classrooms, teaching is done by talking. Students ask few, if any questions. For people to process the spoken language of the speaker, the teacher, parent or trainer's voice needs to be 17db (decibels) louder than the noise in the classroom or environment. +5db to −7db (decibels) is more typical for numerous classrooms. This also goes for listening to other students or people in a meeting. If people do not have a consistently high quality auditory access to spoken instruction, the basis of our current model for educational delivery is undermined. Factors that impact listening at home, at work or in the classroom are:

Room acoustics
Distance from speaker to listener
Room noise (background noise)
Teacher or parent's delivery
Student or person's capacity to hear
Whether the person's native language is being spoken
Attention distracters, such as lighting
Attention distracters, such as a "learning styles" mismatch

"There are approximately 39.5 million school children in the United States, and an estimated 8 million of them have some type and degree of hearing loss," says Debbie Hamilton, a reporter for the Orem-Geneva Times in Orem, Utah. Reasons for hearing problems in the classroom, by those not affected by medical-based hearing problems, were cited as background noises, general on-going conversations and typical noises children make as they shift in seats and move about. Those with even minimal hearing loss suffer even more difficulty distinguishing between audible speech and intelligible speech. In other words, think of the times you may have heard the sounds of what someone was saying to you, but you did not hear clearly enough to understand what was said. "If a child cannot clearly hear the teacher, the entire educational system is undermined. If children don't hear clearly and consistently, the child's academic potential is compromised. Hearing is an underestimated factor in a child's educational progression," according to Flexler.

Do you know of any state or national examinations that evaluate the quality of sound amplification and the teacher's voice in any classroom? What about the quality of the child's voice or others in the class or meeting room? Can you remember drifting off because you could not hear what another participant was saying? Indeed, what "standards" in the standards movement regard the quality of the learning environment at all in assessing learning performance? This is an area that you will want to explore further, particularly if you are an administrator, teacher, parent, or grandparent concerned about children's achievement.

"Classroom noise may be the reason Johnny can't read," says Dr. Carl Crandell. And, "Recent investigations of the acoustical properties of classrooms and their impact on students have revealed disturbing findings. Several groups of children with so-called 'normal hearing' have been identified who experience greater speech recognition difficulties in classroom noise and reverberation than previously suspected. Young children require better acoustical environments than adults with normal hearing to achieve equivalent perception scores." Could this mean that if you mumble as a parent, with limited articulation and enunciation of a broad vocabulary, your children will mumble with a limited means of expressing themselves? It's something to think about!

Also, Dr. Crandell informs us that people whose language is not English have a particularly higher level of difficulty in a degraded listening environment. He points out that: "Children, for whom English is a second language (ESL), exhibit greater speech perception difficulties than native speaking children, particularly in degraded listening environments. Each child (in his study) spent at least 50% of the time speaking

English as indicated by parental report. Specifically, this investigation noted that the speech perception abilities of ESL children were significantly improved with the utilization..."[5] of "sound enhancement" systems that amplify the speaker's voice, whether teacher, corporate trainer, parent or fellow learner.

A solution, then, to the normally degraded learning environment is to provide amplification of the human voice through some type of sound amplification equipment. "The purpose of sound field amplification is to amplify the teacher's voice (or anyone else speaking or training people) throughout the classroom, thereby providing a clear and consistent signal to all pupils in the room no matter where they or the teacher are located,"[6] notes Flexler. She goes on to claim that: "There is a direct relationship between hearing and learning... It could be argued that virtually all children could benefit from sound field systems because the improved signal to noise creates a more favorable learning environment. If children (and adults) could hear better, clearer, and more consistently, they would have an opportunity to learn more efficiently."[7]

A variety of research from many different specialists who have examined ordinary learning environments supports this conclusion. For example, in 1998 the Unitah Public School District presented its findings of enhancing three first grade classrooms with sound amplification equipment. Reading scores on the Utah State Test were examined before and after enhancing the teacher's voice. Prior to the sound amplification, the average test scores were 46%, while seven months later, after sound enhancement, the average score was 75%.

For years our national government leadership has shifted its slogans from "*A thousand points of light*" to "*It takes a village to raise a child*" to the more recent expression "*Leave no child behind.*" These are noble ideas, but take a look at the improvements under a modified sound enhancement environment and one would think that the government would mandate such devices in all classrooms as a "requirement." Here is a proper role of our national government to provide equal protection to all, justified by the research and the equal protection clauses of the Constitution. However, take a trip to your local school and ask to see the classrooms that enhance the teacher's voice. The response might well be: "What?" And that response is likely NOT because they didn't hear you. It is more probable that they just don't understand your question, because the research on sound is not on their radar screen of consciousness. Many will say, "Oh, yes! We provide that for the children who are hearing impaired." But anything further is a stretch, requiring the presentation of the information in this chapter and the references contained herein.

On the other hand, consider the exemplary courage of administrators and teachers who took "sound enhancement" to heart. For example, Mr. Jack Stouten, a principal from Minnesota, has initiated the implementation of sound amplification for teachers under his leadership. He says that: "A teacher's ability to communicate to students is essential to the learning process, and this communication is disrupted when students are unable to hear clearly what the teacher is saying. Such inability can greatly hinder learning, especially for young children, since listening is a key component in learning to read. In both phonics and whole language instruction, they must hear sounds and words clearly in order to reproduce them correctly. Teachers in amplified classrooms report that students become more attentive, less distracted, and require fewer repetitions of directions."

A principal who should be applauded for his insight and courage to implement a change based on solid research, Mr. Stouten conducted a survey of the teachers. The survey "clearly indicates that all the first grade students benefited from electronic amplification of their teacher's voices with:

1. Increased attention or oral instruction.
2. Greater understanding of oral directions.
3. Ability of all students to hear the teacher.
4. Less distraction from outside noises.
5. Increased student achievement.
6. Decreased teacher fatigue.

Because sound amplification is so powerful in increasing learner achievement, we must wonder what teachers would say:

Elementary school teacher, Louise Ortberg, says, "You can take away my desks and manuals, but I'll bar the door if you take my amplification equipment." Another teacher, Martha Hansen wrote, "My microphone is my lifeline between myself and my students. It's an umbilical cord to learning." Ruth Iman, first grade social studies teacher, said, "The system (of sound enhancement equipment) is great! The children can hear and I don't have to try to talk over them!" Berni Mortenses, an upper grade art teacher, noted that sound enhancement "makes my presence known more so discipline is easier. I don't have to struggle to get students' attention after work time, but just quietly ask for their attention. It's amazing – they (the students) respond much more quickly and willingly!" And finally, third grade science teacher, Bryan Crandall, commented that, "The students like having the audio system because they can hear so much better. In one class I forgot to turn on the transmitter before talking, and the students quickly reminded me. They notice the difference."

Yes, and the research consistently proves that there is a noticeable difference. Laurie Allen, a school audiologist, and Donna Patton, a school psychologist, documented a 17% increase in "overall on-task behavior" with audio amplification of teacher voices. They concluded that amplifying the teachers' voices enhanced the students' listening learning environment, which resulted in a positive effect on "on-task" behavior.

I first met Colonel James McGrory, Jr. when conducting a conference leadership seminar for the United States Junior ROTC. Colonel McGrory instructs high school students in the JROTC program in this country's oldest historically black high school in Baltimore, Md., the Frederick Douglas High School. After receiving a grant for which he had applied, Colonel McGrory implemented sound enhancement equipment and told me it has made all the difference in the quality and tone of the learning environment, where learning is now conversational with higher achievement and test scores. He reports that the students use the microphone with increased enthusiasm, articulation and enunciation. I call this the "karaoke" effect, when you hand a microphone to a student and the behavior in speech and motivation is measurably improved and distinctly enhanced than without the microphone.

So overwhelming is the research that "sound field systems, in fact, can make a huge difference in the learning environment, and thus, in the learning potential of children," states Dr. Flexler. As an example, consider the experience of Brigham Young University Professor Paul McCarty, who is also an active elementary school principal: "Before audio enhancement, our kindergarten through sixth grade, 'at risk' elementary school reported negative declines in SAT scores in reading, math, language, and total test battery three years straight. We had tried nearly everything to improve our student achievement. We invested in many new reading and math curricula and texts. We implemented extensive staff development training. We purchased educational software. We hired reading specialists to beef up our reading recovery programs for our Title One students. Unfortunately these programs, methods, and training have shown only minimal improvement for our population composed of poverty, racial minority, special needs, and ESL. We were faced with the reality that our school was not going to show the necessary yearly student improvement required by the *No Child Left Behind Act.*

"The infrared audio enhancement equipment was installed in our school without changing teacher assignments and curriculum instruction from the previous year. The first year (2001) our students had a 10 to 15% grain over the previous year as measured by SAT scores. The second year (2002) of audio enhancement produced the same significant gains. Our greatest student gains came from ESL students with an average gain of 16% as measured by Utah's Criterion Reference Test. I am convinced the problem with student learning today is the learning environment …." Not only did student performance increase in McCarty's research, but student and teacher absenteeism also dropped. These are the words of a courageous university professor who has the tenacity to take on the role of a school principal in a largely "at risk" populated school to implement theories and strategies which work. And the evidence is overwhelmingly in support of audio enhancement. Dr. McCarty's previously unpublished article, *"Listen! Change the Learning Environment to Improve Student Achievement"* is of such value, I have included, at his suggestion, the following excerpt from his article might be useful to reinforce the value of sound enhancement at this point in our discussion:

"Research on Audio Enhancement Effectiveness in Student Learning - An intriguing research study from Brigham Young University (2002) found supporting evidence that learning is really about brain access to information. Changing the learning environment so the student can have the opportunity to access the information through the student's ears thus allowing the student to focus on the spoken word of the teacher, raised student achievement and test scores. The method found to be able to do this was called infrared audio enhancement. The system utilizes an infrared, wireless microphone, a receiver, and at least four strategically placed ceiling speakers that enable the teacher's voice to be disseminated throughout the classroom. The audio-enhanced classroom gives a front row listening hearing advantage to each student, regardless of where they sit in the classroom. The Brigham Young University (BYU) study found that the problem with student learning today can be attributed more to the learning environment than the teacher, the curriculum, textbooks, or educational software. The study supported an earlier Cornell University study that found if students can't focus on the teacher's spoken word, they loose not only the desire, but also the ability to learn (Evans 2001). The multi-year BYU study found student test scores were 4 to 15% higher in audio-enhanced classrooms than in classrooms without the enhancement system.

√   In Florida, Ocoee Middle School was among the first in the nation to employ a comprehensive audio enhancement system that includes built-in amplification for teacher's voices in each classroom. The results? A 10% gain in the first year of audio enhancement (Clark, Orange County Public Schools, Florida, 2002).

√   Anaheim Public Schools in southern California showed significant improvements in 3rd and 4th grade student test scores in reading, math, language, and spelling when using audio enhancement in comparison to previous years' test scores without audio enhancement intervention and implementation. Audio-enhanced schools reported overall gains of 5-15% (Anaheim Public Schools, California, 2002).

√   Reading test scores jumped 17% in seven months of classroom audio enhancement at the rural Uintah Elementary in Roosevelt, Utah (Uintah Public Schools 2002).

√   Phonological and phonemic awareness instruction coupled with the use of audio enhancement systems reduced the number of students identified as 'at-risk' learners (Flexor, University of Akron, 2002).

√   Audio enhancement increased student test scores at high achievement suburban schools as well as schools with students at-risk. Jefferson County Public School District in Colorado reported significant gains in CSAP test scores at its School of Excellence - Maple Grove Elementary School (2002).

Maple Grove Elementary School Principal, Tony Giurado, said of the study, 'audio enhancement has made a significant change in the learning environment at Maple Grove. When I visit classrooms where audio enhancement is in use, I see students who are more actively engaged in the learning process. Teachers are spending more time teaching and less time managing student behaviors. As a result, formal assessments increased by an average of 4 percentage points during the first year of use. In fact, it is remarkable that we made significant growth because our baseline assessment scores were extremely high (8th & 9th stanines) and near the achievement ceiling. On the Colorado School Accountability Report for the baseline year, Maple Grove was designated a "John Irwin School of Excellence" and received the 16th highest academic rating out of 920 elementary schools in Colorado. I believe that the increased scores can be directly attributed to the implementation of audio enhancement because we made no other significant changes in our instructional program or staff'.

√   Oakland County School District now uses audio enhancement systems in its elementary, middle and high schools throughout Region 4, an eight county area in southwest Michigan. Following a highly successful, multiple year assessment called The Oakland County Audio Field Project, district administrators found audio enhancement systems in the classrooms increased academic learning; improvement student on-task behavior; were very teacher friendly to use; and reliable in enhancing all student learning environments (2001).

The Oakland County School District's lead assessment teacher reported how effective audio enhancement was with the students' understanding of language and language development she added, 'Where has this been for the last 20 years of my life!' as teachers no longer have to strain their voices to be heard by students in the back of the classroom. The district's audio enhancement reliability report was summed up with the following, 'The findings are good. Does it work - Yes!; Is it teacher friendly - Definitely!; Is it good for kids? - Absolutely!' (Oakland County Public Schools 2002).

√   Minnesota's Deer Creek and Wadena Schools reported teachers in audio enhanced classrooms found students more attentive, less distracted, and required fewer repetitions of directions. Their study clearly indicated that all the first grade students benefited from the audio enhanced teacher voices. Asked to rank the most noticeable changes resulting from classroom voice enhancement, the teachers listed the following: (1) Increased attention to oral instruction; (2) Greater understanding of oral directions; (3) Ability of all students to hear the teacher; (4) Less distraction from outside noise; (5) Increased student achievement; (6) Decreased teacher fatigue (Wadena County Schools 2002).

√   Dr. Thomas Heck, Superintendent of the Litchfield School District in Arizona reported of his district's positive assessment of audio enhancement, 'I have received very favorable reports from my principals, teachers, and parents on how audio enhancement helps all students. It moved every child to the 'front row' in the classroom to learn and listen better. Yes, I'm sold on audio enhancement as an exceptional educational method to help our children excel and succeed.' (Litchfield School District 2002 and Dr. Paul McCarty, 2003).

Sound enhancement includes both using microphones and music. Use a microphone instead of raising your voice so you can be heard. When you raise your voice, it is harder to convey a positive and supportive tone of voice.

As discussed in **Chapter Five**, where "music" is considered in some depth, there are several ways to use music at home or at work and many reasons to use music in your class. Avoid rock music and other high beat genres or music with words. Use musical instrumentation only for relaxation or classical music to generate positive emotions during:

√ Storytelling
√ Test taking
√ Class assembly
√ Giving instructions
√ Reviewing anything learned
√ Lecturing

It remains a mystery to me why every classroom in the United States is not equipped with a sound enhancement amplifier and wireless microphones. They range in quality, as well as price (from $30. to $2500), as well as music devices, such as a portable "boom box" or "karaoke" stereo systems that costs from $50 to $300.

In summary, studies too numerous to mention have reported the benefits of enhancing the listening environment in the classroom. Studies of students with normal hearing and those with mild and unilateral hearing losses have shown impacts on the relationship between "hearing" and academic performance and behavior. Teachers report that students are more attentive, less distracted, and ask for instructions to be repeated less often, when they use a sound enhancement system. Teachers themselves report reduced fatigue on their part. A classroom sound field amplification system can equalize the teacher's voice throughout the classroom. Wherever the teacher is or wherever the students are, the teacher sounds the same way and can be heard without exhaustion by the listener. Also, and equally valuable for high performance, is that other people or other children can be heard among the group for maximum participation and benefit.

One young child told me, after using the microphone to speak to his classmates, that he had never before heard himself. The feedback from amplification increased his own perception of his voice projection, articulation and enunciation. I have personally spoken with teachers and administrators who required surgery to remove "voice polyps" that grew from straining the voice to speak. We must hold ourselves to higher standards than either mumbling or yelling. If we, with a national policy focus of "leave no child behind," are serious in our intent, then we had better pay close attention to the effect of amplifying the voice and provide the devices that equalize the learning opportunities in all environments at work, at school and at home. This will have far more meaning than the current notion: "I am all ears!"

For information on research and equipment, contact Mr. Jeff Anderson, jeff@audioenhancement.com or www.audioenhancement.com

H2O – Hydration – The One Drink that Lets You Think

Any journey requires a water source for a cool drink. Remember the song "Sons of the Pioneers" sang, *"Cool, Clear, Water?"* One refrain in the song tells us that "ole Dan and I, our throats so dry (Dan was his horse), thirst for *cool, clear, water.*" We are not in the desert, as they were, but the song applies to us, no matter where we live. Clean water is hard to find, although it can be purified, and believe it when I say that water is important to life, as well as health, hardiness, and learning. Realize too that it is *water*, not soda pop, that is critical for the brain, the heart and all living functions, including thinking and learning.

"Water again enters the picture as a crucial player in assisting oxygen distribution to the brain. It keeps the surface of the air sacs of the lungs moist so oxygen can dissolve and move into the blood. Researchers at the National Institute of Diabetes and Digestive and Kidney Disorder have also discovered *that increased water intake increases the capacity of hemoglobin to carry oxygen by one hundred to one thousand times*. Hemoglobin is the iron-bearing pigment in red blood cells that carries oxygen. Similarly, water assists digestion of foods in the digestive tract by dissolving them so enzymes can easily break them down producing the end products needed for oxidation," writes Dr. Carla Hannaford in her book, *Smart Moves.*[8.]

Even though we are part of the "Pepsi Generation™," don't allow yourself or your children to drink soft drinks or sodas, and most especially not "diet" sodas. (Notice the first three letters in the word "diet.")

If you want the details on diet sodas, enter the Internet debate and discussion on the dangers of "aspartame." Check it out and you will find that aspartame, which is in virtually all diet sodas and other sundry products eaten every day, converts to wood alcohol at 85 degrees F. and then to Formaldehyde. Sugar based sodas (containing about *40 grams* of refined sugar in one 16 oz can– note that one packet of sugar you see on a restaurant table is *one* gram) not only dehydrate the body, but also the caffeine in them causes false energy highs that may actually decrease a person's attention span. Remember that fluorescent light bulbs also dehydrate the body.

Under the exceptional leadership of Dr. Janet Aikele, Superintendent of Schools in Arco, Idaho, we implemented the installation of water coolers in every classroom, as well as installing full spectrum lights, while also training teachers in *The Seven Secrets of Learning Revealed*. The year following implementation, the elementary school enjoyed a two-thirds reduction in "special education" referrals. This is a hallmark of success in turning around the slippery slope of labeling children in the misty sea of disabilities. The local Board of Education voted to eliminate soda machines, causing a financial hardship for their athletic programs, but they claimed that doing the right thing for children was worth the loss of revenues paid by the soda machine vendors. As a result, the vendors switched to juices and water.

"Drink water!" – that is the antidote and is the best thing for you and for those you care about. Make water easily accessible and encourage your family or co-workers to drink the recommended 8-10 eight ounce glasses a day. As clinical nutritionist Carol Simontacchi instructs, "Gradually reduce the amount of non-water beverages you consume each day, so that within two weeks you are drinking only eight to ten large glasses of water per day. Addictive symptoms are decreased if you progress slowly. You may also enjoy hot or warm herbal teas for variety, or you may squeeze a fresh lemon or lime into the cool water for added flavor. Serve water with your meals. Sip water throughout the day to keep your body hydrated."[9]

F. Batmanghelidj, M.D. (pronounced: *"Bat-man-ghee-lidge"*) has written the seminal book on a new paradigm of disease and its prevention. In the book, *Your Body's Many Cries for Water*, Dr. Batmanghelidj has set forth a framework for health and hardiness with proper water hydration. He writes that: "The simple truth is that dehydration can cause disease. Everyone knows that water is 'good' for the body and brain. They seem not to know how essential it is to one's well being.

They *do not* know what happens to the body if it does not receive its daily need of water. After readubg his short book, you will have a clearer understanding of this issue. The solution for prevention and treatment of dehydration-produced diseases is water intake on a regular basis."[10]

Go to www.watercure.com where you will find a wellspring (no pun intended) of information on the importance of water on health and learning. When you explore www.watercure.com, you will find sources of valuable information, which claim that we live as a nation of dehydrated people, although we are drinking lots of fluids. You will see how people with Asthma, Allergies, Lupus, High Blood Pressure, and other ailments are remarkably cured with water and sodium, while maintaining the proper alkaline balance.

The importance of hydration cannot be overly emphasized, as it is the tool the body uses to cleanse itself, power its cells and carry nutrients to the cells. Your brain cells are 90% water and your heart cells are 85%, perhaps because of the hydroelectric power generated. Take a diversion on our field trip and go to the web site, order and read Dr. Batmanghelidj's brilliant, practical and meaningful books on the subject of the value of "water" to your life and to your learning capability.

Your brain, and you as a learner, function measurably better with the proper water hydration at the cellular level. So do not rely on the *old deluder* thirst. If you wait till you are thirsty for water, you probably won't get enough. Make drinking H2O a habit! You won't know you are dehydrated until damage is done and you start feeling aches and pain, as in the case of lower back pain and joint pain. So, the miracle compound water, which behaves like no other compound, is necessary for life on this planet and is critical to the quality of your life. Drink up! And if you don't like drinking it, carry a "designer" water bottle and just "sip it" all day long.

ADHD, Learning Disabilities, Food Allergies, and Environmental Illness

Sometimes on trips, we see monuments of leaders who have stood out and done the right thing. I wish to dedicate this section to the tireless energy of my old and good friend Stan Meyerson, founder of the Nutritional Ecological Environmental Delivery Systems (N.E.E.D.S.). This is an organization Stan envisioned to help "improve the quality of life for the health conscious person by bringing resources directly to the consumer through a health, information and learning distribution network in Syracuse, New York." He has helped countless people over the thirty-eight years I knew him by bringing the right health resources, at the right time, in the right proportion. He was an example of "justice" in Aristotle's sense, a model of "shalom" to everyone and an ambassador of his Jewish heritage.

His passing in 2002 has been felt around the world. Stan introduced me to two of the most active and brilliant physicians who stepped out of the traditional American Medical Association mold and spearheaded new initiatives in treating ADHD, Learning Disabilities, Food Allergies and Environmental Illnesses: Doris Rapp, M.D. and William Crook, M.D. They have published several books, two of which I feel you should know about for yourself, your family and your community.

Stan knew of my broad interests and work with a wide variety of people, from head injured patients to engineering and medical students, as well as from Head Start children to corporate executives. He thought I might benefit from the research of Drs. Rapp and Crook. Now, you might be humored a bit by the name "Dr. Crook," thinking to yourself: "Aren't they all?" As it turns out, the venerable Dr. Crook, from Jackson, Tennessee, was my wife's childhood pediatrician when her father was the pastor of the Presbyterian Church in Jackson. My wife, Mary, remembers vividly Dr. Crook's hearing of her brother's infection and temperature and leaving a formal dinner with her father to rush to the hospital where family lore tells of Dr. Crook saving the boy's young life. That is standard for Dr. Crook – leaving the routine of life to provide extraordinary medical help to others.

In his book, *Help for the Hyperactive Child*, Dr. Crook discusses his concern with early childhood ear infections and the common prescription of antibiotics. His concern was that "the broad spectrum of antibiotic drugs (including those commonly used in children to treat ear infections) cause alterations in the flora of the gastrointestinal tract, leaving the over colonization of *Candida albicans*. This organism, generally considered to be benign, has been shown ... to produce both high and low molecular weight toxins. Clinical reports suggest that such *candida toxins* may cause wide systemic and nervous system, including immune system changes that may reduce the child's resistance and lead to a vicious cycle of infections."

A research team consisting of Randi Hagerman, M.D. and Alice Falkenstein, M.S.W. corroborated Crook's claim by showing the relationship between "recurrent otitis media in infancy and later hyperactivity." Further, since 1991, additional research supported Dr. Crook's view that "repeated use of antibiotics for ear infections were much more apt to develop neurological problems, including ADHD, pervasive developmental disorders and autism."

ADHD and other related learning disabilities have skyrocketed, with a corresponding increase in prescriptions of Ritalin to treat ADHD, with a 600% increase during the decade of the 1990's. According to one report, by John Lang, in the *Nashville Tennessean*, "Americans would be horrified to learn that 2 million children across this nation are being given cocaine by their parents and doctors to make them behave better in school." Moreover, Lang, the former Deputy Assistant Administrator of the Drug Enforcement Administration (DEA) said: "We have become the only country in the world where children are prescribed such a vast quantity of stimulants that share virtually the same properties of cocaine."

Why do physicians prescribe this "kiddy cocaine?" Because it relieves the symptoms. And, according to Dr. Crook, physicians are generally unaware that:

1. "Double-blind, placebo controlled studies that document the role of *food sensitivities* (and other dietary factors) *contribute to ADHD*.... In addition, getting a child to comply with dietary recommendations is difficult.

2. Physicians are unaware of the clinical reports and ongoing scientific studies that support the relationship of *repeated antibiotics* and resulting yeast overgrowth to neurological *problems in children*...."

In addition to early antibiotic usage is the general relationship between diet, food allergies and brain dysfunction. Dr. Crook, in his experience and research claims that "During the past 75 years, numerous reports in the medical literature describe the relationship of food allergies to brain dysfunction. Yet, most physicians have remained skeptical. Here's why:

1. Other studies that concluded that dietary changes played little, if any, role in causing ADHD (some of these negative studies were funded by the Sugar Association and other food industries).

2. Most food sensitivities cannot be identified by the traditional allergy prick test.

I'm happy to report that since 1985, double-blind, placebo-controlled studies published in the peer-reviewed literature provide documentation for the relationship of food allergies to ADHD...."[11]

In 2001, I had a graduate student, John, whose grandson was diagnosed with Tourette's Syndrome, with involuntary physical movement and vocalizations. I recommended to John that he call a pediatric allergist for a review and consultation. The family did seek consultation and they discovered, after a few tests, that the eight year old was severely allergic to chocolate and dairy products. That was in August and by November, the boy was 85% recovered according to a very happy grandfather.

Two other graduate students, who were also special education teachers in the Georgia public school system, each had a child with a diagnosis of "bi-polar" personality disorder. After suggesting that they read Doris Rapp, M.D.'s book, *Is This Your Child's World*, they sought treatment from a pediatric allergist. Both children made measurable and observable improvements in all categories. The health and hardiness of both moms improved, along with that of other family members affected by the negative behavior prior to treatment for food and chemical allergies.

All physicians take the "Hippocratic Oath," which has one phrase that stands out, namely, "Do No Harm." Dr. Crook is one physician who prescribed Ritalin before he knew of the research and now avoids it altogether when possible. He writes: "I've found that Ritalin and/or related medicines (including Cylert, Benzedrine, Dexedrine, Tofanil, Tegretol and Mellaril) are *rarely needed* if and when...

1. The child is given a better diet – less sugar and "junk food," including processed and packaged foods that contain colors, flavors and additives. (Such foods are usually deficient in essential nutrients, such as vitamins, minerals and Omega 3 and Omega 6 fatty acids.)

2. The environment is 'cleaned up.' This means avoiding tobacco, smoke, formaldehyde, insecticides, lead, cadmium and other toxic environmental substances.

3. Foods the child is sensitive to are identified using a carefully designed elimination diet. Following identification, such foods are avoided or consumed infrequently.

4. Anticandida therapy is prescribed for the child who gives a history of repeated or prolonged courses of antibiotic drugs for ear and/or other infections.

5. The child's psychological needs are appropriately managed

so that his self-confidence and self-esteem increase.

6. A consistent program of management and discipline is established. This includes setting limits and making reasonable rules.

7. The educational needs are taken care of. This may include one-on-one tutoring and appropriate placement in school.

8. She is given nutritional supplements, including B Complex vitamins, magnesium, calcium, zinc, selenium and essential fatty acids."[12]

In addition to Dr. Crook's perceptive, Dr. Rapp assures us that despite the rise in environmental illnesses, "as parents, educators, and physicians, we can tip the scales in favor of our children's health. How? We can help them by avoiding unnecessary exposures to chemicals, dust, molds, pollen, and known problem or pesticide-containing foods. No, we don't have to live in a glass house atop a windy mountain – but we should clean with safer products and improve our personal environment as much as possible. Dr. Rapp's book, *Is This Your Child's World*, provides the insight you will need to cope with schools that are not up to par environmentally. The same recommendations are also applicable in the home (an environment that is infinitely easier to control than schools or workplaces). For the vast majority of children, teachers and families, such changes do not need to be extensive or expensive."[13]

And, as pointed out by Jean Carper in her national best selling book, *Miracle Cures*,[14] Ritalin and other prescription drugs can be drastically reduced or eliminated altogether with homeopathic alternatives, such as OPC Grape Extract or Pycnogenol combined with other antioxidant supplements and diet strategies. Of course, none of these major breakthrough strategies in health and learning deal directly with the boredom that is often experienced in classrooms and training seminars.

This book and the entire Model of *IntelliLearn*® described in **Chapter Seven** meet that challenge to say: "bye, bye boredom." (Dr. Rapp's books, along with those of Dr. Crook are available through - www.needs.com. As I was writing this section, I got a call to inform me that Dr. Crook, a long-standing collaborator and friend of Stan Meyerson, passed on just two days ago. His life as a physician, researcher and family member will long be memorialized in his pledge to "do no harm" and to have the courage to find a way "less traveled" to help thousands of children, included among them are my wife and her brother. Mary and I were sad when we heard that Dr. Crook would no longer be serving children on this earth. Two standard bearers have departed this world, leaving it a better place because of their steadfast love for people and a thirst of knowledge to do the right thing.

Food for Thought

The title of Carol Simontacch's book is **The Crazy Makers**. However, it is the book's sub-title that catches your eye and "gut wrenching" attention. It raises a seemingly unthinkable specter, namely, **How the Food Industry is Destroying our Brains and Harming our Children**.

When I was a kid living in New Hampshire, my brother Wayne worked for the Fish and Game Department and my dad worked for an engineering firm. On occasion at the end of the day, we would go fishing in the broad, cool rivers that run through the mountains of New England. Catching the limit of trout, we'd clean them and bread them with flour for a fish fry you would never forget. The potatoes for the potato cakes came from the garden about fifty yards from my mother's stove (and it was her bountiful stove). The freshly cooked pie setting on the kitchen counter was filled with the pumpkin from the seeds my older sister Shirley and I had planted months earlier. The juicy, plump tomatoes, ripe from the vine, filled the salad bowl that also contained the lettuce from the seeds we planted and watered that season. My dad used to eat those tomatoes right off the vine, and he would carry a box of salt to season them. As the juice rolled down his jaw, he would laugh and say in his unmistakable "New Hampsha" dialect, "Thar's nothing betta than a ripe tamata with atasta salt in thah hot sun." (This was Dad's "Yankee" version of standard English, which would be: "There is nothing better than a ripe tomato with a taste of salt in the hot sun.")

The milk we had came from the Renfors' farm down the single lane, country road, as did the eggs, which my sister and I collected from the chicken coops. We bought wheat flour, but it was grown and ground at the New Hope Mills in upstate New York where former President Millard Fillmore played as a child. This was a happy time for our family with a wonderful, fresh garden every year that supplied many jars of canned or "put up" vegetables and fruits for the winter season.

Food is different today. Simply ask people what they ate last night for dinner, where they got it and how it arrived into their house. Carol Simontacchi says that: "Now, we are sold packages, boxes, artificial flavors, coloring agents, and pseudo-foods that strip the body and leave the brain poverty-stricken. The product is colorful and flavorful, but not from natural goodness. The colors come from a chemist's beaker, from FD&C Blue No.1, Red No. 40, and Yellow No. 5, or from cochineal (from the female insect, coccus cacti from the West Indies). The flavor comes from allyl anthranilate or isopulegol or linalyl benzoate or methyl delta-ionone, while gravies and sauces are thickened with wood fiber and emulsified by dioctyl sodium sulfosuccinate. (Do we really want to consume things we can't even pronounce?) While some of these agents have been tested for carcinogenic properties, virtually none have been studied to learn their impacts on brain chemistry."[15] Little research exists to show the relationship between food chemistry and learning and behavior.

Perhaps we should not eat anything we cannot name and pronounce. Certainly, physician and health food advocate Dean Ornish, M.D. would agree that we should avoid "anything" that has a face on it or anything that is synthetic or cultivated with artificial treatments. Simontacchi continues, "Instead of being eaten when we are physically hungry, food is now consumed to satisfy artificial cravings generated by a brain that isn't working right and whose receptor sites beg for synthetic stimulation from chemicals. We eat, but we're never satisfied. We're full, but we aren't contented."[16]

Simply look at the statistics on heart disease and diabetes, along with the national increase in child and adult obesity and raise the question: "Is the quality of our food contributing to our health crisis and learning crisis as a nation?"

"Looking with a careful eye," says Simontacchi, "there isn't much dissimilarity between environmental rapists and certain food-manufacturing companies. Industrial polluters spill toxic waste into the soil and water. Some food manufacturers slip toxic products into our cereals, our soups, our breads, our beverages, our fish, and call it progress. We carve a culture out of our favorite food icons and we don't link the food artifacts with the depression, the anger, and the heartbreaking assortment of mental illnesses that beset us."[17]

Although a great deal of research is being conducted in a wide range of areas on health and health related products, no one has looked at the rapacious industry that has altered our consumption of basic nutrition so that our *brains* are deprived of its essential building blocks.

You can't think right if your brain is deprived. Remember the famous "Twinkie defense," where a murderer excused his killing because his brain was dysfunctional as a result of eating mega packages of Twinkies?

I think it is useful for us to read a bit of Carol's personal story that led her down the path of clinical nutrition and health food advocacy. She writes: "The issue of brain health first led me into the health food store and started me on the road to better health through better nutrition when I was in my twenties. I suffered from severe emotional illness in the form of deep depressions, hostility, fatigue and confusion. Then I read how sugar is a poison, and I greatly reduced my intake. I learned that the B complex is required for enzyme activity in the brain and started eating foods rich in B complex. I learned that I needed amino acids and essential fats to build neurotransmitters and neurohormones, and replaced my nutrient-deficient diet of breads and pastries and cakes and ice cream with wholesome forms of protein and beneficial oils. I started eating vegetables. I read about brain nutrition and made drastic changes in my diet and became convinced that it was impossible to be contented and emotionally stable while poisoning my brain with the Standard American Diet (SAD)....

"Parents today can't count on school districts to help teach their children. Many of the people managing the school are in on it, too, earning millions of dollars each year by inviting fast-food chains and soft drink dispensers into schools. *(As an important aside here, let me interrupt Carol and have you remember my earlier reference in this book to the Arco, Idaho Superintendent of Schools, Dr. Aikele, and her Board who eliminated soft drinks and replaced them with low sugar juices and water, resulting in a two thirds drop in special education referrals and an increase in grades, attendance and parental satisfaction.)* They perform a vital function in the marketing scheme of these mega-companies. The schools end up being complicit in 'teaching' that it's okay to drink pop instead of water, to eat candy bars instead of fresh fruit, to load the body up on artificial this-and-that as long as money can be made. Meanwhile, students' test scores are dropping, and the administrations cry out for more funding." *(I should also mention that the custodial staff in Arco said that trash from candy wrappers dropped by 70% after soda pop was removed. They said that, initially, the students were in an uproar, and then settled down into a habit of drinking water.)*

In concluding Carol's story, she prophetically warns, "Mind-altering pharmaceutical drugs are one of the leading industries of this country and growing rapidly. Yet no one is making the association between what we are putting into our mouths and the toxic thoughts and feelings that pour out of our brains. Instead, we blame the breakdown of the family, parents, teachers and political administrations."[18]

Perhaps the Columbine High School tragedy, along with the other nearly twenty shootings at schools in the past five years, can be revisited in terms of the link between food, prescription drugs and brain dysfunction. To illustrate the point beyond the "Twinkie" defense, consider the case of sodium lactate, which is an additive used in many meat products. When sodium lactate enters the body's bloodstream, it elevates adrenal hormone levels, which can induce panic attacks.

"In a study of patients who were diagnosed with multiple chemical sensitivity syndrome (symptoms typical of panic disorders, chest tightness, shortness of breath, palpitations, paresthesias {abnormal touch sensation in the absence of touch, such as tingling or burning}, lightheadedness, and mental confusion) they were given either a normal saline solution placebo (*a fake with no substance*) or an infusion of (*the real thing*) sodium lactate, which is known to produce symptoms of panic disorders. Every patient who received the sodium lactate infusion experienced a panic attack."[19]

Since the amounts of additives are not listed on the package, who knows how much of a negative thing we are ingesting? Perhaps only the chemists at the food packaging plants know. (For a real thriller novel about the meat packing business, you might "enjoy" reading *Toxin* by Robin Cook, M.D., or pick up a copy of Jeremy Rifkin's *Beyond Beef: The Rise and Fall of the Cattle Culture*).

There is a very positive and hopeful note for us to conclude this section on food and nutrition. An emerging field of "glycobiology"and glyconutrients is gaining both wide spread recognition, as well as collecting a few Nobel Prizes in Medicine. I will be brief and give you a web site for further information that you can download, ranging from medical miracle stories to improvement in autism to learning disability recovery. But for now, consider the story of an elementary school principal in Dallas, Texas. Although she had tried many methodologies, except and excluding those outlined in this book, Denise Hampton's school was one of the *lowest performing* schools in Texas, with far too many discipline problems from children within the impoverished neighborhood. There were both academic and social problems through the various grade levels.

Hampton's own ten-year-old niece was having trouble paying attention in school, much like several of the other students. A local physician introduced this principal to "glyconutrient" food supplements to bolster the child's mental function and strengthen the immune system. After two weeks, according to Denise Hampton, her niece's concentration improved, as did her grades in school.

Courageous and confident with medical advice about "glyconutrients," (these are critical sugars that operate at the cellular level to dramatically improve results of all kinds, which you can explore, as well as an extensive research base on the web site) a Dallas foundation that works worldwide to help children in crisis made the "glyconutrients" available to the school children. According to Hampton, *"within two weeks my staff and I started to notice results...* It was a miracle. The children retained information; they began to focus. The school's test scores went from being among the lowest to the *highest in the state* of Texas... I attribute what happened in our school to the glyconutrients that our students began to take... I believe that they are as important as a student learning the alphabet." You can learn more about glyconutrients in the book *Sugars That Heal* by pediatrician Emil Nondoa, M.D. Denise Hampton's story is called *"Miracle in Dallas"* and is available in its entirety at: www.createlight.com.

I do not wish to overexpose you with either the vastness or the seriousness of the issue of food and nutrition at it relates to your brain, your heart and your happiness (as well as those of your family and friends). I can only hope that it is helpful, meaningful and motivating to you in your journey of learning with health, hardiness and abundance.

Other questions that you might have about nutrition and health related issues can be addressed with Wellness Consultant Laurie Lynch, ND., Ph.D., C.Ht. at 910-426-5159 or DrLLynch@allvantage.com.

EMF (Electromagnetic Fields) – Force Fields that Can Hurt You

What would a field trip be without examining the electromagnetic fields along the way?

Do you see the power lines that hover above, or that big satellite dish next to the motel? What about the microwave in your house or the smoke detector and the cell phone you use? Electromagnetic Fields run throughout the planet in both natural and artificial forms. Every cell in your body vibrates with an electromagnetic field that emits a low frequency. When we measure the brain, what we observe is the electrical activity recorded on an EEG or electroencephalograph, while we measure and observe the heart on an EKG or echocardiograph. These recordings are only possible because the cellular activity is generating an electromagnetic field within the liquid, living cell. This might be called our *internal* electromagnetic field (EMF).

For the past fifty years, our bodies have been increasingly bombarded with external electromagnetic fields, the results of which are in serious question. We have all heard of the debate about cellular phones causing brain tumors from electromagnetic field radiation. But few of us have heard of the general relation of EMF on learning, concentration, health and personal performance. To what degree do external EMFs interfere with the more gentle EMFs of the human body?

"High tension wires, electrical line transformers, radio and television transmitting antennas, and electrical power stations all emit an immense amount of electromagnetic energy. Yet surprisingly, emissions from regular telephone power lines can be greater at times than emissions from certain high-power lines. Your child (and you) can also be exposed to varying amounts of EMF energy emitted by computers, lighting fixtures, television sets, microwave ovens, refrigerators, and electric dishwashers. Localized electric fields can even be found around certain small electrical appliances at school and at home (like clocks, stoves, hair dryers, and electric razors) *even when they are not in use.* In certain individuals, this minor degree of exposure can cause symptoms," says Doris Rapp, M.D.[20] She further says that, for example, "In some exquisitely sensitive people, seizures have been produced repeatedly from exposure to beepers, microwave ovens, computer screens, and fluorescent lights." She continues, "…there is even increasing evidence that EMFs can increase the toxicity of chemicals by allowing them to more readily access the sensitive nerve cells in the brain," which can generate low level magnetic fields which permit particles to enter the brain which can interfere with brain function.

Dr. Dee Coulter conducts research on newborns and EMFs. Coulter's research shows that "more newborns in technologically advanced cultures are exhibiting an 'excited' state – almost a state of shock at birth. They lack the natural rhythm and coordination that, in previous generations, was established in the womb. The fetus lies in amniotic fluid, a fluid/electrolyte bath that easily transmits external EMFs to the fetus. Outside EMFs may interfere with the fetus' own natural EMFs. If we consider the constant bombardment of EMFs that pregnant women are exposed to, we can understand why babies are born 'excited' and may remain that way throughout life."[21]

Dr. Hannaford claims that: "Bone and fat (low water content tissues) are less affected by external EMFs than high water content tissues like the brain, muscles, heart and kidneys. Considering that the brain is approximately 90% water, external EMFs must have some effect on its efficiency."[22]

An inexpensive gaussmeter measures EMFs, and generally, the closer you are to the object, the higher the milligauss(mG). A reading of 10 mG is a concern, but in Sweden scientists warn that a 2.5 mG is cause for concern. Also, there are preventative products designed to dramatically reduce the effects of EMFs. (For a list of such products, including the amulet discussed below, contact www.needs.com. And to contact physicians who have had expertise with patients with EMF symptoms, Dr. Rapp suggests the American Environmental Health Foundation in Dallas, Texas. Dr. Rapp's books are available from www.needs.com.)

I have an extensive travel and lecture schedule. In 1999 I learned about the "Q-Link" amulet and its properties from Anthony Robbins, an internationally recognized leader in personal improvement. I was introduced to Tony's work from a friend and mentor who was a former Chairman of the Joint Chiefs of Staff. In passing, my friend said, "Have you ever explored that fire walk?" It was much later that I connected Tony to his famous "fire walk" and attended one of his trainings during a period when his foundation and our non-profit organization, The National Academy of Integrative Learning, Inc., were developing a student-teacher training summer camp. I began to wear a "Q-link" amulet, designed by scientists at Stanford University and have had tremendous results in my own energy levels, concentration and endurance. My personal physician gave me an EKG three months after beginning to wear the EMF medallion and was surprised at the positive change in my EKG from the previous reading. After the reading, he asked, "What in the world are you doing?" Your EKG is stronger and improved over the one we took a year ago! (Research about the Q-link and other EMF devices can be obtained through www.needs.com.)

Remember that knowledge is power, and the more you *learn* and *do* something about those potentially negative influences, as well as the helpful ones, in your environment, the more able you will be to make intelligent choices for you and your family members.

Air Quality – The Quality of the Air Can Influence Your Thinking

Any journey would be short lived if we couldn't take a deep breath and smell the air and natural aromas that nature provides around us. Indeed, breathing is critical for life. Oxygen is among the essential ingredients for life. If you are swimming and are trapped beneath the water, you drown – no "ifs, ands, or buts" about that fact of life. Likewise, if the air you breathe is filled with carbon monoxide (e.g. cigarette smoke), you will suffocate since carbon monoxide is forty-four times more aggressive than oxygen in competing for space in your blood stream. But even in the best of circumstances with clean air, only about 20% of the air you breathe is oxygen. Therefore, it is important to pay attention to the quality of air in your environment, and to make sure it is filled with oxygen and, is free from pollution!

"The brain makes up only one fiftieth (1/50) of the body's weight and yet it uses an amazing one fifth (1/5) of the body's oxygen. The first artery coming out of the heart carrying freshly oxygenated blood, the carotid, goes directly to the brain. The whole system tends to take care of the brain's needs first," asserts Carla Hannaford, Ph.D.

To get oxygen, you must breathe, and if you walk briskly for twenty minutes a day for at least three days per week you will dramatically increase mental function, blood flow and oxidation. Yet, only one third of our children in schools, according to one national study, have physical education classes for students. Very few classes have bodily activities associated with learning as we discussed in the chapter on Multiple Intelligences. Obesity is on the rise at all age levels and suggests people are becoming couch potatoes. If you are one, you probably are not getting the oxygen your body needs to function properly.

Dr. Hannaford adds that: "Movement has also greatly decreased in adult populations in the United States. Robert Dustman found that getting inactive men and women in their fifties and sixties on a four-month brisk walking program increased their performance on mental ability tests by 10%." [23] She also cites studies that have proven that physically active mammal brains (without much strain or Olympic Medal training) had *20% more blood vessels* than "couch potato" inactive mammal brains. (Although the mammals in this case were rats, it is a reasonable inference to suggest the same with humans.) By the way, this is why the bodily/kinesthetic Intelligence (**Chapter Five**) is so critical to oxygenation in daily classes and to the successes portrayed in Chapter Seven.

We have a major "standards" movement across the United States, with each state adopting its own achievement tests. But what are the standards for daily exercise and for air quality?

Doris Rapp, M.D. states that: "Although local, state, and federal government agencies have established general guidelines to protect human health and safety, most were established for adult males working in industry, not for children, teachers, or pregnant women in schools. Existing legislation, unfortunately, typically takes the form of suggestions, guidelines, or policies, not mandates or laws that would be much more substantive and require enforcement."

I live on Hilton Head Island, surrounded by nature's bountiful water and beautiful marshes. That beauty brings with it problems, such as mold infestation. We know that mold is evident everywhere, however, there are specific things we can do to prevent or reduce mold, as well as limit its negative impact on the health of children. Of course, mold and air quality have to be a routine concern of the District Board of Education and the administrative leader. But, as an editorial recently lamented, scratching its proverbial head, "Why do we have to face the problem of mold in each new school, as if we didn't learn our lesson years ago with other schools in crisis with air quality problems? Prevention does not seem to be part of the planning process." And we don't plan ahead, but rather wait until enough parents are upset before another 'study' is done. We've had enough studies in the past – enough for us to make sure that preventing mold is a condition of the contract to both design and build the building.

By the way, no air quality systems were ever planned in the new buildings, and carpets were installed as if the previous, high priced studies that condemned the use of carpets did not exist. Several schools have been both built and expanded with a seemingly mindless approach to "air quality" as essential to student performance, never mind public health issues. Another contributor is the ineffectiveness of leadership on this issue. The structure of management is "site based management." No success in solving a problem at one place has any impact on another place. Site based management does not need to be so ineffectual. However, if you are organized as a "system of schools," rather that a "school system" you leave yourself vulnerable to "niches" of excellence or "pockets" of success emerging because there are no common vision, purpose, direction and process to achieve the mission. In other words, everyone is "doing their own thing."

"In 1994, the New York State Education Department formulated policies affirming that *every child has the right to a safe and healthful learning environment.* Educators there believe that parents have the right to know about health hazards in schools, and that schools should serve as role models for environmentally responsible behavior. Thus, the state's schools are developing plans to conduct research about current and emerging school environmental and safety issues. For example, New York State schools will be required to report various environmental health matters and actions to the state health department. For details about the policies, contact The State University of New York, The New York State Department of Education, Office of Central Services, Albany, NY 12234. (518) 474-3852."[24]

The Maryland Example

"What can states do to reduce school environmental problems? In 1987, the Maryland Department of Education implemented a statewide indoor air quality program (IAQ), setting an exemplary gold standard for the rest of the nation. A number of Maryland publications describe the state's efforts, including:

☑   Indoor Air Quality in Maryland Public Schools

☑   Indoor Air Quality Management Program

☑   Guidelines for Controlling Environmental Tobacco Smoke In Schools

☑   Guidelines for Controlling Indoor Air Quality Problems Associated with Kilns, Copiers, and Welding in Schools

☑   Air Cleaning Devices for HVAC Supply Systems in Schools

For further discussion on policy in Maryland, write to: Maryland Department of Education, 200 West Baltimore Street, Baltimore, MD 21201. 410-333-2508."[25]

ACTION ITEM:

Whether you are on the couch right now or on a treadmill, here is a simple breathing technique you can do that is commonly used in Tai Chi and Yoga. The idea is to breathe in through your nose, hold your breath, and then exhale slowly through your mouth. There is a counting process to all of this. The ratio is "one to four to two." So if you breathe in through your nose for a count of four, you would hold your breath for a count of four times that number (sixteen in this example) and then exhale for a count two times the original count (eight in this case). So try it. A helpful way to keep count is to lift each finger on the left hand and then the right hand as you count. So, for "one," lift one finger; for "two," lift two fingers; and so forth. (I know you only have ten fingers, so when you get to eleven, start with the first hand again.) Begin by using the 4:16:8 count. Breathe in through your nose for a count of four. Hold your breath for a count of sixteen. Exhale for a count of eight. Repeat this process five times, three times a day, and monitor the difference in your mental performance.

If possible, conduct this in an environment where the air quality is good. MENSA Society member Dr. Win Wenger, author of *The Einstein Factor*, first told me about the relationship between holding your breath and improved mental performance. His strategy recommended holding your breath under water in a pool or bathtub for increasing lengths of time. This particular version of breath-holding was introduced to me by Anthony Robbins who is one of the outstanding leaders in personal training and improvement. After learning the process, it was reinforced in one of his "Power Talk" series; a very useful "audio magazine" that I encourage you to consider as a resource, along with his audio series "*Unleash the Power Within*." These can be obtained through the Anthony Robbins Research International, Inc., at 1-800-898-8669.

The remainder of this section is an important discussion about air quality and includes an excerpt from an article written by Pharmacist and Nutritional Leader, Stan Meyerson. I include it as a tribute to his passion for learning and health. Stan was a personal friend for 38 years. His passing leaves us saddened at the loss of this gentle force for the improvement of mankind; but we can be firm in our resolve to carry forward his mission of health through continuous learning.

Fact: We Spend 90% of Our Day Indoors
By Stan Meyerson, founder N.E.E.D.S. Inc.

We are saving money on our heating and AC bills each month with our energy saving, technology efficient homes. Then why are we all feeling so unhealthy indoors?

Indoor air pollution is the major pollution problem facing the nation. Since we spend 90% of our time indoors, we would like to think the quality of the air we breathe is safe and healthy. The sad truth is that we are being continually subjected to inhaling a huge number of indoor pollutants, both airborne and chemical.

Construction techniques have changed. All types of buildings, homes, offices and schools are now sealed more tightly. Energy may be saved, but at the expense of our health. Tight buildings have the indoor air re-circulated and trapped indoors, with little or no air exchange.

√   **Reviewing the Pollutants**

Dust: Did you know that a 2,000 square foot house will yield approximately 60 pounds of dust per year, as well as a host of different types of dust mites (40,000 dust mites live in one ounce of dust)? Additional airborne pollutants found in your ventilation system, cleaning materials, household pets, walls, carpets, bathroom, basements, garbage and everywhere in your home are bacteria, viruses, mold spores, pollen and tobacco smoke. Symptoms of airborne pollutants included are allergies, eye irritation, throat infections, asthma, fatigue, behavioral problems, colds, flu, eye and respiratory infections, headaches and depression.

Bacteria and Viruses: Bacteria, commonly known as "germs" are found to live virtually everywhere. One reason diseases caused by bacteria spread rapidly is that unlike viruses, they have the ability to reproduce themselves by dividing and multiplying every 20 minutes. To reduce the bacterial population, be sure to store all foods properly and keep the house, work place and schools as clean as possible. Remove standing water and lower humidity levels. Clean and disinfect the dehumidifier regularly.

Viruses: Extremely minute and contagious, viruses are unable to function or reproduce completely on their own and must invade host species cells. Once inside the compatible host cells, the virus injects its nucleic acid, which allows it to reproduce within the cell. Ozone generators may be able to destroy certain viruses by producing reactive oxygen.

Chemicals, Chemicals, Chemicals: More and more we are being subjected to new chemicals. They are found in our clothing, carpets, drapes, furniture, stoves, water heaters, paint particle-board, etc., damaging health. Symptoms are headaches, eye and skin irritation, fatigue, asthma, nausea, dizziness and cancer.

Gases: Combustion gases are the result of burning substances, heating systems, gas or oil, fireplaces, wood stoves and tobacco. (Twenty-five percent of children who live in homes with cigarette smoke contract cancer from "second hand" smoke. I don't believe that there is such a thing as second hand smoke because when you breathe it, it is for the first time and the effect is infectious.) The most prevalent of these gases are Carbon Monoxide and Sulfur Dioxide.

Volatile Organic Compounds (VOC): These are compounds that are dangerous to breathe. Exposure to VOCs has been linked to Central Nervous System damage, respiratory problems and even cancer. VOC exposure appears to be a main reason for the onset of MCS. The most common VOCs are Formaldehyde, Benzene, Toluene, Caron Tetrachloride and Tricholroethylene.

Air Filtration Systems: The Choices

Prior to our discussion in choosing the appropriate air filtration system, please be aware that the air filter will not solve all indoor air problems. They are not magic bullets, but superb tools helping to reduce and remove many of the toxins that we are exposed to. Before purchasing an air filtration device, it is paramount that one reduces as many of the contaminants in the environment as possible. First check your furnace and cooling systems. Change the furnace filter. Remove as many of the known sources of toxic contaminants, e.g. out-gassing carpets, paints, noxious cleaners, etc.

Air filtration systems work by letting air pass through a material (media) designed to trap the pollutants and then exchanging for pollutant free air.

√   **HEPA Filters**

HEPA (High Efficiency Particulate Arresting) are a very special extended surface filters, also known as absolute filters that are designed to trap 99.97% of airborne particles as small as 0.3 microns (a micron is one millionth of a meter). These include dust, mold, animal dander, bacteria, mildew and pollen.

√   **Activated-Charcoal & Activated-Alumina Filters**

Activated charcoal (activated carbon) is charcoal from coconut shell, coal or wood, which has been subjected to a special process, creating an extremely large surface area that is extremely porous. This produces a greater ABSORPTION of the polluting gases, volatile organic compounds (VOC) but not for formaldehyde.

√   **Activated-Alumina Filters**

Formaldehyde requires a special media for efficient removal. Activated alumina is heated; alumina granules impregnated with potassium permanganate. This media is able to absorb an even wider range of gaseous contaminants, including formaldehyde.

√ **Ozone Generators**

Ozone does not mask odors, but sanitizes and deodorizes. Ozone is activated oxygen, having the ability by means of a chemical process, to attach to all molecules in the air. Ozone breaks down, destroys or oxidizes pollutants in the air. These include mold, mildew, bacteria, odors, formaldehyde, and chemical gasses. The ozone reaction created works instantaneously by breaking the bond between the unwanted molecules, converting them to oxygen and water vapor." (For a complete reprint of Stan's article or for further information about air quality systems, contact: www.needs.com.)

Dr. Rapp suggests ways to improve air quality, which you might wish to know. I recommend that you obtain her book, *Is This Your Child's World*. Here are some of her recommendations about what you can do right now at home, at work or at your child's school.

"Ways to Improve Indoor Air – to help right away in most cases:

☑   Clean the entire building more thoroughly and more often. Vacuum heavily used areas often and well.
☑   Have an HVAC engineer thoroughly evaluate each school or home ventilation system.
☑   Be sure all ductwork is clean and free of chemicals and molds.
☑   Filters must fit properly, be clean and not be laden with molds or germs. Install ancillary ventilation hoods and supplementary exhaust systems in heavily polluted areas.
☑   Use room air-purifying machines in localized poor-air-quality areas.
☑   Use central air-purification systems to enhance air quality throughout the building.
☑   Check for mold and germ contamination in rooms with a high incidence of illness.
☑   Use only environmentally approved, safer cleaning material and mold-retardant agents, such as Borax.
☑   Install and maintain dehumidifiers to eliminate excessive humidity. Check the ventilation system.
☑   Stringently reduce the use of chemicals.
☑   Do not allow bus engines to idle while waiting for

students to enter or leave the school, or in garages or drive-
ways at home.

☑   Be sure drain traps contain water to decrease sewer
gas.

☑   Request and read Material Safety Data (MSD) sheets
for every chemical used in or around schools and homes.
Check for chemical contamination.

☑   Replace routine pesticide use with safer biological
forms of insect and pest control. Do not use pesticide
control unless there are pests.

☑   Offer less pesticide-contaminated, more natural foods
and water in schools.

☑   Stop or restrict the use of perfume, tobacco, fingernail
polish, offensive glues, cements, etc.

☑   Use natural light and full-spectrum lighting.

☑   Store all flammable materials in OSHA-approved fire
cabinets.

☑   Install exhaust fans in storage closest/rooms where
maintenance and art supplies are kept.

☑   If carpets must be installed, inexpensively check for
chemicals and health hazards.

☑   When indicated, carefully raise the temperature to at
least 90° F. for a day or two to "bake out" the molds and
chemicals."[26]

Within *Is This Your Child's World*, Dr. Rapp sensitively portrays
"air quality" through the feelings of a six-year-old during her dancing
lessons, which were held in a mold filled building. The six-year-old wrote
the following poem that is entitled: *Dancing Day*. If you have the occasion, read it aloud to another person and glean the dramatic story told in
the words of this struggling child. Her poem is below:

DANCING DAY

"I was sad, I was crying,
I felt in my tummy like nobody loved me.
It felt like I was gonna cry more.
That made me sadder and sadder.
It feels to be scared,
Like I'm a dumb person that nobody likes.
I feeled like I had a nonlistening brain.
I thought I was nothing,

Every time I go dance,
I feel like I want to go home."

Aroma Therapy (Smell) –
A Rose by any Other Name

Do you wear cologne or perfume? What about aftershave lotion? How does your house or your classroom smell? What is the odor of your building or workplace? (Please don't say that it depends on who is there.)

Some odors are pleasing to people and draw them into positive feelings and a mental state of alert concentration. However, for chemically sensitive people, the aroma of a particular smell coming from a particular aftershave lotion or from the scent of hair shampoo can set off an allergic reaction, which could range from minor skin or eye irritation to a rush to the hospital with a full scale asthma attack. About 70% of asthma patients react negatively to perfumes, shutting exhaling capacity by as much as 60% within moments of exposure. Also, see the section about $H2O$ for the relation of water to asthma cures www.watercure.com.

On the positive side, I have had several teachers and administrators buy bread-making machines, and they have reported that baking bread twice a week in school creates a different culture of positive emotions and well being. Additionally, other natural aromas, such as eucalyptus or pine extract, are touted by the aroma therapists as stimulating attention, concentration and cognitive function, notwithstanding the fact that some persons might be hyper-sensitive to such aromas and, if that is the case, those should be avoided.

Synthetic chemicals producing fragrances in electric "plug-in" dispensers should be avoided for a variety of reasons because many people are chemically sensitive.

Pets and Parasites –
Your Pet Might Not Be Your Best Friend

Remember when your parents said, "Don't let that pet kiss you," or "Don't get your face near that pet!" Well, you don't have to kiss the pet to connect with the varmints you might get at this stop on our journey.

I want to draw your attention to an audio cassette circulating throughout the United States called "The Silent Epidemic," which discusses the general maladies, such as ADHD, arising from parasites contracted from household pets and other environmental sources.

Several years ago, a couple came to me indicating that their child had just been diagnosed with Hyperactivity and ADHD with the prescription for Ritalin. The family, who had read Peter Breggin's book *Talking Back to Ritalin*, was opposed to this remedy and was concerned about alternatives. I asked, "How many pets do you have?" They were somewhat taken aback and replied, "What do pets have to do with our son's hyperactivity and ADHD? By they way, we have three – two dogs and a cat." With that, I suggested that they read a pamphlet I had on the negative impact of parasite infestation and how to remedy it with an inexpensive, natural "de-worming" kit found in most health food stores. I also suggested that they pick up a copy of Jean Carper's anthology of research studies on natural remedies, *Miracle Cures*. In that book is an extensive section, research based, on alternatives to Ritalin. Three weeks later, a pair of elated parents called to talk about the turn around in their son's school and learning performance.

Dr. Rapp indicates that, "Teachers, as well as parents, should learn to watch for dark eye circles, red earlobes, nose-rubbing, skin-scratching, wiggly legs, yawning, and various throaty sounds. Try to correlate these changes in appearance with exposures or the ingestion of certain foods or beverages. Problems with sitting still, learning, walking, and speaking definitely can be associated with any of the above changes in how environmentally sensitive individuals look."[27] And, she continues, "A white-coated tongue is a common indication of excess yeast. This condition is different from the mottled "geographic" tongue, which suggests a possible food allergy in children or adults... A bloated abdomen sometimes occurs with food allergies, but other digestive problems, such as chronic yeast infections and parasites, are also common causes."[28]

What I am suggesting is that you consider all of the possibilities that your Pediatric Allergist might advise when taking the path of least harm and go forward on the path of greatest success for you, your child or your family. (Please don't read this and then suggest to anyone who is particularly disagreeable with you, such as your mother-in-law or boss, that a "de-worming" treatment might improve them.)

Color – Somewhere Over the Rainbow

The next stop on our field trip is the wonder of color. Certain colors affect the human brain and therefore influence human learning, performance and achievement. Research indicates that bright yellow is a very harsh and disturbing color, which is often in kitchens where arguments typically occur. Contrasting bright yellow or bright red is pastel pink (Pepto Bismol™ pink), which is a most soothing color, especially for calming aggravated people. Many police departments are painting their interrogation rooms this color pink, as it dramatically and instantly reduces testosterone levels that foster aggressive behavior in males and females. Having a few "pink" colored cards around the house to show at the start of an argument might be helpful.

In addition, the long wave length of violet and indigo are soothing, along with forest green and sky blue. If you can, paint your office or classroom off white or another neutral color, while featuring other colors in posters, paintings and pictures that you can change frequently. There are many references to color and color therapy that you can seek out. However, as a primer, I would refer you to Dr. Jacob Liberman's book, *Light: Medicine of the Future*. Also refer to Helen Irlen's book: *Reading by the Colors: Overcoming Dyslexia and Other Reading Disabilities through the Irlen Method*. As the discoverer of "scotopic sensitivity syndrome" Helen Irlen has experimented with a variety of challenges ranging from mild to severe motor coordination, bi-polar behaviors and emotional management issues. The colored lenses she has invented provide a resource for more than the wonderful improvements in reading, depicted earlier in this chapter.

Room Design – Some Need a Beanbag; Some Need a Hard Chair

The next turn in our field trip takes us into room design. In order to increase the learner's comfort and performance, whether the learner is you or someone else conducting a class, training session, or a meeting, arrange chairs in a large horseshoe-shaped semi circle, with a large space in the middle for activities and presentations. Position tables around the walls for space to place books, materials, and displays. Make it easy to move chairs for large group activities or for a change in scenery. Allow students to sit in different locations, instead of having an assigned seat. This should also include beanbag chairs or a "chemical free" rug and pillow for the few who can't concentrate unless they are in a contorted position. Also, a few people in a class, and perhaps someone in your family, needs to be highly mobile when learning. This means the environment must provide for the opportunity to get up and walk or pace on the side or rear of the room (without interfering with others).

Research shows that some people will concentrate better while sitting on the floor, while others need mobility. Make a flexible environment to accommodate the learning of new and difficult information. (Reference: Rita Dunn, Ed.D.; The Center for the Study of Teaching and Learning Styles; St. John's University- www.learningstyles.net).

Temperature –
Some Like It Hot; Some Like It Cold

Sometimes when we take trips, it is wise to bring a jacket or sweater, just in case. Research is quite clear that temperature significantly affects the learning performance of students and adults. Some people prefer it warm while others prefer it cool when learning new and difficult information. About thirty-five percent of the body heat loss is through the top of your head, and some people may be dysfunctional if it is too cold or too warm for them when learning or concentrating. Simply determine for yourself whether you prefer a warm or cool room. When working with others, seek to achieve optimal body temperatures by having adults or children wear sweaters or extra clothing if they prefer it warm. Wearing a hat also reduces heat loss.

For those who prefer it cool, have them sit next to the open window or an air conditioner. Perhaps a small fan that makes very little noise might suffice. Have the people, including yourself, note the classes or work environments where they have been uncomfortable and urge them to take responsibility to achieve the optimal temperature for their individual learning style. (Reference: Rita Dunn, Ed.D.; The Center for the Study of Teaching and Learning Styles; St. John's University-www.learningstyles.net.)

Instructional Design – The Fun, the Joy, and the Excitement of Learning

Field trips sometimes have a guide who talks and talks, while others help you interact. Traditional classrooms are conducted in a manner that has the instructor talking most of the time, with language that is declarative, exclamatory or commanding. For effective learning to occur, active student participation in creative thinking, analysis and question raising must take into account seven intelligences, learning styles, music, skits, role playing, group exercises and individual and group performance. (Reference: see **Chapter Seven - *IntelliLearn® Strategies, Tactics and Tools***, in addition to reviewing other chapters in this book.)

The traditional lecture/note taking/exam-taking model for the delivery of information causes a steady decline in classroom energy as the class period progresses. The last 20-30 minutes (or more) usually tend to suffer a decline and depletion of energy that is manifested in a sharp decrease in interest and motivation. This decline and depletion of energy results in very little learning of new information, if any at all. This is why memory researchers claim that in traditional instruction, we only remember the first five to ten minutes and the last five minutes of what is being talked about. In many cases, some individual learners shut down in their learning abilities and interest much earlier, creating boredom and the opportunity for misbehavior to occur.

With the traditional lecture-listen approach to learning, there is little value for the forty-five or ninety minute period. There is a current effort to lengthen the class period and the school day, as well as the school year. But what sense does that make if you don't improve the flow of energy from what is often boredom to high performance achievement? The *IntelliLearn®* Model includes several strategies, tactics and tools revealed in this book to create an energy flow in the classroom. This energy flow varies from high energy to low energy, creating a "dance of energy" during the learning and teaching process in a given class period. (Reference: see **Chapter Seven** – *The IntelliLearn® Model.*)

Feng Shui (Pronounced "Fung Shu-way") – Bring Balance and Harmony to Your Life

An analogy for the Chinese "feng shui" might be the math subject of "geometry." When you organize all the points and lines so that the angle is a 90-degree angle, you get a "right triangle." And, by the way, you get a right triangle no matter where you are – in Europe, Asia, North America, or on the moon. Similarly, organizing the directions and points of energy that emerge from the elemental forces of nature provide both balance and maximum health, happiness and prosperity, according to worldwide Feng Shui Masters.

Have you ever said, "I need more balance in my life!"? Do you remember a family member stressing out because of "over work" or "over schooling?" One of the key issues in many of the TV "infomercial" shows and magazine advertisements for "self-help" products is helping people develop a healthy relationship among the competing responsibilities that make up their lives: e.g. "family," "work," "school," "church," "friends," "hobbies and recreation". All compete in the modern world for your attention, loyalty, time and energy. We need balance.

Do you recall seeing someone wear plaids with stripes? We usually tell that person, "That clashes; I don't think you want to wear that." Or imagine someone wearing two colors that conflict with each other. What about perfume that "hangs" and lingers on the verge of nausea?

The same concern about "balance" applies to office buildings, houses, hospitals, classrooms and schools. We can arrange the furniture, wall hangings and plants in such a way that the energy flows to create positive climates for humans or, in a way that establishes a negative energy.

During a visit to a hospital pediatric section a few years ago, I had a hard time imagining anyone getting well in that space. The organization of the space – the color, the lighting, and the drab pictures – were overly dark and dreary. The "earth tone" emphasis gave a negative energy from floor to ceiling. A simple change of wall colors, a shift from cool-white fluorescent lights to full-spectrum lights, and an aquarium filled with fish would provide an alternative of harmony with the blues and greens in nature.

You, too, may have gone into a house or restaurant and just "felt" a positive balance of energy. Likewise, you have probably gone into locations where you felt a negative disturbance of the energy in the environment.

As one explanation, over three thousand years ago the Chinese began to develop the process of "Feng Shui," which literally means "wind and water." All the forces of nature are understood in terms of the forces of these two fluid and dynamic elements, both of which make up the basic unifying force of nature: "Ch'i." Whereas the early Greek philosophers identified basic *substances* (Water, Air, Fire and Earth), the Chinese looked at identifying basic *processes* of the universe that emerge from the actions of one substance on another. These basic substances are wood, fire, earth, metal, and water. They each have a positive and negative force on one another.

On the positive side, wood produces fire. Fire produces earth. Earth produces metal. Metal produces water. Water produces wood. On the destructive or negative side, wood destroys earth. Earth destroys water. Water destroys fire. Fire destroys metal. Metal destroys wood. They are separate processes unified by the flow of energy forces that are either in or out of balance.

In modern physics, we speak of four forces. Albert Einstein's last quest was to find the fifth force of nature that unified the four forces of nature (gravity, electro-magnetic energy, the strong and weak forces). He was not successful in identifying the "Ch'i" or "unified field theory."

The modern version is "Yin" and "Yang," which is understood as the feminine and masculine forces in nature. In the Western cultures, "left brain – right brain" are often used to express the same different and often competing energies that require balancing. Feng Shui has evolved over the years, initially designed as an effort to arrange a respectful burial setting for Chinese ancestors. Since then, Feng Shui has evolved into an art and science, practiced by trained Feng Shui Masters. These Masters are "energy flow" experts who organize the environment in such a way as to bring happiness and prosperity and to avoid pain and agony.

In cities on the west coast of the United States, Honolulu, Hong Kong and Singapore, I have been in buildings where architects and building contractors hired Feng Shui Masters to engage in a strategic and systematic process of examining the geometry, geography, wind flow, neighbor buildings and terrain, north, south, east, and west directions for the front door and the relationship to streets, streams, mountains and intersections. Such buildings, as well as personal houses or classrooms, have a unique "feel" to them, where the flow of energy from the five substance relationships, wood, fire, earth, metal, and water is uninterrupted and flows easily.

Modern physicists speak of a "field" of energy and an energy flow that is both positive and negative. Indeed, Dr. Rupert Sheldrake wrote a book entitled *A New Science of Life,* in which he depicted "morophogenic" energy fields that enhance or detract from living organisms. We have cited above some of the serious energy detractors to living tissue, such as EMFs, fluorescent lights and certain colors and smells. Fredric Schiffer, M.D. has written a recent book entitled, ***Of Two Minds: The Revolutionary Science of Dual-Brain Psychology,*** in which he writes of his clinical psychiatric and neurological research, revealing that 66% of the population responds positively to one side of the brain or the other having a dominant and controlling voice over the other competitive, but less dominant brain. His therapy, which controls the way the environment is perceived through only one eye or the other, helps people bring balance between the conflicting forces of the two.

The idea of Feng Shui is to minimize conflict and to maximize health, happiness and prosperity. It provides you with a set of principles to study your environment and to organize it on the principles of Feng Shui, which have developed with both science and religion over 3,000 years. The purpose of Feng Shui is to align the real and symbolic forces of opposites and relationships of water, fire, wood, metal and earth to bring balance, beauty, energy and personal well being into your physical world.

For example, a Chinese American friend of mine was having trouble sleeping in the evening. She and her husband, who has worked with me on transforming schools and corporations, live in a high-rise with a beautiful view of the city, ocean and mountains. She has a stressful job, as does her husband. She described her problem as insomnia. I asked her husband if they had done a "feng shui" analysis of their high-rise apartment. He said, "No." I recommended a popular book, *Feng Shui For Dummies*, which is available at most bookstores, and they picked up a copy.

As it turns out, their bed faced west, so that the tops of their heads were facing toward the west, and their master bathroom door opened to face the headboard side of the bed. Well, they could not move the bed, because of limited space, so they reversed the sleeping arrangements and put the pillow where their feet were. Then they made sure to cut off the flow of positive energy from the bedroom through the open door in the bathroom and down the commode. What they did was to close the commode lid and close the bathroom door. From the first night of this alteration, four years ago, my friends claim that they have had uninterrupted, peaceful and quality sleep through the night.

Perhaps the "power of suggestion" was at play here. Perhaps not. Three thousand years of Chinese wisdom might have some useful contribution to the ergonomics of your living environment. I can only say that your brain, your heart and your happiness will improve if you study your environment, bring all of the energy forces in alignment, and bring balance with opposites in your environment expressed through art, plants, music, lighting, fabric, pictures, and furniture. For example, if you have a hard chair and a desk, also have a beanbag in a corner. If you have a painting of a water scene, place a cactus flower nearby. An aquarium filled with water or a desktop waterfall works wonders to provide the energy of water.

In terms of our Western Culture's view of intelligence theory, Howard Gardner at Harvard University has added his version of an "eighth" intelligence that is different from what I have included here as the "Spiritual, Ethical and Aesthetic" Intelligences, and is called the "naturalist" intelligence. Perhaps, Feng Shui would be a close definition of what Gardner has in mind in aligning with the beauty and forces of nature and the spirit of well-being. Whether East or West, we all seek what the Chinese call the three great blessings that are enhanced through Feng Shui: health, happiness and prosperity.

The Sixth Secret Revealed

What have you learned here and how can you apply this information to improve the quality of your learning and your life? What we reviewed is that given all the most effective teaching and learning processes in the world, you still might suffer the slings and arrows of a hostile environment. Whether it is chemical poisoning from carpets in your child's first grade class or constant aggravation from fluorescent lights, we all must be mindful and diligent. What we must *not* do is to blame children and others for *not* learning or *not* doing well in school or on the job, without first and foremost looking at all of the possibilities that could be impacting the learner's deficiency.

Thus, study your environment and arrange it for your good fortune and the well being of yourself, as well as for those around you! You will not be disappointed and the Miracle of Learning will be enhanced.

Refererences

[1] Rosenthal, Norman E. M.D., *Primary Psychiatry*, p. 31.

[2] *op cit*

[3] *op cit*

[4] Irlen, Helen, *Reading by the Colors: Overcoming Dyslexia and Other Reading Disabilities through the Irlen Method*, Turtleback Books, 2001, p.x.

[5] Crandell, Carl Dr., *The Volta Review,* 96, pp 291-306.

[6] Flexler, Carol, *Decisions in the Selection and Management of Classroom Amplification Systems,* 1992.

[7] *ibid.*

[8.] Hannaford, Carla, Ph.D., *Smart Moves: Why Learning is Not All in Your Head*, Great Ocean Publishers, 1995, p. 146.

[9] Simontacchi, Carol, *The Crazy Makers,* New York: Tarcher/Putnam, 2000.

[10] Batmangheldi, F. M.D., *Your Body's Many Cries for Water*, 1995, p. 4.

[11] Crook, William, M.D., *Help for the Hyperactive Child*, Jackson, TN: Professional Books, 1997.

[12] *ibid*, p. xxi.

[13] Rapp, Doris, *Is This Your Child's World: How You Can Fix the Schools and Homes that Are Making Your Child Sick,* Bantam Books, 1997. p. xv.

[14] Carper, Jean, *Miracle Cures,* Harper Collins, 1997.

[15] Simontacchi, *op cit,* p. 2.

[16] *ibid, p. 2.*

[17] *ibid, p. 3.*

[18] *ibid*, p. 4.

[19] *ibid*, p. 118.

[20] Rapp, *op cit*, p. 229.

[21] Hannaford, *op cit.*

[22] *ibid, p. 150.*

[23] *ibid*, p. 147.

[24] Rapp, *op cit.*

[25] *ibid*, pp 120-121.

[26] *ibid*, p. 133.

[27] *ibid*, p. 68.

[28] *ibid*, p. 78.

SECRET #7
Revealed.

The IntelliLearn® Model
For
High Performance Learning & Achievement

Building the
"Quality Learning"
Community

A
NEW
PHILOSOPHY

Achieving
Quality & Excellence

Better Learning

Positive Climates

Building Linkages

Putting It All Together

Removing Barriers with
Authentic Learning

A New Learnership Model
"Learnership - The Human
Side of Quality Learning."

Human Side of Quality:
A Forward Path for Educational
Reform & Achievement

Changing Structure &
Governance Toward
Empowerment

Diversity's Strength & Capacity

Chapter Seven

Secret #7
Building a
Learning Community

**Using a "human quality" focus -
All you want and need for learning is waiting for you
right here. Some assembly is required, but you have the
Power Tools.**

In the previous chapters of this book, we revealed six secrets of learning. This **Seventh Chapter** pulls those six secrets together into a system of learning and organizational culture that is a *learning community*. Such a community is best accomplished with a focus on the human side of quality. In this chapter, you'll learn how to implement the secrets into a successful Model, whose culture embraces the unification of the diverse principles outlined in this book. You might be surprised to know that the learning community can be as small as a family, as diverse as a public school, as complex as a corporation or as large as a nation or world community. To foster optimal personal and individual lifelong learning and growth, common principles must favor an acknowledgement of and respect for diversity, such as "e pluribus unum" ("out of many, one"), while also sustaining the common social culture of a learning "community."

This concept is often expressed in the African expression: "It takes a village to raise a child." As intuitively obvious as this is, it prompts the questions: "What does this village look like? Who is building the village? And on the basis of what principles and standards?" For a worse case example, consider that Hitler built his entire German Nazi Party around his "Hitler youth corps," where unswerving loyalty and blind "brainwashing" led to millions of deaths. More recent, the Mullahs of Islamic Fundamentalism who advocate the "Jihad"(holy war against infidels or non-Muslims) have built schools of "terror" around the world since the deposition of the Shah of Iran. Those schools took in infants and grew a generation of young men pledged to carry suicide bombs into the public places where innocent women, children and grandparents gather in peace.

In opposition to a culture of "hate" and elitism, if you want to optimize the development of people's brains, their hearts, their productivity and their happiness, you need to establish new mental models and build a common culture of the learning community on the highest standards and principles of truth, love, dignity, integrity, respect, diversity, hope and opportunity.

However, this is not without its challenges, particularly in the face of individual "self interests" and the "public interests" of the group. For example, Plato wrote about the essential problem of the "one and the many" 2500 years ago in *The Republic,* where the interests of the "self" are often in conflict with the interests of the "many." Mobocracy never led to happiness, nor did its opposite, Totalitarianism. The world is filled with gardens of gravesites as tributes to both. The natural tendency in the evolution of governments is to expand economic wealth in direct proportion to the investment in the education, skill and learning of its people. In terms of political process, the organizational structure has been to evolve toward a democratic form of government. As governments evolve, the fragile notion of democracy is expressed as: "of the people, by the people and for the people." This is a tribute and triumph for a culture of learning and economic prosperity.

In anticipation of the tyranny of the few controlling the lives of the many, without representation, the Democracy in the United States was organized with a Constitution, whose First Amendment protects citizens from forces that would prevent them from telling the truth. Contrary to popular opinion and some court interpretations, the First Amendment was never intended to protect "free expression and free experience;" rather it was to protect free "speech" so that people could speak the truth as they saw it, argued about it and defended it without persecution. Notice that the framers of the Constitution did not refer to "freedom of expression" or "freedom of seeing" (so you can be unwittingly exposed to suggestive photos in magazines or borderline pornography on television or in movies) or "freedom of "hearing" (so you can be exposed to any debasing smut on the streets, radio or television). Thus, if you yelled "fire!" in a crowded theatre, when there was none, you could be arrested and prosecuted, since you lied to incite and hurt people. It was not the truth. And the pursuit of truth requires freedom to explore, learn and think.

The metaphors that provide the overarching framework for the *IntelliLearn®* Model allow serious-minded people who truly desire high learning achievement to speak with a *new language* about a "community of promise" rather than the current "community at risk." These metaphors are grounded in scientifically validated processes and are: "The New Science of Learning;" "Learning as a Performing Art;" "Diversity as Capacity;" "Teacher, Parent or Leader as Orchestrator and Coach;" "Empowerment;" "Total Quality;" and "Learnership."

To build a learning community that incorporates all of the secrets revealed in this book, I, along with my colleagues, have designed a strategic "system" of learning, whose results have been both wonderful and staggering. Schools reduced learning disability referrals by two thirds while doubling standard test scores. Some schools saw a reduction of discipline referrals at the same time the scores rose in standard exams from 34% to 90% on or above grade level.

"Putting it all together" could be a mighty task. But to save you the effort and energy of "inventing the wheel" for yourself, I have created a strategic system and Model for you as a guideline to replicate high performance and learning achievement at home, at work and in your community.

Research has validated this Model. It has won several awards for supportive training processes and products designed to successfully replicate the Model in any community; and the point of entry in any community can vary from a school or community agency to a business, church or family. These services and products (see **Appendix B**) are designed with individual learning styles in mind and include mixed media products of video, audio, print and computer CD.

This chapter depicts the Model of *IntelliLearn®* in three parts:

Part One-
Purpose: Overall Purpose Statement of the Model

Part Two-
Structure: Building the Quality Learning Community

Part Three-
Function: The Human Side of Quality

IntelliLearn™ is a System

Much like the Circulatory System in the body.
Heart Å Neurosciences
Vessels Å Multiple Intelligences
Body Organs Å Components of IntelliLearn™

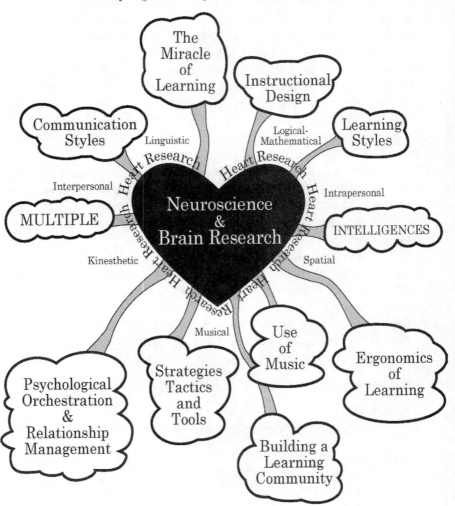

Part One – PURPOSE: The *IntelliLearn®* Model for High Performance Learning and Achievement

"Learning More, in Less Time, with Increased Memory and Greater Creativity"

The purpose of the comprehensive *IntelliLearn®* Model is to provide a coherent system of quality learning processes to enable individuals and families, as well organizations such as corporations, government agencies, public and private schools, and colleges and universities, to successfully learn more in less time with increased memory, creativity and application of new knowledge and skill. Initially developed while I was teaching, administering and conducting research at Syracuse University, I refined and implemented the Model in collaboration with several colleagues: Professors Rita Dunn, Ken Dunn, John Grassi, Leo Wood, and Howard Gardner and with other universities under the leadership of the *National Academy of Integrative Learning, Inc.*, which is a non-profit organization, founded while I was at Syracuse University.

Award winning research supports the quality learning, with a validation by the New York State Department of Education. The Honorable Regent Emlyn Griffith and Adelaide Sanford supported its presentation to the Regents of the State of New York in various forums. The United Nations selected the National Academy of Integrative Learning, Inc. to represent its worldwide literacy initiative. Various components of the system have won a variety of awards for high achievement. Many foundations, government agencies and local school districts have supported the *IntelliLearn®* Model for Faculty and Staff Development. Government agencies endorsing the Model include Cadet Command for Army Junior ROTC, The United States Department of Energy and the United States Air Force and the State of New York Legislature. In addition, corporations, such as Kodak, Intel, Sara Lee Knit Products, Hillenbrand Industries and Shell Petroleum have also incorporated the Model as their "core competency" in learning. From increased performance, these and other companies have saved millions of dollars, from which they have sponsored their partnerships with schools and communities (See **Appendix D** for a list of participants).

The *IntelliLearn®* Model incorporates all the "secrets" revealed in the previous six chapters in a variety of unique training seminars, self-directed learning products, curriculum and course design processes.

The Model also includes organizational leadership processes and Quality Leadership consultative strategies to dramatically increase the likelihood of personal and organizational success and performance. These services apply to all of the stakeholders involved in an organization. For example, in a school, this would include parents, board members, teachers, administrators, students, bus drivers, custodians, food service staff, secretarial and clerical staff, teacher aides and other support staff in the "Vision" and "Implementation" processes. This is why a School District like the one in Arco, Idaho could have a significant increase in reading performance at the elementary school and a two-thirds reduction in special education referrals.

The *IntelliLearn*® Model demonstrates how to successfully:

√ Present more knowledge, skills and information in less time;
√ Increase the climate and culture with positive tools of learning;
√ Tap the diversity of learners with new strategies;
√ Improve learner performance in all subjects and courses;
√ Increase memory and retention rates;
√ Engage learners in active, creative and reflective learning;
√ Drastically improve learner skills as "self-directed" learners;
√ Increase communication, cooperation and reduce discipline problems.

Presented in a way that participants learn and experience the values and benefits of the positive strategies, tactics and tools of *IntelliLearn*®, the implementation format can vary, whether it be a keynote address, conference workshop, seminar, or personal interaction.

Participants explore and examine the innovative philosophy of learning and learning processes that orchestrate and coach for high achievement. Active participation relates these orchestrating and coaching processes to the individual, classroom and to organizational management through a demonstration of specific heart-brain teaching, learning and management techniques across various curriculum subject areas including: Leadership and Learnership, Developing a Positive Climate and Culture, Application of Theory and Neurosciences, Building Emotional Intelligence and Caring Relationships, Role Playing, Movement, Dramatization, Use of Music and Rhythmic Activities, use of Art, Video and Spatial Presentations, and so forth. These are demonstrated by dynamically activating the Secrets, including the seven intelligences, learning modalities and communication styles.

This learning experience is also accomplished in a way that one develops proven strategies, tactics and tools to create effective personal learning achievement, as well as optimal and effective classrooms, where the instructional climate and culture assures that all students learn more in less time with greater depth, breadth, retention and joy of learning. In addition, participants involved in *IntelliLearn*® explore how to reduce burnout through the increase of individual performance, personal enthusiasm and positive outcomes. Educators, parents and employees have a full plate, but the *IntelliLearn*® Model strengthens their plates, rather than adds more.

Research has validated the successes in a variety of observable and measurable ways. These measurements include locally determined results as evidenced by gains in standardized national, state and local instruments, as well as personal goals and results.

For example, in Arizona, Leo Wood's chemistry class increased from 52% passing with Cs or better to 93% passing with Cs or better, simply by utilizing the strategies contained in the new systems approach: the *IntelliLearn*® Model. In addition, Mr. Wood's class saw a huge shift from 28% dropout to 7% dropout, as well as a shift in gender enrollments from 8 out of 10 enrollments being males, to an enrollment mix of 50% males and 50% females. Mr. Leo Wood's success is an example of a national treasure. If there were a "Hall of Fame" for teaching, Leo Wood would be in it. Students in all grade levels can far exceed current performance.

One parent, who was an engineer at a chemical plant, participated in the seminar Supervisory Management Training utilizing the *IntelliLearn*® processes. After a period of three months I saw him in the Control Room and he said, "I wanted you to know that my fifteen-year-old son has gone from grades of "D" to grades of "B" based on what you taught me." Not only are these processes applicable to schools and work, but they are also transferable to the home.

High school biology, math, English and chemistry classes using *IntelliLearn*® tools found students accelerating in performance. For example, reading is a critical area for all learning success, and virtually all first graders can leave the first grade reading at the third grade level with the *IntelliLearn*® Reading Component. Moreover, with the strategies, tactics and tools contained in the secrets revealed, we could anticipate at least 90% of our nation's students passing all subjects with a C grade or better. Further, employees engaging in the millions of hours of training could cut those hours, while increasing memory and performance.

From the schools in Harlem, New York to the Apache Reservation Schools; from the communities of Upstate New York to the villages in Hawaii; from the large corporations such as Eastman Kodak to small family businesses like the auto body shop in Idaho; from hospitals in Louisiana to Police Departments in Honolulu; from single parent families to intergenerational families; from teachers to students; from parents to children, PEOPLE have enjoyed the benefits of high performance and achievement through learning to learn, learning to choose, learning to relate and learning to create.

All people within an organization participating at all levels of the organization with learning performance as a priority can benefit, such as school board members, administrators, teachers, parents, trainers, instructors, instructional designers, supervisors and staff who are interested in enhancing learning outcomes and processes.

In addition to new metaphors and a new linguistic framework for high performance, the Model is grounded in key principles and core concepts - *corecepts*. These "corecepts" include the following principles as the core of all strategies, tactics and tools:

1. "THE MESSAGE RECEIVED IS THE MESSAGE SENT!"

This is the *"First Law of Communications"* identified by Marshall McLuhan. It anticipates that you might have the most well thought out message, teaching style or curriculum. However, if the message you wish to have sent is not being received the way you want it to be perceived, then you must pay attention to the receiver. In business this is known as "listening to the customer." If a person is a tactile-kinesthetic learner and you deliver your message linguistically, don't feel bad when your message, instruction and communication fail. Thus, the *IntelliLearn®* Model focuses on the learner's communication style, as well as that of the communicator, and is "learner centered" or "customer focused." The former Director of Information Technology for the State of Ohio and principal of the North High School in Springfield, Ohio, implemented staff training in the *IntelliLearn®* Model for faculty who taught nearly 1800 high school students. The results, following the first year of training, showed a 7.3% decrease in student failure rates, while attendance increased, as well as both teacher and student showing positive attitudes toward innovative class instruction.

2. "YOU GET MORE OF WHAT YOU REINFORCE!"

This is the *"First Law of Psychology"* introduced by the Behaviorists. If you can hold onto anything the Behaviorists brought into this world in the last century, it was this principle. Indeed, building redundant systems that reinforce the knowledge and skill you wish for people to learn is critical. Thus, having a useful framework like the Theory of Multiple Intelligences provides a schematic of at least seven intelligences through which to present information and skills, reinforce, reflect and review that information and those skills and create higher performance than the "one size fits all" mode of traditional learning pedagogy. Thus, when Arlene Garcia and Denise Johnson of Belen Middle School, New Mexico, won the U.S. Presidential Award for Teaching, they spoke of how they were trained in *IntelliLearn*® processes, which enabled them to teach math and science with abundant reinforcement using music, art, drama, personal interaction, relationship building, learning styles and cooperative learning.

3. "ANY ACT OF LEARNING IS AN ACT OF CREATING!"

This is a first principle, which is derived from research in brain sciences and neurocardiology. When people learn new and difficult information, whether it is knowledge, beliefs or skills, the act of learning is *not* a simple "transfer." New information requires the making of new connections with knowledge, beliefs and skills. When this occurs, a change in physiology takes place, including the increase of chemicals associated with improved memory. This connection making is an act of creativity within the learner's brain, heart and body systems, and is often accompanied with an "aha" reaction that we have all experienced. As a result of this act of creativity in making new connections between new and existing information, skills, knowledge and beliefs, we often hear people joyfully or gleefully saying: "Oh! I get it now!" Think of the thrill you had when you rode a bike for the first time and you were in control. George Smith, of People Builder's International, has jointly developed an innovative assessment tool with The National Academy of Integrative Learning, Inc. which enables learners to identify where they are on the *map* of those personal skills necessary for anyone to achieve personal career and academic success. His strategic tools allow the learner to be creative in developing a plan of action to strengthen, enhance or develop those necessary skills.(see **Appendix B**).

4. "DIVERSITY IS A CAPACITY!"

The motto of the longest surviving Democracy is *"E Pluribus Unum."* In the last century, we understood it as meaning "one out of many," where the focus was on the "one." The actual Latin translation is "out of many, one" where the emphasis is on the "many" who make up one unity. Diversity is a key to capacity building and this has been proven over and over from science and medicine to literature and invention. It takes different people thinking and doing different things to make challenging competition and to make improvement. We are smarter together than we are independently as individuals. This is not to denigrate a Mozart or Einstein, but it is to state the facts of the village that is needed to raise the child. To leave no child behind requires the best in each and the uniqueness of talent each has to contribute to the whole. *IntelliLearn*® embraces this corecept with a number of research-validated strategies, such as the diagnosis and implementation of various learning styles. Rod Hairston, founder of *Envision U, Inc.,* has had exceptional success with an initiative called the *"45 Day Challenge."* In that telephonic training seminar, people, including students and corporate executives have benefited by a personal reevaluation of the diversity of priorities and commitments required to achieve one's vision. Hairston lays out a strategic path forward for personal achievement.

5. "OUR STRENGTH IS IN OUR CONNECTEDNESS!"

No man is an island, although plenty of people feel helpless, alone and abandoned. The history of human progress is filled with examples, both on a personal basis and on a group basis, that the strength of the individual or the organization is as strong as its weakest link. As mentioned earlier in this book, Buckminster Fuller was noted for his scientific discoveries and inventions. Among his discoveries was the strongest structure known on this planet the "tetrahedron", which gains its strength from the connections of the components, not just in the material used. Thus, even in the world of physics and chemistry, we see that linkages or connections strengthen the structures of things. The same holds true for human beings. The greater we emphasize and focus on the *IntelliLearn*® Learnership Model, the more relationships and connections are fostered with meaning, purpose and depth. Love, loyalty, dignity, kindness, patience, respect and integrity represent the "bonding glue" of connections. Indeed, "love" may be the energy force that unifies all nature – the unifying force that Einstein sought to find until his death. Lt. Kealoha of the Honolulu Police Department revised new recruit police training based on the principles of **IntelliLearn®**, particularly in building strength through connectedness with the community. The strategies and tools learned at the Academy increased the Police Officers' capacity to look at the public as learners requiring linkages and connections in order to communicate more effectively.

6. "STUPIDITY IS A LEARNED BEHAVIOR!"

This is a very serious principle. When I first formulated it, I was astonished at the reaction from university professors, school administrators, corporate executives, employees and teachers. The statement seemed counter-intuitive. However, they were surprised because our cultural assumption is that some are "smart" and some are "dumb." And it is the business of education to sort out who is who and which is which. Thus, we have the testing mania across the country. It is almost heretical to ask the question that Psychologist Howard Gardner first posed to me at a lunch we had together in Cambridge a few years ago. He told me the central question in human development is "In what way is each person smart?"

In the United States, our test and measurement strategies are designed to find out "what's wrong" with people or simply "what they do not know." The goal of state and national standardized exams is, as one young ten-year-old told me, to find out "who is stupid and who is not." However, if you look at any three-year-old in the world, including the children in your family, would you call him or her "stupid?" Now, there are hungry children; there are abused children. But you can search the world over and you will not find children at three years of age who are "stupid." Could they be called "stubborn," "silly," "foolish," "lazy," or "mean?" Of course, but you won't find children of this age falling into the "stupid" category.

Stupidity is a learned behavior that emerges from the current traditional school's purpose, which is not to build citizens and transfer what is best in our culture; rather, it is to sort and select between those who do well in a dutiful world of teachers talking while children listen inactively and where paper-pencil tests determine one's life chances. The *IntelliLearn®* Model utilizes those processes that determine "in what way are you smart," assuming the giftedness in each individual's potential for outstanding achievement. This includes the nearly one third of the children in schools who live below the poverty guidelines and the masses of nearly illiterate adults in the workforce. Dr. Jesus Martinez, who has a Ph.D. in chemistry and is a scientist at the world renowned Sandia National Laboratories, took the *IntelliLearn®* Model with its emphasis on the giftedness of people and built the *"GANAS"* program, designed to help teachers improve science teaching to children, and the SCIAD Program for scientists and engineers, who volunteer in the public schools, to bring new knowledge and confidence to both teachers and learners. According to Dr. Martinez, "With *IntelliLearn®*, SCIADs and teachers can create an environment where it is safe to learn, learners enjoy hands-on activities, movement is allowed, and everyone learns more naturally, in less time, with less stress and with better retention."

7. "EVERYONE IS BORN A GENIUS!"

This key corecept draws heavily on the "Pygmalion" research at Harvard University and elsewhere around the world. The Pygmalion studies show that what people in authority (supervisors, administrators, teachers, parents) or what people engaged in learning, achievement, performance or health recovery *"think"* about their chances of success will influence the outcomes. People who think students will fail will experience failure among those students. What you expect of people and your anticipated outcomes will affect outcomes. If you think students or children will do well in your family, workplace or in school, they will tend to do far better than if you think otherwise. Well-substantiated by research, this psychological orchestration or mental state of positive affirmation applies to health and wellness, too. Looking for the "giftedness" in each person provides a baseline for capacity planning and capability building as opposed to deficit intervention. Norman Vincent Peale's book, *The Power of Positive Thinking*, along with Norman Cousin's *The Anatomy of an Illness* and Napoleon Hill's *Think and Grow Rich* are based on the principle that *thinking influences outcomes*. These books have positively changed the lives of thousands, because by changing your *thinking*, you can change your life. And the path-forward to changing "thinking" is through "learning."

What is required to implement these corecepts is a high interest in learning to implement the strategies, tactics and tools that manifest these corecepts in real life experiences. It includes a strong commitment to increasing the effectiveness of instruction and learning, whether that is in a family, school, corporation or for your personal use. It also requires an interest in systems change, process improvement and high performance. Also required is a commitment to a state of inquiry I refer to as: *"open minds, open hearts."*

The structure and context for implementing the Model is the "Quality Learning Community" structure, which is discussed below in Part Two, with a number of case studies demonstrating the processes and results of implementation. Part Three will detail the positive climate and culture relationships of the human side of quality learning, which is a key *functional* process for successful implementation.

Part Two – STRUCTURE: Building the "Quality Learning" Community

Pulling the secrets together as one unified whole in the Learning Community Model provides new meaning, purpose and direction for educational reform of our schools, economic development and wealth generation and for personal success and happiness for our children and families. However, since there appears, on the surface, to be nothing in common among them, what incentive is there for the head of quality initiatives at a major corporation, an elementary school teacher, high school parents, a superintendent of schools and the head of training at the local hospital, among many others, to create a learning community?

The answer is in the growing awareness that *innovations in the science of learning apply equally well* to corporate management, industrial training, staff development, and classroom teaching and, are critical for economic growth. By applying a new systems approach to learning, unprecedented successes are being recorded in businesses as well as public schools across the country.

Since the 1983 Nation at Risk report, we have heard many pleas for new partnerships to deal with the crises in American education. Spearheading the new alliances are various organizations such as the National Governors' Association, the U.S. Chamber of Commerce, the U.S. Department of Education's America 2000, and the National State Standards Movement. From all walks of life, we hear a call for new leadership to bring the wide range of segments together to establish successful *learning communities*.

The strategic purpose of the "learning community," as a part of new vision or enhanced learning across all sectors of society, is a focus on integrating organizations, institutions, and people to produce more in the global economy. The old question of finding out "Who is smart and who is dumb?" falls away to the enlightened question: "In what way is each person smart?" In the global, information economy of the knowledge worker, capability building through continuous improvement, learning and linkages replaces the sorting, selecting and segmentalism of the industrial age.

In her book **Change Masters**, organizational management consultant Rosabeth Moss Kanter claims our society is known for its "segmentalism." We have our schools, our industries, our community agencies, all of which are further divided into departments. We have our professional associations, service clubs, our professional organizations, political parties, and governments. As for education, levels and functions are further divided into early childhood, primary, middle, secondary, post-secondary, and adult. This does not even include the variety of specializations across these divisions.

Under the guise of improvement, "site based management" efforts often create a poor "system of schools" that compete with one another, rather than an improved and successful "school system." I know of an example in Florida where the individual school gets a financial reward from the state for test score performance, and the teachers and administrators in the various schools don't even talk to each other about the things that work for them. Not to blame the schools for this organizational factionalism, industry has plenty of similar examples. One corporation I consulted with to create a "learning organization" was initially structured as a "holding company," with several different entities whose responsibility was to deliver a designated "return on investment and equity" to the parent corporation in exchange for being left alone. As it turned out, through the insight of the new chairman and CEO, by building a "learning organization" in which common, shared activities led engineers of one division to talk and collaborate with scientists of a different unit, they came up with new products as a result of the "merger of ideas." Some even began to think that the new *niche* products would outperform the entire holding company in expanded revenues. This is one example when the whole is greater than the sum of its parts, but it starts at the top with the "leader as learner" – or what I call "learnership."

Dissimilar to the shared culture of the learning community, our traditional, industrial economy communities are most often segmented, with opportunities limited to respective boundaries imposed from our perspectives or from those who supervise, govern, and legislate with the latest "flavor of the month." "Competition of ideas" prevails over the more productive "merger of ideas," pulling the best forward. Survival demands the "merger of ideas" which surface in a culture which permits connectivity, mutual collaboration and affection.

The Whole Picture
of the
IntelliLearn Model of Learning & Teaching

One must focus on the processes that produce the outcomes.
The core process is the interaction between student and teacher.
Begin at the center, the heart (core) of learning and work out.

A New Philosophy

Imagine sitting in a training room at Eastman Kodak in Rochester, N.Y., or at Gulfstream Aerospace in Savannah, Ga., with about 40 other representatives from schools, hospitals, local governments, businesses, community agencies, the police department and the local Chamber of Commerce. Corporate executives and business owners are seated randomly, along with teachers and parents.

Unlike a usual meeting for fundraising or civic projects, these people are engaged in a common desire to learn about our new systems approach to building learning communities with strategies that drastically enhance learner achievement. Each is interested in shifting away from segmentalism into new levels of "connectedness," drawn together to create learning communities within their classrooms, schools, industrial plants, and communities, as well as their families.

In recent years, organizations have asked me to help them enhance individual and organizational performance using our successful seminars, along with products, strategies, tactics and tools that present a new philosophy found in the *IntelliLearn®* Model. Initially I assumed teachers and managers in schools, corporations, community agencies, and universities would have different needs and concerns. After all, even the study and education of people is segmented – pedagogy for children, adolescent psychology for teens, and androgogy for adults. But I found that all organizations are in the same boat with respect to creating the learning community. That boat is our common need and opportunity to enhance learning performance greatly, at every level and in every sector of society, if we are to survive economically, socially and personally.

Cooperation alone isn't enough. Our most pressing leadership challenge is to tap the *full* mental capacity of each individual and evoke the highest levels of quality, performance, and productivity. It is becoming increasingly evident from research that we must *not* hold on to an outmoded "uniformist" view and reinvent individuals into "the one best model" of teaching, training, and instruction. The "one size fits all" approach to processes that produce outcomes has been proven woefully inadequate to the tasks of a learning community and economic prosperity.

The *IntelliLearn®* Model is based on a new regard for the importance of diversity as a capacity in "the learning community boat," where there's an oar for everyone, regardless of where they are located within the community or at what level. No one is excluded, as all are crucial for survival and prosperity. In the past, we have approached the issue of learning as if it belonged almost exclusively to schools – a supply-side view. Today, the information economy has made effective learning a core activity that must occur throughout living, working, parenting, civic involvement and recreating – a demand-side view. Beyond the major growth in trade book publication in the past thirty years, take a look at the vast growth in specialty and hobby magazines, as well as the proliferation of information-learning channels on cable, such as the Discovery Channel and WEB MD. Vast expanses in learning web sites have emerged to meet the demand of people's curiosity and need to know.

To achieve "learning on demand," leaders of schools, businesses, communities, and post-secondary institutions must call for a new, collaborative vision, purpose, and direction – one that focuses on and fulfills the common need for learning far more effectively throughout one's lifetime. Consequently, when considering the creation of learning communities, the needs, and solutions were unusually consistent among the different sectors and included the following issues:

1) Quality and excellence;
2) Governance and restructuring toward improvement;
3) Building linkages;
4) Diversity as capacity;
5) Better performance through better learning;
6) Creating positive climates; and
7) Removing barriers to authentic learning.

Each of these issues emerge as common considerations when developing learning communities.

Achieving Quality and Excellence

To achieve systemic change and community success, schools and corporations are focusing not just on excellence, but also on the quality of the work or teaching processes that allow people to succeed. The Voyager Charter School in Honolulu has "quality process" as one of three legs it stands on for its success with inner city children. One mother remarked that her child never liked school, but the Voyager School has been an inspiration to the entire family. "My child loves school now," she said. The school is also based on principles of cognitive growth as the second leg and the *IntelliLearn*® Model of quality instruction and leadership as the third.

Also, the Leander School District in Texas, where I recently delivered a keynote address on "Quality Instruction," has been a leader for nearly nine years in assimilating the Malcolm Baldridge quality focus and creating a culture of positive support and high achievement. When I was addressing the 2000 or more employees, the climate and culture of the people felt more like a close family than it did like a bureaucratic school district. On the other hand, in some states that have initiated the Baldridge Award process from the State Education Department down to the local district, as in Ohio, many faculty have told me that the training for them is like another imposition, seemingly unrelated to the needs of the classroom and more to do with record-keeping. These teachers who are speaking have full plates and they see the plate getting over-burdened, because they don't make the connection from quality data recording to quality instruction to the quality of performance and productivity.

Just like the Hawaii and Leander examples, representatives from all sectors seem convinced that a focus on how to achieve "quality" in teaching, learning, managing, supervising, communicating and performing is a key to enhanced individual and team performance. Within the corporate sphere, Mr. Joe Braidish, Director of Corporate Consulting Services, Kelly Executive Partners at the University of Indiana, whose customers include Fortune 100 companies, has been consistently faithful to the notion that developing "quality" relationships is the cornerstone to high performance in the workplace and productivity in a nation's economy. At the factory floor level, Mr. Jim Flynn, plant manager for Sara Lee Knit Corporation witnesses major reductions in defects, increased employee enthusiasm, reductions in training time and improved performance at every level through the implementation of quality processes with *IntelliLearn*® instructional strategies.

"Total Quality Leadership" (TQL) and "Total Quality Management" (TQM) are not mere slogans, especially for those schools like the one in Mt. Edgecombe, Alaska, where learner performance is remarkably high with community service as a bonus. TQL and TQM are "vision" phrases for a world in which communities provide the strongest collaborative support for the learning process, which produces high achievement and potential economic prosperity for everyone. The Total Quality Model includes guideposts as well as processes for re-thinking how we want our schools and other organizations to be structured and how they are to function. Dr. Sally Anderson led the charge in Idaho for "quality leadership" as a structure and process for the Albertson

Foundation's significant contributions to the public schools. In one district, Butte County #111, dramatic increases occurred at all levels of measurement after the administrators, faculty, parents, community leaders, bus drivers, food service personnel, and students were trained in the various quality processes of the *IntelliLearn*® Model.

Quality and excellence are natural outcomes of the learning community, which brings community and business partners together with schools and parents, precisely because the focus of the learning community is on the quality of life, quality of work, quality of learning – in short, a total quality focus. Do not discount the importance of a common language to describe that common purpose as a unifying principle that brings people together. An example of common interest working across sectors to pursue high standards in both industry and education is exemplified in the Malcolm Baldridge National Quality Award. Many enlightened school officials are adopting process improvement plans that follow the Baldridge Award process. However, implementation of these processes vary with the commitment of the leader at the local level to modeling the required learnership behavior and to the "empowerment" of people, as opposed to implementing just another "mechanical flavor of the month."

Changing Structures and Governance Toward Empowerment

If we want quality and excellence, we will achieve it when leaders and organizations adopt the principles of "Theory R 'Relationship' Management" and empowerment as discussed earlier in **Chapter Four**. This requires different operating structures and procedures than those we have inherited from the old industrial "management" model of top-down, hierarchical, segmented structures of modern corporate and school management. The most promising structure that applies at the classroom level, the school building level, the corporate level, and the community agency level is a framework that permits team learning, effective site-based management, self-directed teams and high performance management – namely, "Theory R" as a component of the *IntelliLearn*® Model.

Dr. Christopher Eaddy, who runs the Governor's "Save our Students"(SOS) program in North Carolina has had independent research verify his exemplary model of developing "relationships" as the cornerstone to student achievement, as well as reductions in discipline problems. Dr. Janet Johnson, President of the independent research and evaluation firm EDSTAR, Inc., has conducted extensive research on the SOS program with exceptional results from this "after school" initiative. Dr. Eaddy has written a recent book about leadership, entitled *The Greatest Teacher – Understanding How to Use your Power as an Educator* (A study of 150 "Teacher of the Year" winners, available at www.ChristopherEaddy.com. David Lockett, in Toronto, Canada initiated a program with youth offenders based on tapping the emotional intelligence of learners and creating new empathic relationships between victims and their families and the aggressor youth offenders and their families, thereby reducing the one year recidivism rate from forty-two percent to zero.

The innovative use of mixed media, distance learning and computer CD learning can help make high achievement and performance happen. A training CD has won a coveted international award under the innovative production leadership of Donna Rice, Bureau Chief at the National Cadet Command, Army Junior ROTC Programs in high schools together with the development team headed by John Shultz at American Management Systems, Inc, and our organization, with Leo Wood and me as the instructional design team. It is a product called "Quantum Learning," which incorporates the *IntelliLearn*® technologies to support individual training and staff development in the Secrets of Learning. The CD is a useful companion to this book (see **Appendix B**).

Another example, developed through shared needs and success, is Oklahoma State University's Telecommunications Institute, where I served on its Board as a founding member. Under the leadership of Dr. Marshall Allen, the Institute has bridged the resources of business, universities, government agencies and schools to create new telecommunications structures. Also, *IntelliLearn*® consumer products that we produced for students, parents and family members, as well as for professionals, have supported accelerating the learning and achievement process. Award winning products like *"Amazing Grades"* empower learners and families by helping them learn how they learn best and what to do to obtain higher achievement (see **Appendix B**).

In addition to the innovative use of technology to support the learner, organizational structures need to also be responsive. The entire goal of changing the governance and structure of existing organizations is to achieve better results. Corporations are building new structures and processes around the decentralized quality processes with a customer focus. Schools are increasingly emphasizing site-based management and shared governance where bringing parents into partnership can help in the shared decision-making processes. Neither is successful if they go too far on either side of the continuum – too top down on the management company side or too loose on the confederation of holding company units or site based schools. "If you don't know where you are going, any road will get you there," is an old expression for direction. We might add, "If you don't know what to DO, any structure will get you there!"

A close parallel exists. Learner-centered environments in schools are emerging as similar to customer-focused businesses. Dr. John Grassi, Vice President of Cambridge College, pioneered the first innovative master's degree completion program that focused, under his leadership, on training teachers and administrators in results-driven, accelerative learning processes that are learner-centered, team-based and emotionally positive.

One example of decentralized team-based governance in the schools is in Springfield, Ohio at the South High School. Under the leadership of Mr. Rick Butler, the faculty and students implemented staff development training using the *IntelliLearn*® Model with its focus on relationships. Building relationships across all sectors, during the first year following training from The National Academy of Integrative Learning, Inc., South High School, with an enrollment of 1600 inner-city students, enjoyed a 17% drop in discipline referrals, while having a 10% increase in grades across the board.

By integrating the diversity of perceiving and processing information in a stress-free, non-judgmental learning community environment, elementary schools like Principal Margaret Bradley's P.S. 223 in Queens, N.Y., shifted in two years from 51% on or above grade level in reading and math to 80%, as measured by CAT Tests. Award winning research has documented that when utilizing components of the *IntelliLearn*® system in all settings, through focusing on individual participation in decision making and work processes, as supported by the broader team or group, the concept of empowerment has surfaced – empowering the workforce, empowering teachers, and empowering the learners.

Restructuring within organizations and across institutional boundaries already has achieved strong impetus. Peter Drucker is known for writing about the "knowledge worker," whose success will be diminished unless corporations build learning organizations. Ted Sizer, who founded the Coalition of Essential Schools (the Re-Learning organization) at Brown University, and W. Edwards Deming, a guru in "quality leadership," as well as many derivative groups, like the "Baldridge Award" process initiative for companies and schools, are focusing on organizational transformation.

The desire for collaboration and synergy within organizations is expressed through initiatives such as quality circles at Sara Lee Knit Products in North Carolina or in the work of educators such as Cliff Bailey, the late principal at Kapaa Elementary school in Kuaii, Hawaii, where the school has been divided into clusters of schools within schools with the teams functioning around themes and self-directed management.

New paradigms such as *"systems thinking"* are spoken in enlightened organizations attempting to increase communications and cooperation among previously disconnected departments, divisions, areas, or employees and students. Learning communities become models for teams and teamwork through the conscious effort of communication, shared visions, personal mastery, and team learning, as advocated by Peter Senge in his book, ***The Fifth Discipline***, as well as by Congressional Medal of Honor recipient Wayne T. Alderson who, along with his daughter Nancy McDonnell wrote the book, ***Theory "R" Management***, which reinforces the ***IntelliLearn***® Model of love, dignity, respect and positive relationships among all levels within an organization. This is a key to building linkages and connections (see **Chapter Four**).

Building Linkages

As noted earlier, Buckminster Fuller identified that the strongest structure known to mankind is the triangle-looking *"tetrahedron"*. You have seen geodesic domes made up of several tetrahedrons as gym structures on school playgrounds. It is strong because it is made up of triangles, whose strength comes not only from what they are made of, but also from their linkages or connections. The same is true with families and organizations. Our strength is in our connections or relationships with each other, with the group being smarter together than any one individual. And because of the diversity of individuals, with husbands and wives different in their learning styles, and children within the same family different in how they learn best, it takes new "mental models," communication processes and consistent work to get along with others and to have positive relationships.

This is one of the principles of quantum physics, as well as of other new areas of science and medicine, namely that the linkages and connections throughout the system are crucial to understanding, growing, or healing the system. Margaret Wheatley brilliantly explores this point in her book, ***Leadership and the New Science***.

The climate and culture of linkages, connections and relationships hold true for people to survive. The days of isolation and segmentalism are passé for those who hope to survive, because many now recognize that enduring quality, excellence, and performance can only be enhanced through collaboration across and between sectors, be they people, organizations, or countries. Economic trade is the key to interdependence, prosperity and peace.

Many new efforts to link the school to the broader community of business, parents, agencies, and colleges and universities have taken hundreds of forms, ranging from adopt-a-school programs and gifted and talented programs to science advisor programs, mentoring programs for at-risk youth, school-parent councils, youth entrepreneurship, and dropout prevention programs and "service learning" through the Junior ROTC programs across the country. Several communities have begun to adopt a "learning community" perspective to assemble and add capacity to their assets, provide joint venture initiatives across the community, and maximize resource utilization through combined partnerships among schools, companies, and community agencies.

Of course, those creating the learning community criticize the school as an island, a concept especially important in low-income communities. A key ingredient is that there must not be just changes in the classroom but also growing capacity in the community to influence education.

The parent-driven "College, Here We Come" program in a large Washington, D.C., public housing complex is a sterling example. White House Policy Analyst and Board Member of the National Academy of Integrative Learning, Inc, Morgan Doughton, shared with me that the program, led by Carol Hall, encouraged educational success by *all* kids in the complex, whether or not college bound. The organization, which operates its own study center and builds mutual support among parents, has reduced dropouts to near zero. The number going on to college has multiplied from five to nearly three hundred (with one hundred more going on to skill academies) – this with no outside funding. In addition, the initiative has changed the way schools view these youngsters (youngsters to whom the teachers previously didn't even bother to give homework assignments, knowing they wouldn't be done).

System-wide collaboration is needed to create a learning community. This requires reaching out from your own territorial imperative or turf, building relationships, and seeking advice, counsel, support, and cooperation of other community stakeholders. It requires a strategic plan and commitment to building the kinds of "people relationship" skills required to guarantee your capacity to succeed in your mission. This applies to classroom students as empowered shareholders as well as to the organization itself, whether that organization is within a school building, district, corporation, municipality, or state government agency. Once again, far too often, we assume that the stakeholders in the effort to improve the results have the "relationship" skills or "people skills" *to create and deliver the processes that produce the results.*

The use of telecommunications technology and distance learning can extend the boundaries of communication to cities and states of common purpose to expand the order of magnitude and to replicate good processes that research has determined work and work well. Oklahoma State University's Telecommunications Institute has created new pathways for establishing distance learning to build learning communities in the United States and abroad by using mixed media – combining the use of distance learning and CD computer instruction with audio and video.

It is precisely the connectedness and seeing the linkages that stimulates creativity, critical thinking, analytic thinking, team cohesion, and valuing diversity of perspectives. Why should math be learned only in a math class, English only in English class?

Diversity's Strength and Capacity

Leaders of corporations, school communities, colleges, and universities speak about problems associated with an increasingly diverse population. That can mean anything from increasing dependence on employees for whom English is not the primary language to soaring numbers of non-English Laotians and Latin Americans in Lowell, Massachusetts; from foreign national enrollments in engineering at Oklahoma State University to increasing numbers of first-generation children from many cultures at Principal Mike Arcuri's elementary school in Utica, N.Y. It can mean diversity in family structures, as in the case of the student body of P.S. 27 in Brooklyn, where more than 40% of pupils now live in foster homes.

Diversity in learning, however, is not ethnic or domicile governed, but individual. Research confirms that each individual performs significantly higher when learning in his or her own way. Regardless of our particular view of diversity, learning organizations – whether school, workplace, or neighborhood center – no longer can emphasize or impose uniformity on the one best way of teaching, training, learning, leading to bell curves of lower and lower centers. Today we must understand diversity as an asset, not as a deficit in need of remediation. Accordingly, leaders and practitioners can capitalize on the strengths of diversity by assessing, honoring, and recognizing differences that make a difference. (See **Chapter Two**.)

This view is also endorsed by other diversity theorists such as Howard Gardner and David Perkins at Harvard through the theory of multiple intelligences; Robert Sternberg at Yale with his view of the triarchic (three part) mind; Ken and Rita Dunn at City of the New York University and St. John's University with their theories on learning style; John Grassi's accelerated learning theory; Paul McLean's triune brain theory; and Marion Diamond's regenerative brain theory as an application of neuroscientific theories.

Employing the diversity model of learning styles (Dunn and Dunn), which is incorporated into the learning community strategic plan, former Principal Roland Andrews led Brightwood Elementary School in Greensboro, N.C., from 34% of students on or above grade level to 90% on or above grade level as measured by national standardized exams. He also led the school to a reduction in discipline cases from 148 to 8 over the same three-year period.

Better Learning

Getting people to learn more in less time with fewer resources at higher levels of achievement is a common hope. Concerns about individual performance and increased productivity, though common, are often described differently. While corporations like Eastman Kodak and Intel speak about "high performance" and self-directed teams, several school districts are formulating strategies to reduce dropouts, increase graduation rates, improve employability or skills for self-employment, and increase life skills.

New performance criteria require changes in what people know, how they learn, and the mechanisms or technologies through which they learn. Curriculum in schools is changing in ways similar to the shift in industry to learning about work processes and systems linkages, rather than learning short-term or dated skills. Innovative human resource development is the essential theme, about which learning to learn far better is a strategic key. It's so crucial that leading-edge companies like Motorola, Toys "R" Us, Xerox, Sara Lee Knit Products, J.M. Huber Company, Hillenbrand Industries and Eastman Kodak have adopted strategic plans that include far more investment in ongoing learning for all employees.

In addition, private foundations, such as The National Endowment for Financial Education (NEFE), spearheaded by Executive Director Elizabeth Schiever, is devoted to providing innovative and meaningful curriculum and instruction so that ordinary students can learn the value and benefits of financial education. What money and credit, as well as debt and interest do in a person's life can be critical to success or endless failure.

Ginnie Moore, who directs University Outreach Services for Shawnee State University in Portsmouth, Ohio, has reported outstanding success in both the Tech-Prep Consortium initiatives with *IntelliLearn®*, as well as in an innovative "after-school mall" where students who are "at risk" become "at promise." Also, innovative consortial arrangements, such as the academic and career education partnership at Tri-County Technical College in South Carolina, launched tech-prep as an alternative to the general high school diploma, using *IntelliLearn®*. The college won a national award using the instructional strategies embodied in this book. Continuous learning, then, is the key to continuous improvement, and a core concept in the shift from outworn manpower models to mind-power strategies for continually enhancing human performance.

Using instructional design strategies of the *IntelliLearn®* Model, Ed White, a trainer in Kodak's electronics training courses, and Alice Lombardo, a math teacher at Frederick Douglas Middle School in Rochester, N.Y., were at the same training session. White taught a Kodak course in electronics that at one time required forty-eight classroom hours and led to good but not outstanding gains. Ninety days later the engineers would demonstrate seventy to seventy- four percent retention of material on a written test. After assisting Ed White in converting his electronics course into an *IntelliLearn®* format, White taught the same material in half the time (twenty-three hours) and ninety days later his students scored 96% retention (up from 74 %).

Lombardo teaches in an inner-city middle school where 23% of the students are identified as "at risk." She taught her seventh graders using learning community principles of *IntelliLearn®* and as a result, an astonishing 52% of her students passed one year of seventh grade math by mid-year.

To make real progress, several old assumptions must be turned on their heads.

Positive Climates

All organizations, with the people who lead them, want to and must create cultures of positive self-esteem with environments free of mockery, put-downs, abusive treatment, stereotypes, demeaning character judgments, and violence. This culture change toward a positive climate, too, is an outcome of the *IntelliLearn*® process.

At the end of one training session, a corporate manager from Mobil Chemical stood up and apologized to teachers and administrators for industry's misjudgment and underestimation of the professional talent represented by educators in the room. Small innovations can have major impact.

To help achieve such communities for learning, many organizations have used innovative cultural communications tools (see **Chapter Five**), such as the "good and new" or "think and listen." The "good and new" gives each student a few moments to describe something new and positive in his or her life. The "think and listen" gives each learner quality time for someone else (or a pair of learners) to listen to what they have to say, without interruption, for at least five minutes each way. This tool creates a genuine sense of listening in environments that traditionally have little time devoted to being heard and listened to.

Incorporating the "think and listen" and the "good and new" in her classes, Jeanne Panka, who teaches high school biology in North Syracuse, N.Y., often has each student begin the class by saying something "good and new" that has happened in his or her life in the past twenty-four hours. Students focus their attention on the positive expectancy in their lives and, indeed, begin to look for new stories of the good or new things going on in their personal lives. After using these and other *IntelliLearn*® tools to build a learning community in the classroom, Panka's student test scores rose from 76% passing to 96% passing regents biology tests.

Chris Owens teaches a reading class at Paul Robeson High School in south side Chicago. Her fifteen and sixteen-year-old students formerly read below the fifth grade level and had a 40% dropout rate between September and February. Dr. John Grassi and I, along with other members of our training team, worked with Chris to provide new attitudes and tools to build the learning community. Following her first year of creating a new environment that fosters positive interaction and mutual respect, she had **no** dropouts by February, with several students gaining one to two years in reading skill over six months.

Sara Lee Knit Products follows a similar routine with training of employees in statistical quality control process. When employees feel connected to the learning material with an emotional climate of positive inclusion, learning is faster, people remember far longer, and they enjoy learning to the level that it increases corporate and personal success. One plant reduced its turnover rate from 48% to 18%; reduced its orientation course for new employees from fourteen weeks to seven weeks; and reduced its defective material output from four thousand pounds per month to three hundred pounds per month. The net savings in one year exceeded $200,000.

Removing Barriers with Authentic Learning

Traditional teaching and learning is an artificial experience in which students are subjected to verbal-auditory and stimulus-response models. More than seventy-five percent of the time, the authority (the instructor) is talking or directing students to sit and read. In these traditional classrooms, little or no attention is paid to the internal learning environment of each student – how they feel, what they fear, how they learn best, their diversity of learning styles and modalities, the culture they bring to the school or workplace, the dysfunctional behaviors they exhibit through expressions of "I can't" or "I won't."

To turn this around, the *IntelliLearn*® Model includes several processes designed to make the classroom exciting. To the Nintendo generation, the classroom is a boring place. Even the most dedicated teachers focus on discipline first and settle for trying to reach a few.

Approaches to learning must change. They are changing. Indeed, based on the results of the *IntelliLearn*® Model, it is fair to say that we are leading that change in communities across the nation and around the globe.

Toward the goal of creating exciting and engaging classrooms, Dr. John Grassi has developed the Accelerated Learning Program. "The ALPS Method is a process of relating to learners in a manner which enables them to learn virtually anything in a joyful, brain-compatible way. It has been used successfully with learners of all ages, from pre-kindergarten to graduate school. It was developed by Grassi in 1981 and used originally in training bilingual teachers in Boston Public Schools and in teaching adults in the Cambridge College Graduate Program, Cambridge, Massachusetts. It is now used in many schools and school systems throughout the United States, in corporate training, in medical training for nurses and in private schools and colleges."[1] Dr. Grassi's model is a key component of the instructional processes in the *IntelliLearn*® Model.

The Guggenheim School in Chicago, where eighth graders formerly were taught a city-mandated four-week outlining course, used this model. According to teacher (and later principal) Dr. Nancy Ellis, the students hated the lecture course, and 80% failed the mastery test. After creating an *IntelliLearn®* Model learning community environment, where the diversity of student strengths and experiences were incorporated into the communications process with skits, songs, dialogues, and team collaboration, Ellis taught the same course in one week, not four, with all children passing the mastery test with a minimum of 75% competency. The course became an authentic learning experience. Years after her initial exposure to these innovative learning and teaching processes, Nancy told me she used many of them to complete her own Doctoral Dissertation.

Similar results occurred in corporations. In the various manufacturing plants throughout the United States, managers and line workers are jointly incorporating the use of statistics to measure quality of manufacturing processes. (Also, several schools are adopting similar initiatives under the "Baldridge Quality Award" framework.) Success in learning the required material used to be limited. One major firm implemented an *IntelliLearn®* approach that incorporates collaboration and trust. As a result of bringing the learner's culture and personal experience into the learning community, one trainer said, "I can now...consider ways to benefit the business by tapping into some of the hidden talents of all employees; that is, workers who outside of the plant are athletes, artists, musicians, etc."

Tapping into the authentic experiences that people bring to the learning place and incorporating them into the learning process provides an essential ingredient to making learning what Ed Nicholson, retired principal of an internationally recognized vocational high school (BOCES) in Oswego, N.Y., calls "REAL: Relevant, Exciting, Applicable, and Lasting." This is also an example of what French psychologist Jean Piaget meant when he wrote: "You can teach anything to anybody, as long as you establish a real life connection." And, making "new connections" with current experience is the essence of *"creativity, innovation, problem identification and problem solution."* Under such circumstances, the group "becomes" the curriculum.

Part Three – FUNCTION: A New Leadership Model: "Learnership – The Human Side of Quality Learning"

As stated earlier, corporations engage in developing decentralized management and self-directed teams, schools are exploring site-based management and shared governance. The impulse, however, is not yet pervasive and institutionalized. And many examples of "shared governance" are reported as confused decentralization. This can happen when leadership relieves itself of responsibility and accountability under the guise of empowering people and getting people involved (Theory Z). It also happens when one creates a system of disaggregated schools or divisions, as opposed to a "school system," and doesn't model the behavior of "learnership" or doesn't walk the talk. Rather, they often "mock the talk" as if the problem is with those who need the treatment. This applies to the work place as well. Of all the successes I have either seen or been part of creating, it was only in "niches" or specific divisions where excellence emerged *when the leader took the responsibility* for creating the learning organization model.

Too often the approaches are superficial – sometimes put down as "programs of the month." They might be well intentioned, but usually fall into disregard and are abandoned after a year or two, precisely because patchwork intervention does not work for system-wide change and improvement.

A new role for leadership requires shared vision, purposeful cooperation, and common strategies in improving learning. This means that the leaders become learners and every learner exhibits leadership behavior in an environment where people are continuously modeling optimal learning behavior. I call this "*Learnership*."

Learnership focuses on the architecture and construction of systems that feature the "human" side of quality, where empowerment guides leaders. As stated at the outset, it is only recently that we have begun to realize that the conventional separateness of schools from business and communities must be overcome through "learning communities" that meet the one need that binds us together: the need for successful learning over a lifetime to create personal and national performance and wealth. And lifelong learning, along with continuous improvement, demands that we focus on the excellent human processes that produce high standards and high performance – the human side of quality. A recent poll of United States Business Chief Executive Officers indicated that their number one concern was "empowerment" of people.

The Human Side of Quality – The Path Forward for Educational Reform and Achievement

What do we mean by the "human" side of quality? After all, anything having to do with quality involves "human beings." Whether a high school staff is establishing a vision and implementing quality, as in the case of the award -winning faculty at West Mesa High School in Albuquerque, people are actively engaged in establishing a vision and monitoring progress toward improvement. Ms. Marnie Gochenour, principal of the Kenwood Elementary School in Springfield, Ohio, suffered with low performance among students and teachers. The Sheriff's Department was in the school every other week hauling out a student for some drug related event. There seemed to be little hope, especially with aloof parents. After we trained the faculty and staff over a two-year period in the *IntelliLearn®* Model of Quality instructional processes, Kenwood students and faculty went on two years later to win the Ohio Governor's Best Practices Award.

Also, with funding provided by the Albertson Foundation, Dr. Janet Aikele, Superintendent of Schools in Arco, Idaho, reported a 66% reduction in "special education" referrals after implementing the *IntelliLearn®* Model of quality instructional design. It was "the teachers and students" who activated the processes that set new records in the district for high human performance. Indeed, simply bringing the useful framework of "Quality Leadership" to a school district is, itself, an act of human involvement.

This is so intuitively obvious to us that you might wonder: "What could we mean by the human side of quality, anyway?" This is a particularly "odd" question, since the traditional view adopted in educational administration and instruction is that most of the problems in families, in corporations and in "schooling" are people problems. In fact, according to a former Dean at Dartmouth College, Dr. Myron Tribus, traditional leadership starts with "fixing the problem" by first "fixing blame" on someone, finding out what's wrong with them and then remediating people, whether students, teachers, parents, or administrators.

Because of this persistent focus on "blaming" people within any system or organization, very little educational policy or state education legislation focuses on improving the "systems" within the educational system. Nor is there an emphasis on the "processes" that produce the results of the system. Rather, policy, legislation and practice tend to emphasize "doing" things *to* people in terms of reward or punishment.

However, in contrast to this traditional view, which is also the prevailing "modus operandi," Edwards Deming, one of the great economic and organizational change icons of the last century, claimed that most of the "misfires" in managing organizations, including operating schools and teaching in classrooms are "system" problems as opposed to people problems. Moreover, Deming is reported to have said that ninety-five to ninety-eight percent of problems that inhibit achieving high performance in an organization are *not* people problems; rather they are "system" related. And when there are people problems, according to Deming, those problems are usually due to the *interference* of management personnel getting in the way of those who are directly connected with producing the result. (Just listen to any group of teachers in the school lounge about the current "staff development" flavor of the month that has come down from administration.)

For example, if a nation's reading performance is not at the level aimed for, the problems have less to do with the students' inability or the teachers' performance, and more to do with the "system" of reading instruction. Virtually all reading systems guarantee that *some* of the children can learn to read. And there are never any guarantees that students will love reading. That is not good enough for any fragile society where reading is a critical skill for economic, social and political success. Our children and our nation deserve more than current achievement levels, especially since there is a reading *system* component of **IntelliLearn**® developed by Dr. Renee Fuller that guarantees that every first grader can leave the first grade reading at least at the third grade level, with joy and enthusiasm for reading. We have examples of high school students, from Baltimore to Idaho who have been taught to use this system to teach 4th and 5th graders, reading on the first grade level, to read on grade level or above in a short period of time. Thus, we have an apparent paradox between the prevailing traditional opinion that people cause the majority of problems of performance as opposed to the "quality" view that most problems in the "system" lead to at least 95% of the trouble in producing excellent outcomes.

To avoid this seeming paradox, we must steer through the horns of the dilemma: the "people" constraining the "system" versus the "system" constraining the "people." The path forward is found in the "quality perspective" that if we create and establish a human relationship "system" for people's thinking, speaking and acting in accordance with measurable and observable behaviors, then our leadership focus shifts *from blaming people* to *improving the human relationship processes* that improve our system of conduct, responsibility, accountability and performance toward the vision. (Modern thinkers might call this "creating the optimal environment," while Plato and his student Aristotle would see this as something deeper, logically necessary and more lasting; namely, "as building community.")

The *IntelliLearn®* Model began several years ago when I established a clinic for "head injury, stroke and dementia" patients using learning processes I developed while at Syracuse University. In an effort to develop a more "results driven" process for rehabilitation of patients, the origins of this "system" for cognitive rehabilitation and learning performance were built on *four* key principles of the Edwards Deming philosophy of "total quality" leadership. Merged into that Model was recent research from the field of neurosciences, in general, and neurocardiology, in particular (see chapters Three and Four). By combining these principles, we arrive at a new theory of human performance based on the human side of "quality" – The *IntelliLearn®* Model.

The four key concepts of the "human side of quality" derived from Deming's principles are:

1. The high performance organization works as a "system" in which the components cooperate toward the aim of the organization,
2. "Remove fear, threat and intimidation from the climate and culture" of the system,
3. "If you want to improve results, you *must* focus on the processes that produce the "outcomes" of the system, and
4. If it can't be measured and monitored, it is probably not worth doing.

In addition to these four principles, the *three* solid principles from neurosciences, as discussed in previous chapters, are:

1. Physiology determines outcomes and mental states influence physiology. For example, your physical state will dramatically influence how you feel, and how you feel determines results in human performance,
2. The human heart has its own brain that "thinks," "remembers," and "communicates" with others, and
3. There is not one memory, but multiple memory systems and multiple ways of experiencing the world, such as multiple intelligences, multiple learning styles and multiple communication styles.

Let's first consider the Deming Principles. In his book, *The New Economics*, Deming wrote that: "It would be better if everyone would work together as a *system*...What we need is cooperation and transformation to a new style of management."[2] Furthermore, "A *system* is

The Aim of *IntelliLearn*® System - a Flow Chart:

Obtaining Peak Performance
with the Flow of Endorphins

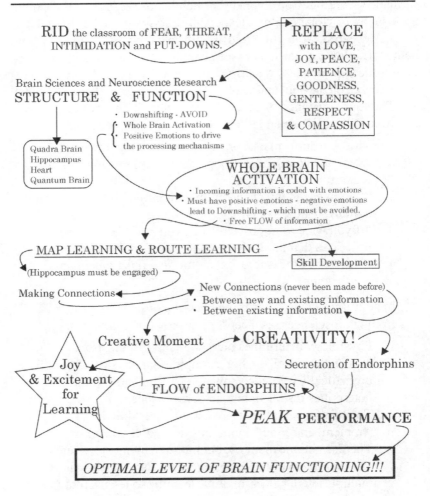

a network of interdependent components that work together to accomplish the *aim* of the system. A system must have an *aim*. Without an *aim*, there is not a *system*. The aim must be clear to everyone in the system. The aim must include *plans* for the *future*. The secret is cooperation between components toward the *aim* of the organization."[3] He also said that a key principle was to remove "fear" (threat, intimidation, put-downs, negative energy) and to recognize that if you want to improve the outcomes, no amount of inspection of the outcomes, by itself, will advance improvement. Only by also measuring, monitoring and inspecting and improving the *processes* that produce the outcomes will you witness significant, continuous improvement toward the results.

I once met a Superintendent of Education for the State of South Carolina who considered herself an expert in quality. During her eight years of service she failed to advocate any processes to improve the results. Her career was spent developing ways to examine results and compare those results from one school district to another. Even though it was in her power to allow districts to take state exams at one of three times during the day (before ten; between ten and noon; between noon and three) she chose to remain focused on results, rather than on processes. If she had implemented this one simple *process improvement* change, it would have resulted in statistically significant increases in student test score results. Instead, eight years went by with no observable or measurable improvement in children's learning outcomes.

Accordingly, a system within a school or within a district across a state should be a system in which various components, such as the different levels of the class and grade system, along with students, teachers, parents, administrators, board members, and staff, work *together* to achieve the *aims* that the community has for the school – its vision of civility and growth and development of children into young adults in preparation for their contribution to the abundance and the prosperity of society.

But on what set of principles or in accordance with what theory can people work cooperatively within the system? I believe that what Deming was implying is that the "human side" of quality requires the establishment of a *"system"* of human relationships and conduct, which lay out the conditions that optimize human connectedness, cooperation and empowerment. Moreover, when establishing that "human system" it becomes one of the components of the broader organizational system, along with other components, all of which include the adopted "vision, mission, purpose, goals and core values, as well as strategies tactics and tools."

Deming was not explicit in his advocacy for a "human" system, or for that matter that there be one; but it is implied. Nevertheless, admitting that he was not a psychologist, Deming hints at what such a "system" might look like by asserting the "driving out" of "fear" and the focus on "processes" that produce outcomes. He would have advocated the *IntelliLearn*® Model, together with its "human side of relationship" management approach. In so doing, he takes a major departure from the current oppressive or disempowering models of management, such as Frederick Winslow Taylor's "top-down" system, as well as management Theory X (people are lazy and need the boot), Theory Y (people are productive if you nudge them), and, to a lesser degree, Theory Z (people perform if they are involved and engaged). For example, in South Carolina one superintendent operated his entire administration on fear, threat, intimidation and oppression of "his" administrators, teachers, staff and students. "No pain, no gain" was his unspoken credo.

This is similar to the current mania of testing across the country. Rather than getting high results by removing "fear" and by focusing on those researched validated processes that produce high performance, state testing is creating high fear and unhealthy stress among all the stakeholders from Florida to Hawaii. For instance, Ohio teachers told me that many children simply put their names on the test and then "doodle" the bubbles on the answer sheet into interesting patterns. The kids simply do not want to participate in high stress evaluations that determine whether they are worthwhile as people and worthy of being loved as human beings. One Massachusetts parent told me she would like to require each legislator to take and pass the eighth grade proficiency test. She was not hopeful of the results, without extensive remediation.

From one Deming perspective then, if we want to achieve the aim of the organization with outstanding results, we must create a system that includes a "human system" as a component whose characteristics include the removal of "fear" and the focus on processes that produce results. This is best accomplished with the "learnership" processes in the *IntelliLearn*® Model.

Without such a Model of human relationships and process improvement, this is not as easy as you might think. Unless you have a comprehensive theory of how to remove fear and which processes of human relationships and conduct must be incorporated, monitored and measured to produce high performance results, an organization's aim and purpose could be left adrift in a sea of competing ideology and "flavors of the month" programs.

To avoid this anarchy of personalities and to move toward a theory of human performance based on solid principles, we can learn from and draw upon the research in neurosciences we discussed previously, which provides a comprehensive biological basis for explaining human behavior. Consider the following three principles derived from cognitive science:

√   **(1)** First, human behavior is a function of human physiology. As mentioned in an earlier chapter, neuroscientist Candace Pert wrote *The Molecules of Emotion* which shows that each of us is a human apothecary with an instantaneous capacity to produce chemical reactions in the brain and body that can have both positive and negative effects in our lives. And we can control many of these states of physiology through such training as biofeedback or choice making. If a person is filled with fear, threat, anxiety, stress, negativity and intimidation, there will be a biological presence of chemicals, such as adrenaline, histamine, as well as a depletion of the positive immune antibody "IgA" (immunoglobulin A), and an increase of corticosteroid stressors that weaken and erode the cardio-vascular system.

Norman Cousins also pointed out in his book, *The Anatomy of an Illness,* that the state of emotion can affect not only behavior, but also disease. He claimed that the more laughter a person enjoyed, the less likely he or she would be afflicted with disease. Extensive research proves that belly laughter increases both T and B killer cells in your immune system and produces endorphins that make you feel better, while you're getting better. An entirely new branch of medical research and clinical practice has emerged in the past twenty years called "psycho-neuro-immunology." Harvard's Herbert Benson is a leader in that field of research that shows that a person's state of emotions and state of "mental" attitude can strongly influence disease causation and cure. Thus, a person's state of awareness, state of emotion and state of mental attitude can determine the outcomes of behavior, as well as physical disease, such as cancer and cardio-vascular disease.

Indeed, Harry Emerson Fosdick and Norman Vincent Peale, along with their student Steven Covey, have shown the power of "positive" thinking on behavior, results and achievement. The important point to be made here is that, with training, you can learn to choose the particular "states of mind and emotion" you elect, rather than being a victim of the forces and pressures of life. William Glasser, M.D. has had a brilliant career in psychiatry on the "Choice Theory" principle. Moreover, an entire branch of therapy called "neuro-linguistic programming" (NLP) has helped millions of people get beyond the mindless reactive state of stimulus-response to a "proactive" state of personal choice in selecting the state of physiology in reacting to most any circumstance.

Anthony Robbins has developed his "brand" of neuro-linguistic programming, with several strategies that help change the physiological state of the person who wishes to change behavior. I have personally seen Tony engage people in a process that allows them to change their *physical* state and to then transform their behavior from years of helplessness, regardless of the cause, (as in the case of phobias as a result of "rape" or physical disabilities due to financial disaster) into a positive, pro-active physical state of "I can handle this and move on with my life!" My view is that what NLP developers Bandler and Grinder uncovered, when they invented NLP, is a language that communicates to both the heart and, thereby the limbic system in the brain. Simply put, "change the heart and you can change your world!" If you don't change your heart, you'll continue making the same old mistakes with your brain making excuses.

√   (2) Second, the human heart has its own brain and memory system located in the physical heart, pumping information to every cell in the body. In the book, *The Heart's Code*, as we reviewed in **Chapter Four**, Dr. Paul Pearsall documented from the field of neuro-cardiology and heart transplant research that two thirds of transplant recipient patients take on some characteristics of the heart donor. This occurs without the transplant patients, their families or the medical team having any knowledge of the identity or geographic region of the heart donor. The range of behaviors varies from taking on donor hobbies, never before entertained by the transplant recipient, to having specific personality characteristics parallel to the donor. I have created a bumper sticker that says: "Live your life as though you are going to be a Heart Donor" (It will be interesting to review the research on the recent mechanical heart transplants, when it is available).

Emotional states and behaviors associated with fear, threat, intimidation, anxiety, stress, anger, mean-spiritedness and "put-downs" are correlated with not only heart disease, but also poorer performance and achievement. Therefore, an organizational system that focuses on the "human" side of quality will focus on "heart" enhancing processes, which include "loving, kind, caring and affirming" thoughts, speech and actions. In psychology this is known as an "affiliative motive." People who are loving and caring, and who, for example, follow the "golden rule," wish to establish warm and caring relationships with others. According to Harvard's David McClelland, this social or interpersonal motive has physiological consequences for people and organizations. McClelland and his colleagues show, for example, that "loving and caring" people who act from the "heart" and who are "light-hearted" have decreased levels of stress hormones, high levels of immune function IgA, increased levels of norepinephrine, which increase hardiness, as well as a general reduction in disease and illness compared to the general population.

The optimal "human system" in any organization requires core values, processes and behaviors that foster love, kindness, peace, honor, respect and a high regard for the dignity, diversity and uniqueness of individuals. Indeed, human advance has been a history of "E Pluribus Unum" – "Out of Many: One - Unity"

√   (3) Third, and finally, research in Cognitive Psychology has led to a major breakthrough in Intelligence Theory, building upon the work done by Dr. Carl Jung, early in the last century. The writings of Professors Robert Sternberg at Yale, Howard Gardner and David Perkins at Harvard, and psychology journalist, Daniel Goleman, suggest that there are four examples of what I call "diversity theorists." They have each held that traditional Intelligence Theory is too narrow to account for the tremendous potential and variety of human behavior and performance. In short, these leading psychologists and researchers each condemn the "one size fits all" mindset of current intelligence theory, which focuses on a single construct of intelligence, comprised of logical-mathematical and linguistic performance. Furthermore, they are quite critical of the narrow measurement of this construct through the popular exams, such as standardized national or state timed, pencil-paper tests that are blind to personal growth in performance, as well as to the variety of processes that demonstrate knowledge, skill and performance. They are critical of the fact that by limiting our tools of measurement, we restrict our view of reality.

The general theme of this research is that "diversity is our capacity," requiring a "system" of education and learning that accommodates the differences between and among people's multiple intelligences, variety of learning styles, variation in communication styles and the broad band of ways of experiencing the world, including music, drama, art, reading, writing, speaking and creating. The operating principle of justice here is that "there is nothing more unequal than treating unequals equally." We must have an inclusive system with principles, strategies, processes and measurements that accommodate everyone within the system; not just the few of an outmoded "one size fits all" system.

The Seventh Secret Revealed

Let me conclude this chapter with the reminder that when "putting it all together," these core principles provide a comprehensive and strategic framework for the *purpose, structure and function* of the "human" side of quality. Establishing a "system" with a vehicle for positive human relationships can abolish fear, threat and intimidation. The new *IntelliLearn®* Model focuses on processes that foster love, respect, dignity, loyalty and integrity and produces outcomes that move us toward the path forward to personal, organizational and economic success. Adopting processes that pay attention to the physiology of health and hardiness, while combining the "heart" needs of Emotional Intelligence with love and kindness are requisite to the *"human side of quality."*

The components of the "human side of quality" are both expressed and achieved through the implementation of the secrets revealed, including the "Miracle of Learning" perspective, the diversity of learning, the heart's new role in learning, the function and structure of the brain, the multiple intelligences, the ergonomics of learning and the learning community. These all come together in the *IntelliLearn®* Model, along with its variety of strategies, tactics and tools (see **Appendix B**). One can obtain support in implementing this Model through seminars and self directed learning materials, publications and products.

Moreover, the strategic focus on designing and implementing a quality learning community, whose climate and culture embrace the high regard for the diversity in how people learn and process information, provides the final empowerment component in the *IntelliLearn®* Model. We should judge any Model by its application and successes. Throughout this book I have provided numerous case study examples of high achievement and success (see **Appendix D** for a list). By implementing the *IntelliLearn®* Model for yourself, your community, your local school district or your company, it can provide you with high achievement and success, as well as the joy of learning and happiness as it has for so many others.

References

[1] Grassi, John R., *The ALPS Method: Whole-Brain Learning and Teaching Techniques for Teachers and Trainers. Training Manual*, Framingham, MA: ALPS Products, p. xx.
[2] Deming, Edwards W., *The New Economics for Industry, Government and Education*, MIT Press, p. xv.
[3] *ibid*, p. 50.

Conclusion

Unlike most books, this conclusion is actually a commencement – a celebration! This is the time for acknowledging the things you have learned from reading this book. It is also a call to go forward and make use of what you have discovered about *The Secrets* for yourself, your family, your work-mates, your schools and your community. You have taken the trip along the path of uncovering the *The Seven Secrets of Learning Revealed*. Having taken this trip, while along the way reinforcing old ideas and learning new information and skills, you can now write your own conclusion, reflecting new beginnings and, perhaps, a new plan for the future.

So, dear reader, compose your own narrative of what this book means to you and in what way has it helped you. Also, if you wish, you can complete the following **"action item"** which we call "*expand-a-story*" as a portrait of your fresh, new perspective, as well as of your vision for a future that is filled with the *Miracles of Learning*. And please send me a copy, if you wish, so that I can learn from you. And, if you permit me to share your story with others in our training seminars and on our Web site, I will be pleased to consider doing that.

Thank you for investing your time and energy and I hope the rewards will continue to be bountiful. Also, I welcome you to visit our WEB site and peruse our products and services, which might assist you in your continuous journey on your personal "miracle of learning." If we can be of assistance to you, your company, or your school district feel free to email or call for additional assistance www.intellilearn.org.

Thank you,
Laurence Dean Martel, Ph.D.
The National Academy of Integrative Learning, Inc.
P.O. Drawer 5784
Hilton Head Island
South Carolina 29938

ACTION ITEM: EXPAND-A-STORY (Take the lead sentences
and complete them by filling in the blanks with your own story or, construct your own story of success in any way you wish. Feel free to use
the "expand-a-story" as a tool for learning with your family, co-workers or others with whom you wish to communicate. Simply pick the
topic and create a story line to be completed. *Have fun with it*!)

I have always been concerned about improving learning and I bought
The Seven Secrets of Learning Revealed book. I read the book
and began to get excited. What I discovered which was most
important to me was_____

_____
Another thing that surprised me about what I learned was_____

_____

I didn't realize that _____

_____

I applied the following to (myself or my family or friend) and began to
see an improvement in   _____

_____

I feel empowered now, because of_____

_____

which I learned as a secret in Chapter_____

However, I was disappointed because I wanted to learn more about

_____

_____

_____

Nevertheless, what I have learned has armed me with the following new information_____

_____

_____

which helped me_____

_____

_____

Signed:

_____

The Gifted Genii in Us All

Why Do People Rush Around
With Trouble,
and Worry So?

When To Their Problems,
Solutions Await;
In Hearts and Minds of Every Soul.

For In the End, When All is Bright,
And Happiness Regains,
The Cause is Simple, My Dear Friend:

Tis Thinking, Love, and Prayer That Makes It So!

L.D. Martel

The
Seven
Secrets

Bibliography

Bibliography

Adler, Mortimer J.   Reforming Education: The Opening of the American Mind. MacMillan Publishing Co., 1977.

Alderson, Wayne T. & Nancy Alderson McDonnell
Theory "R" Management, Thomas Nelson, 1994.

Amen, Daniel G., M.D.
Healing the Hardware of the Soul. The Free Press, 2002.

Aristotle   The Nicomachean Ethics. 1984

Armstrong, David M.
Managing by Storying Around, Armstrong International,

Asha,   37 Suppl. 14, 15-19 American Speech-Language-Hearing Association

Barzakov, Ivan Ph.D.
The Essence and Impact of OptimaLearning®. 2002.

Batmangheldi, F. M.D.
Your Body's Many Cries for Water. 1995

Baum, Frank   The Wizard of Oz

Bennett, William J. (editor)
The Moral Compass: Stories for a Life's Journey. Touchstone Books, 1996.

Benson, Herbert M.D.
The Relaxation Response. Wholecare, 1995, 2000.

Berg, F.S.   Facilitating Classroom Listening: A Handbook for Teachers of Normal and Hard of Hearing Students. 1987.

Berger, Kathleen The Developing Person through the Life Span. Worth Publishing, 1993.

Bloom, Allan   Love and Friendship. Simon & Schuster, 1993.

Breggin, Peter R. Talking Back to Ritalin: What Doctors Aren't Telling You About Stimulants and ADHD. Perseus Book Group, 2001.

Bible   The Bible. King James Version

Campbell, Don G. Mozart Effect. HarperCollins Publishers, 2001.

Campbell, Don G. Introduction to the Musical Brain. St. Louis. MO: Magna Music-Baton, 1983.

Campbell, Don G. The Roar of Silence: Healing Powers of Breath, Tone and Music. Wheaton, IL: Theosophical Publishing House, 1989.

CampbelL Don G.   100 Ways to Improve Teaching Using Your Voice and Music. Tucson, Arizona: Zephyr Press, 1992.

Carnegie, Dale   How to Win Friends and Influence People. Pocket Books, 1994.

Carper, Jean   Miracle Cures. Harper Collins, 1997.

Chiazzari, Suzy   The Compete Book of Color. New York: Barnes & Noble, 1998.

Churchland, Paul M.   The Engine of Reason, the Seat of the Soul: A Philosophical Journey into the Brain. MIT Press, 1995.

Cousins, Norman   The Anatomy of an Illness. Bantam Books, 1993.

Conroy, Pat   The Water is Wide. Bantam Books, 1972.

Covey, Stephen R.   The 7 Habits of Highlv Effective People. New York: Fireside Books,1989

Crandell, Carl Dr. & J. Smaldino   The Volta Review, 96, 291-306

Crook, Robin M.D.   Toxin. Penguin USA, 1999

Crook, William, M.D. TN: Help for the Hyperactive Child. Jackson, Professional Books, 1997

Damasio, Antonio R.   Descartes' Error; Emotion, Reason and the Human Brain. New York: G.P. Putnam's Sons. 1994.

DeBeauport, Elaine   The Three Faces of Mind: Developing Your Mental, Emotional, and Behavioral Intelligences. Illinois: Quest Books, 1996.

DeBello & Guez   Principal, November 1996.

Deming, Edwards W.   The New Economics for Industry, Government and Education. MIT Press, 2000.

Dennison, Paul   Brain Gym, Teacher Edition. 1994.

Diamond, John   Your Body Doesn't Lie: How to Increase Your Life Energy Through Behavioral Kinesiology. Warner Books, 1994.

Diamond. Marion Cleves   Enriching Heredity: The Impact of the Environment on the Anatomy of the Brain. New York: The Free Press, 1988.

Dossey, Larry   Healing Words: The Power of Prayer and the Practice of Medicine. San Francisco: Harper, 1985.

Dossey, Larry   Healing Beyond the Body: Medicine and the Infinite Reach of the Mind. Random House, 2001.

Dunn, Rita and Kenneth Dunn and Donald Traffinger   Bringing Out the Giftedness in Your Child. New York: John Wiley and Sons, 1992.

Dunn, R. & Griggs. S.   Learning Styles: Quiet Revolution in American Secondary Schools, National Association of Secondary Schools

Eaddy, Christoper   The Greatest Teacher: Understanding How to Use Your Power as an Educator. www.Christoper Eaddy.com, 2002.

Epstein, Herman   A Strategy for Education. Oxford University Press, 1992.

Family Circle Magazine   October 7, 1997.

Ferguson,   Science, 1997

Flexler, Carol   Decisions in the Selection and
                            Management of Classroom Amplification
                            Systems. 1992.

Gallway, Timothy W.   Inner Game of Tennis. Bantam Books,
                            1982.

Galyean, Beverly-Colleene   Mind Sights. Zephyr Press, 1984.

Gardner, Howard   Frames of Mind: The Theory of Multiple
                            Intelligences. New York: Basic Books,
                            1983.

Glasser, William, MD   The Control Theory Manager. Harper
                            Business, 1994.

Glasser, William, MD   Schools Without Failure. New York:
                            Harper & Row, 1969.

Glasser, William, MD   Control Theory: A New Explanation of
                            How We Control Our Lives. New York:
                            Harper & Row, 1984.

Glasser, William, MD   The Quality School. New York: Harper &
                            Row, 1990.

Glock, Jenna   Discovering the Naturalist Intelligence:
                            Science in the Schoolyard. Zephyr Press,
                            1999.

Goleman, Daniel   Emotional Intelligences. New York:
                            Bantam Books, 1995.

Goodlad, J.,   A Place Called School. McGraw Hill, New
                            York, NY, 1984.

Gowan, J.C.   "The Production of Creativity through
                            the Right Hemisphere Imagery"

Grassi, John R.   The ALPS Method; "Whole-Brain
                            Learning and Teaching Techniques for
                            Teachers and Trainers". A Training
                            Manual. ALPS Products, Framingham,
                            MA 1993.

Hale, Jonathan   The Old Way of Seeing. Houghton Mifflin
                            Co., 1994.

Hannaford, Carla, PhD.   Smart Moves: Why Learning is Not All in
                            Your Head. Great Ocean Publications,
                            1995.

Hart, Leslie   Human Brain, Human Learning. Brain Age
                            Pub., 1999.

Harvey, Dr. Arthur and Marcy Marsh and Ole Andersen
                            Learn with the Classics. LIND Institute,
                            1999.

Hawkins, David R.   Power vs. Force: The Hidden
                            Determinants of Human Behavior. Hay
                            House, Inc., 2002.

Healy, Jane   Endangered Mind: Why Our Children
                            Don't Think. New York: Simon and
                            Schuster, 1990.

Hermann, Douglas   Super Memory: A Quick Action
                            Programme for Memory Improvement.
                            Blandford Press, 1997.

Herrman, Ned   The Creative Brain. Lake Lure, NC: Brain
                            Books. 1989.

Higley, Connie and Alan and Pat Leatham
　　　　Aromatherapy A-Z. Hay House, Inc.,
　　　　1998.

Hill, Napoleon　　Think and Grow Rich. Fawcett Books,
　　　　1990.

Hollwich, Fritz　　The Influence of Ocular Light Perception
　　　　on Metabolism in Man and in Animal.
　　　　Springer-Verlag, 1979.

Irlen, Helen　　Reading by the Colors; Overcoming
　　　　Dyslexia and Other Reading Disabilities
　　　　through the Irlen Method. Turtleback
　　　　Books, 2001.

Joseph, Dorothy Duckett　　A Tale of Two Systems. Brooklyn, NY:
　　　　CKDJ Publishers, 2002.

Kanter, Rosabeth Moss　　Change Masters: Innovation and
　　　　Entrepreneurship in the American
　　　　Corporation. Touchstone Books, 1985.

Kennedy, David Daniel　　Feng Shui for Dummies. John Wiley &
　　　　Sons, 2000.

Liberman, Jacob　　Light: Medicine of the Future. Santa Fe,
　　　　New Mexico: Bear and Company. 1991.

MacLean, Paul　　A Mind of Three Minds: Educating the
　　　　Triune Brain. 77th Yearbook of The
　　　　National Society of Education. Chicago,
　　　　IL: University of Chicago Press, 1978.
　　　　(pp. 308-342).

MacLean, Paul　　The Triune Brain in Evolution. Plenum,
　　　　New York, NY 1990.

MacLean, Paul　　A Triune Concept of the Brain and Behavior. Toronto:
　　　　University of Toronto Press, 1973.

Martel, L. and Rita Dunn and Andrea Honigsfeld
　　　　Learning-Style Characteristics of JROTC
　　　　Cadets and Instructors: Implications for
　　　　Training and Instruction. Virginia:
　　　　Department of the Army, 2001 and ERIC
　　　　Clearinghouse on Information &
　　　　Technology, Syracuse University, 2003.

Martel, L.　　"The Human Side of Quality", QED News, ASQ
　　　　Education Division, Spring/Summer, 2002, (pp.8-12)

Martel, L.　　"Unlock Your Child's Brain Power", Family Circle
　　　　Magazine. Sept., 12, 2000, (pp. 59-60).

Martel, L.　　"Making the Most of Family Differences: The Quiz that
　　　　Tells You How", Family Circle Magazine. Feb. 17, 1998,
　　　　(pp.48-50).

Martel, L.　　"Different Strokes for Different Folks," Family Circle
　　　　Tennis Magazine, May, 1997.

Martel, L.　　Quoted extensively in Perelman. L
　　　　"Kanban to Kanbrain", Forbes Magazine
　　　　ASAP Technology Supplement, June 6,
　　　　1994.

Martel, L.　　Producer, Personal Learning Success. A
　　　　consumer and adult assessment product for
　　　　personal skills. Maxim Communications,
　　　　1994.

Martel, L.   Producer, Personal Skills Program,
                                  developed by Dr. Darwin Nelson, Dr. Gary
                                  Low and George Smith, ED.S., Hilton
                                  Head Island: IntelliLearn. 1994.

Martel, L.   Producer, Successful Learning Style.
                                  Written by Dr. Kenneth J. Dunn. Hilton
                                  Head Island: Center for Adult
                                  Productivity, Integrative Learning
                                  Systems. Inc., 1993.

Martel. L., Dunn, K., and Sullivan, M.
                                  Personal Success Style. Hilton Head
                                  Island: IntelliLearn, 1994.

Martel. L.   Empowerment - Personal Ownership of
                                  Work. Hilton Head Island: Intellilearn,
                                  1994.

Martel, L.   "Building a Learning Community', School
                                  Administrator. June. 1993.

Martel, L.   Producer Personal Learning Power. (A
                                  multi-media package designed to assess
                                  how learners learn.) Unlimited Learning,
                                  Dallas, Texas. 1991.

Martel, L. and Major General Harold W. Todd (USAF ret.)
                                  "Integrative Learning: Multiple Gateways
                                  for Lifetime Learners", National Academy
                                  of Integrative Learning, Inc., 1992.

Martel, L & Ward .R.   Revitalizing American Competitiveness.
                                  "The Learning Enterprise", 1990.

Martel, L.   "The Effectiveness of the Integrative Learning System
                                  as Perceived By New York State Teachers and
                                  Administrators", A study of 300 people commissioned by
                                  the State Education Department, New York 1990.

Martel, L   "The Integrative Learning System" A Review of
                                  Theoretical Foundations. National Academy of
                                  Integrative Learning, Inc. in partnership with Syracuse
                                  University, 1991.

Martel, L   "From a Nation at Risk to a Nation at Promise" The
                                  Journal of Continuing-Higher Education. The lead article
                                  in the 50th Anniversary Issue, 1988.

Martel, L   "The Implications of Advanced Learning
                                  Theories on Education". A Commissioned
                                  Article for the New York State
                                  Board of Regents, The National Academy
                                  of Integrative Learning, Inc., 1989.

Martel, L   "The Validation of `Integrative Learning'
                                  as a Staff Development Model". The New
                                  York State Department of Education.
                                  1988.

Martel and Colley   "Ethical Issues in Marketing Continuing
                                  Education" — A chapter in Marketing
                                  Continuing Education Programs. Beder.
                                  H.. ed.Jossey- Bass Publishing Co.,
                                  California, 1986.

Martel and Richman   The Role of Self-Concept in Predicting
                                  the Success of Academically and
                                  Financially Disadvantaged Students within
                                  Higher Education Opportunity Programs.

	New York State Education Department. ERIC, ED 26481 1. 1985.
Martel, L.	"The Nation at Risk. A 1 Challenge for Continuing Education". The Journal of Continuing Higher Education. vol 32. No.1, Winter 1984.
Martel, L.	"The Adult Learner in Continuing Education", by S. Gabor, The Journal of Continuing Higher Education. Vol 30, No.1, Winter 1982.
Martel, L ed.	"Federal Policy for Adult Education: A Review of Approaches and Positions", by W. Rivera : The Journal of Continuing Higher Education. vol 29. No. 4, Fall 1981.
Martel, L	"Tax Credit as Subsidy for Lifelong Learning", The Continuum Vol. XLV-No. 2, Fall 1981.
Martel, L ed.	"The Exclusiveness of Continuing Education: Social and Political Ramifications", by R. L. David, The Journal of Continuing Higher Education. Vol. 29. No 2. Spring 1981.
Martel, L ed.	The Itinerary of the Concept Equal Educational Opportunity, The National Institute of Education. ERIC ED 208097, 1980.
Martel, L Pub.	Basic Algebra Series, by D. Hakim. A 13 chapter Series in Intermediate Algebra produced in cooperation with the Center for Instructional Development, Syracuse University, 1978.
Martel and Seebring	"The Implication for Public Policy and Social Service Worker Characteristics Toward Social Service". The College for Human Development. The Penn State University, 1976.
Martel, L	"Central New York Training Activities". A Published Report for the New York State Division for Youth, 1974.
Martel. L.	"University and Community: Partners in Change". A Published Paper delivered at the President's Seminar- State University, Dayton, Ohio, 1973.
Martel and Benzel	Project Start: Manpower Development in Human Services. A Published Research Report for the College for Human Development, Penn State University, 1972, 1971.
Martel, L.	A Study of the Feasibility of the Refined Syracuse University Specifications for a Comprehensive Undergraduate and In-service Teacher Education Program for Elementary Teachers. U.S. Office of Education, Bureau of Research, Published Project No. 9-0422, 1970.
Martel, L.	"The Role of Liberal Arts in Teacher Education", Chapter III in Specifications

for a Comprehensive Undergraduate and
In-service Teacher Education Program for
Elementary Teachers. U.S. Office of
Education, Bureau of Research, Published
Project No. 8-1108, 1969.

Martel, Leon
Mastering Change: The Key to Business
Success. Simon and Schuster, 1986.

Moir, Anne & David Jessel
Brain Sex: The Real Difference Between
Men and Women. New York: Lyle Stuart
(Carol Publishing), 1989.

Montessori, Maria
The Montessori Method. Massachusetts: Robert
Bentley, Inc., 1964.

Neilson, Stefan
Communication Skills for Leadership:Team Building,
Self-Esteem and Conflict Resolution in Character
Education. (Conflict Resolution: A Workable Process
for Resolving Personal Differences such as Hostility,
Anger, Miscommunication, and Agendas) Seattle: Aeon
Hierophant, 1999.

Neilson, Stefan & Shay Thoelke
Winning Professionally and Personally. Aeon
Communications.

Neilson, Stefan & Joe and Nora Hutton
Character Education: Secrets for Character Revealed.
Aeon Hierophant Publishing.

Neilson, Stefan
Careers Unlimited, To Be or Not to Be. Your 21st
Century Blueprint for Selecting a Career Through the
Winning Colors Process. Aeon Communications, 1999.

Neilson, Stefan
Winning Professionally and Personally: How to Use
Easy and Successful Skills to Dramatically Improve
Your Leadership, Team Building and Communication
with Groups and Individuals. Aeon Communications,
2001.

Nondoa, Emil, I.
Sugars that Heal: The New Healing Science of
Glyconutrients. Ballantine Books, 2001.

NSSE
Education and the Brain. The National Society for the
Study of Education, 1978.

Ortiz, John
Weiser,
The Tao of Music:Sound Psychology. Red Wheel/
1997.

Ott, John N.
Health and Light: The Effects of Natural and Artificial
Light on Man and Other Living Things. ArielPress,
2000.

Ott, John N.
Light, Radiation, and You. Devin-Adair, 1982.

Palmer, Parker J.
The Courage to Teach: Exploring the Inner Landscape
of a Teacher's Life. San Francisco: Jossey-Bass
Publishers, 1998.

Pearsall, Paul
The Heart's Code. Broadway Books, 2000.

Peale, Norman Vincent
The Power of Positive Thinking. Ballantine Books,
1975.

Peat, David F.
Synchronicity: The Bridge Between Matter and Mind.
Bantam Books, 1987.

Peck, Scott
The Road Less Traveled and Beyond. Simon & Shuster,
1997.

Penfield, Wilder
Epilepsy and the Functional Anatomy of the Human
Brain. Little Brown Medical Div., 1985.

Penfield, Wilder   Mystery of the Mind: A Critical Study of Consciousness and the Human Brain. Princeton University Press, 1978.

Penfield, Wilder   No Man Alone: A Neurosurgeon's Life. Little Brown and Company, 1977.

Pert, Candace, B.   The Molecules of Emotion: Why You Feel the Way You Feel. Scribner, 1997.

Plato, R.   The Republic. Armont Publishing, 1977.

Pribram, Karl H.   Brain and Perception: Holonomy and Structure in Figural Processing. Lawrence Erlbaum Assoc., 1991.

Pribram, Karl H.   Brain and Behavior. Penguin.

Pribram, Karl H.   Freud's "Project" Reassessed: Preface to Contemporary Cognitive Theory and Neuropsychology. Basic Books, 1976

Pribram, Karl H.   Languages of the Brain: Experimental Paradoxes and Principles in Neuropsychology. Brandon House, 1982.

Purpel, David E.   The Moral and Spiritual Crisis in Education: A Curriculum for Justice & Compassion in Education. Massachusetts: Bergin & Garvey Publishers, Inc., 1989.

Radio, Myron J. and Rod N. Johnson
                                    Inside Out – Using Classic Children's Stories for Personal and Professional Growth. Beaver's Pond Press, 2003.

Rapp, Doris J.   Is This Your Child's World: How You Can Fix the Schools and Homes That Are Making Your Child Sick. Bantam Books, 1997.

Restak, Richard, M.D.   The Brain, New York: Bantam Books,
October, 1984

Rifkin, Jeremy   Beyond Beef: The Rise and Fall of the Cattle Culture. Plume, 1993.

Robbins, Anthony   Awaken the Giant Within: How to Take Immediate Control of Your Mental, Emotional, Physical and Financial Destiny, Fireside, 1993.

Robbins, Anthony   Unlimited Power: The New Science of Personal Achievement, Fireside, 1997.

Rosenthal, Norman E. M.D.   "Primary Psychiatry", Sept.-Oct., 1994.

Rosenzweig, Mark   Annual Review of Psychology. Annual Reviews, 1975.

Rosenzweig, Mark   Annual Review of Psychology 1974. Annual Reviews, 1974.

Rosenzweig, Mark   Annual Review of Psychology, 1985. (etc. for 1988, 1990, 1992.) Annual Reviews

Sarason, Seymour   Anxiety in Elementary School Children: A Report of Research. Greenwood Publishing Group, 1978.

Sarason, Seymour   American Psychology and Schools. Teachers College, 2001.

Schiffer, Fredric   Of Two Minds: The Revolutionary Science of Dual-Brain Psychology. Free Press, 1998.

Senge, Peter   The Fifth Discipline: The Art and Practice of the Learning Organization. New York: Currency Books, 1990.

Sheikh, Anees, Dr.   Imagery in Education: Imagery in the Educational Process. Baywood Publishing Co., 1985.

Sheldrake, Rupert   A New Science of Life. Inner Traditions Int'l Pub., 1995.

Siegel, Bernie	Love, Medicine and Miracles: Lessons Learned About Self-Healing from a Surgeon's Experience with Exceptional Patients. Harper Perennial, 1990.
Siegel, Bernie	Peace, Love and Healing. Bdd Promotional Book Co., 1992.
Shakespeare, William	Romeo and Juliet. Pocket Books, May, 1988.
Sills, Judith, Ph.D	Biting the Apple: Women Getting Wise About Love. Viking Press, 1996.
Sills, Judith, Ph.D.	Excess Baggage: Getting Out of Your Own Way. Penguin, USA, 1994.
Sills, Judith, Ph.D.	A Fine Romance: The Passage of Courtship from Meeting to Marriage. Ballantine Books, 1993.
Sills, Judith, Ph.D.	A Fine Romance: The Psychology of Successful Courtship: Making It Work for You. St. Martin's Press, 1990.
Simontacchi, Carol	The Crazy Makers. New York: Tarcher/Putnam, 2000.
Sperry, Roger	"Some Effects of Disconnecting the Cerebral Hemispheres," Science. 1982.
Sproul, R.C.	Stronger Than Steel: The Wayne Alderson Story. Harper & Row, 1980.
Steingart , Irving	A Thing Apart: Love and Reality in the Therapeutic Partnership. Jason Aronson, 1995.
Steingart, Irving	Pathological Play in Borderline and Narcissistic Personalities. Aperture, 1983.
Sternberg, R.	Successful Intelligence. Yale University Press, 1996.
Stone, Rhonda	The Light Barrier: A Color Solution to Your Child's Light- Based Reading Difficulties. St. Martin's Press, 2002.
Titoff, William	Doctoral Dissertation. Bay City, Michigan, 1999.
Tiller, Veronica E. Valerde	The Jicarilla Apache Tribe: A History. University of Nebraska Press, 1983.
Too, Lillian	Feng Shui: How to Apply the Secrets of Chinese Wisdom for Health, Wealth and Happiness, Barnes & Noble, 1996.
Toffler, Alvin	Future Shock. Bantam Books, 1991.
Wallas, Graham	Men and Ideas. Ayer Co. Pub., 1977.
Wallas, Graham	Our Social Heritage. Ayer Co. Pub., 1989.
Wallas, Graham	Great Society: A Psychological Analysis. Peter Smith Pub., 1987.
Wenger, Win	The Einstein Factor: A Proven New Method for Increasing Your Intelligence. Prima Publishing, 1996.
Wheatley, Margaret	Leadership and the New Science Revised: Discovering Order in a Chaotic World. Berrett-Kohler Pub., 1999.

Wilber, Ken   A Brief History of Everything.
Shambhala,   1996.
Wood, Leo M. & Fisher, Cinda Use of Music. Hilton Head, SC:
                               IntelliLearn, 1997.
Zukav, Gary   The Seat of the Soul. Simon & Schuster, 1989.

The
Seven
Secrets
of
Learning
Revealed

APPENDIX

Appendix A

Case Studies of
Research & Comments
About *IntelliLearn*®

EDUCATION – Case Studies of Success

In **North Carolina** students in Brightwood Elementary School improved from **34%** on or above grade level as measured by National Standardized Tests to **90%** on or above grade level following training in the *IntelliLearn*® Learning Styles components. During the same time period "actionable discipline"cases fell from 108 to 8.

In **Upstate New York**, Ms. Panka's High School Regents'Biology Class increased passing rates on quizzes from **74% to 96%** in one year following *IntelliLearn*® training.

The Butte County Joint School District #111 in Arco, **Idaho** reported that "A" grades in a secondary English class have increased by 33% as a result of the strategies of *IntelliLearn*®; math and phonic scores have increased at the elementary school; attendance has increased from **92% to 98%** in one semester at the elementary school; reading proficiency has increased measurably for some elementary school students.

In evaluating *IntelliLearn*® training, staff in the Williamsburg County, **South Carolina** School District said "Caring instructors provided a no fail or win-win environment." "New knowledge, skills and joy." "I can use everything I learned in my classroom."

Administrators in the **Springfield, Ohio** City School District reported: one of the Elementary Schools had achieved a 50% reduction in failures over the previous year using *IntelliLearn*®;

the Middle School improved a total of **54%** in over-all test scores as a result of teachers being trained.

INDUSTRY – Case Studies of Success

Crag Erickson's Division at **Eastman Kodak** achieved "Class A status" in **50%** less time with a rating of **99.5** using the *IntelliLearn*® **MRPII** process. "A new record high at Kodak."

Gulfstream Aerospace Corporation with $1 billion in sales, a net profit of $47 million and 5,000 employees redesigned their Quality Course with *IntelliLearn*® projects of QLP and SPC. The result was the course reduced from 24 hours to 8 hours; savings of thousands of hours and reduced oxygen line production from 31 days to 3 days; airplane wing assembly reduced from 8 days to 2.5 days.

Hillenbrand Industries employs 9,800 and has sales of 1.7 billion and a net profit of $140 million. Through *IntelliLearn*® new product technical training they saved $100,000 with a significant time reduction.

Intel Corporation by using *IntelliLearn*®, HAZCOM SAFETY TRAINING was able to achieve a rating of 3 to 4.7 (out of a possible 5.0) with their 48,500 employees and achieve a **43% to 89%** effectiveness; thus saving thousands of employee training hours and maintaining $21 billion in sales and $5 billion in net profit.

NEW HIRE SKILL QUALIFICATIONS based on the *IntelliLearn*® Process saved **Sara Lee Knit Products** $200,000 and reduced turnover from 48% to 18%. The training time was cut from 12 weeks to 3 weeks. Products with defects were reduced from 4,000 pounds to 300 pounds.

Eastman Kodak Company with *IntelliLearn*® MANUFAC-TURING PROCESS for their Black and White Electronics Division saved $20,000,000 by being able to train employees in 1/3 less time and **50%** ahead of schedule.

COMMENTS about *IntelliLearn*® Workshops

From Gary E. Morgan, Colonel U.S. Army, Director, Junior ROTC (Retired):

"Our (Army JROTC) instructors from across the United States who have received IntelliLearn® ...Training are very excited about the instructional strategies you have introduced to them and are already starting to use them in the classrooms. We are convinced that it is only a matter of time until these methods begin to manifest themselves into higher student achievement, especially in those schools where they radiate from Junior ROTC to core subject classes. We also believe that student accomplishments will increase as a result of applying your instructional approach to our service learning effort as cadets will increasingly and more effectively begin to serve other students and the greater community."

From Sandra Thompson, Executive Director, Georgia Association for Career and Technical Education:

"On behalf of the GACTE and the Georgia Department of Education we want to thank you for participating in the 55ᵗʰ Annual GACTE Conference In-service...your presentation provided pertinent information concerning teaching strategies, tools and materials for our teachers and administrators. Your educational expertise was a contributing element to making this year's conference a success...You are helping to **"Make a difference for all our students..."**

From Janet Aikele, Superintendent Butte County School District #111, Idaho:

Butte County School District has been engaged in a partnership with **IntelliLearn**®...*This partnership has been most beneficial to our school District...Our district has many barriers yet to cross, and many miles to travel. It is with confidence that I recommend* **IntelliLearn**® *to anyone who desires assistance in an entire change project. I have con-*

fidence that our partnership with this group of leading professionals has only just begun."

From Julie Dwyer, North Carolina Association of Educators, Inc.:

"On behalf of the NCAE Center for Teaching and Learning, I want to thank you for your presentation at our Good Teaching Conference...those who were there benefited tremendously from this wonderful opportunity...The responses from your session were overwhelmingly positive and I have selected a few...to share with you:

"Exciting – ideas I can begin using with my kids on Monday morning."

"Dr. Martel validated my practices and gave me new strategies. I loved it!"

"He was a wealth of ideas."

"The bomb! Dr. Martel took the audience through many possible barrier/remedies to learning problems. He left us with so many thoughts to ponder."

From Barb Bode, PTA Idaho State Convention Program Chair:

"...tell Dr. Martel how much we appreciate him coming and presenting at our PTA convention. He was the hit of the convention. Everyone...must have attended his workshop and some of them twice. He made a lasting impression..."

From Edgewood School District, Ohio:

*"I would ...like to expend my deepest appreciation to all who contributed to this **Intellilearn®** workshop. I appreciate all the...strategies, tactics and tools!...I will definitely incorporate what I have learned into what I do in both my personal and professional life."*

From Hawaii Elementary Schools:

"Dr. Martel's workshop made me feel energized, that learning is fun with lots of smiles on faces, and easy ways to remember and apply content."

From Springfield City School District, Ohio:

"IntelliLearn® *has helped me realize that students' individual needs must be met in order that true education is present."*

From Williamsburg County Public Schools, South Carolina:

"Caring instructors provided a no-fail or win-win environment." "New knowledge, skills and joy."

From City Schools of Oswego, NY:

"...Our teachers, parents and students have nothing but positive statements to make about their experience with *IntelliLearn®."*

"I had a boy the first semester...who came to me with many bad behaviors. I used a constant positive approach and within weeks he became a kinder and more helpful boy."

From Vista Middle School, Las Cruces, NM:

"Super insights on Joy of Learning through use of what we have!!!"

From Independent School District, Penasco, NM:

"I was surprised to learn that if you really want to you can make all lessons fun and students can learn."

From Heritage High School, Leander, TX

"Dr. Martel reinforced my belief that student emotions are a valid concern for me as a teacher and that I can do a tremendous amount by caring enough about kids to take time to really look at each of them."

Appendix B

Products, Workshops & Services

For ordering and pricing information, please visit our WEB SITE: www.intellilearn.org

To schedule a workshop, call *IntelliLearn®* at **843-686-4050 or e-mail us at martel@intellilearn.org**

LEARN TO LEARN

"Amazing Grades" Video Package – includes 4 booklets, audio tape and video tape. Discover each student's personal learning power. By Dr. Kenneth Dunn. Published by Unlimited Learning, Inc. Distributed by National Academy of Integrative Learning, Inc.

Successful Learning Style – Draw your own learning power profile after taking the simple test provided in this 42 page booklet. Written by Dr. Kenneth Dunn; produced by Laurence D. Martel, Ph.D. Published by National Academy of Integrative Learning, Inc.

Quantum Learning CD – An internationally, award winning self-directed training CD on the principles and processes of the *IntelliLearn®* Model. Produced with American Management Services, Inc. for the United States Army JROTC Leadership program and also modified for the Air Force JROTC. As it stands, the CD is applicable to all learners, trainers and teachers who wish students to learn more in less time with increased memory.

LEARN TO CHOOSE

Personal Learning Skills Program, Your Personal Map to Success – A step by step journey to achieve your own personal success. 140 page book. Produced by the Maxim Group in conjunction with George

Smith and Laurence D. Martel, Ph.D. Published by Integrative Learning Systems, Inc. Also available with instructional video and audio tapes.

"Integrative Learning: A Case Study of Success" – Video Tape. Classroom vignettes of Integrative Learning in action. Produced by National Academy of Integrative Learning, Inc., and New Channels, Syracuse, NY.

School Success - By Laurence D. Martel, Ph.D. and Peter Kline. A 129 page book designed to help students learn better, study better and do better at school or at home. Published by Learning Matters, Arlington, VA.

Personal Success Style – Conceived and written by Laurence D. Martel, Ph. D., Kenneth Dunn, ED.D., Mary Sullivan, Ed.D. A 106 page book – how to use your personal success styles to achieve excellence on the job and enhance the quality of your life.

Personal Ownership of Work, Seven Keys to Empowerment – By Laurence D. Martel, Ph.D. Provides you with personal, practical guidance to increase your empowerment capability at home or at work. 81 page book.

LEARNING MATH FACTS, CREATIVE THINKING

Multiplication Facts By Leo M. Wood and Tiffany Wood. Teaching the multiplication facts using a totally new approach called "Multiplication Circles." Stories, songs, drawings, games and other activities (for 3rd grade). Published by National Academy of Integrative Learning, Inc.

Number Line Activities and Number Town By Leo M. Wood and Tiffany Wood. Math lessons dealing with activities introducing both positive and negative numbers and their uses. Also introduces addition and subtraction of simple whole numbers using a holistic, real-life, hands-on-brain activating approach (for Kindergarten and 1st grade). Published by National Academy of Integrative Learning, Inc.

Fraction Triangles by Leo M. Wood and Tiffany Wood. Teaching fractions using Fraction Triangles. Polygon creatures in polygon land become involved with triangles to build holistic, hands-on, brain activating models for developing the understanding of fractions (for 4th grade). Published by the National Academy of Integrative Learning, Inc.

Fraction Jugs by Leo M. Wood and Tiffany Wood. Teaching fractions, using the "Fraction Jugs" – recycled gallon milk jugs and 2 liter plastic soda pop bottles. These jugs become cheap and excellent props for demonstrating a hands-on practical application for the teaching of fractions. The fraction jugs are also used to introduce the addition and subtraction of fractions (for 4th grade). Published by National Academy of Integrative Learning, Inc.

Proportion Activity By Leo M. Wood and Tiffany Wood. Introduces the Complete Mathematical statement as a concept for improving mathematical communication. Maps are used to provide a real life scenario to develop the concept of proportions. Scale models of a picnic table are built and then the building of a life size picnic table can be done (for 6th grade). Published by the National Academy of Integrative Learning, Inc.,

Great Mathematicians (B.C. to 20th Century): By Leo M. Wood and Tiffany Wood. Includes the life histories of 11 great mathematicians, identity cards, scripts and information cards of titles and items of interest (for any grade). Published by the National Academy of Integrative Learning, Inc.

LEARNING TO RELATE

Winning Color Cards Created by Stefan Neilson and Shay Thoelke. Discover within five minutes the incredible secret to successful communications with others. Set of four heavy stock color cards identifying the personalities of others. Distributed by the National Academy of Integrative Learning, Inc.

Your Winning Color Power Pack Created by Stefan Neilson and Shay Thoelke. In seconds identify yours and others present behaviors, present self-esteem, present motivation. Insights are given into understanding self and others. 22 page booklet distributed by National Academy of Integrative Learning, Inc.

"Family Relating Styles" - An article and assessment tool to increase family rapport and communications. Written by Laurence D. Martel, Ph.D.

INSTRUCTIONAL DESIGN AND *IntelliLearn®* CURRICULUM UNITS

Out of the Box Units. Eight ready-to-use teaching units involving students' seven intelligences: "Creative October", "Holiday Magic", "Ancient Egypt", "Ancient Greece", "Fantastic Fractions", "Web of Life", "Novel Ideas", "Journey into Geometry." Conceived by Out of the Box Instructions, Inc. Distributed by National Academy of Integrative Learning, Inc.

INFORMATIVE

"Rap Video" on Learning Styles

WORKSHOP, SEMINAR, TRAINING TOPICS

√ Leadership and Organizational Change
√ Total Quality Learnership
√ Instructional Design
√ Multicultural and Diversity Enhancement
√ Learning Styles
√ Cooperative Learning
√ Multiple Intelligences
√ Communication Styles
√ Personal Skills Development
√ Organizational Transformation and Development
√ Teaching and Learning Strategies
√ Superintendent, Administrator and School Board Training
√ Parent Awareness Training
√ Teacher Staff Development
√ In Service Student Awareness and Mentor Training

For ordering and pricing information, please visit our WEB SITE:
www.intellilearn.org
To schedule a workshop, call *IntelliLearn®* at 843-686-4050 or
e-mail us at martel@intellilearn.org

Appendix C

An Example Prototype to Obtain Funding for Your Community or School

PREFACE - The following proposal outline contains an architecture and working Model to achieve a School District's vision, mission, goals and guiding principles. This architecture is based on a combination of the well-researched *IntelliLearn®* Model of instruction in combination with the unparalleled Deming Quality Leadership Process. There are four dynamic phases to this approach which include the critical activities of assessment, planning and stakeholder "buy in," support and ownership. In addition, what is often the most difficult phase is the "doing" or "what to do" to achieve the vision, mission and goals, as well as to express the values. That is addressed in Phase II, Implementation. Finally, the important process of verifying the observable and measurable results, tangible and intangible as established by the community of stakeholders is addressed in Phase III, along with issues of replication. Phase IV treats the important aspects of technology as a tool for supporting the process and continuous improvement generally. This architecture and model has room to negotiate the customer's (school and community) current and emerging needs by substituting or adding additional parts to these phases. Also sensitivity to timelines, resources, commitment to change and current culture and climate of each school is a critical success factor.

Deliverables & Expected Outcomes

This is a general framework for deliverables and expected outcomes as they relate to the customer's current needs and emerging needs. There is always flexibility to customize this effort while in progress in order to address either unanticipated circumstances or emerging needs. Although not limited to the following list, among the major Deliverables and Expected Outcomes are:

Deliverables:

☑   Validated training sessions with predicted validity in achieving the established learning performance goals;

☑   Skills that have been widely demonstrated to enhance performance in leadership, instruction and learning;

☑   Models for instructional design and sample curriculum units as guides for teacher production;

☑   A working strategy for change and success in achieving student learning;

☑   An unparalleled level of expertise in transforming classrooms and schools into high performance learning environments;

☑   A set of award winning assessments to diagnose different learning, communicating and personal skill styles;

☑   Ongoing support and follow-up to assure success; Technology support to build new staff development linkages and replication;

☑   An Evaluation and Assessment Model for continued improvement.

Outcomes:

☑   Measurable and observable achievement toward School and state goals;

☑   Building of "community" at different levels;

☑   Establishment of models for continuous improvement in policy, administration, instruction, parent involvement, student service and community guiding principles;

☑   Improvement of instruction and learning;

☑   Development of curriculum units;

☑   Establishment of High School Club to support mentoring and instructional assistance;

☑   Demonstrated competence in using *IntelliLearn*® strategies, tools and technologies;

☑   Application of management and instruction which supports a wide range of learning styles;

☑   Achievement of professional goals established by individual staff members;

☑   A demonstration conference on successful performance, showcasing innovation;

☑   Customer satisfaction which leads to raving fans.

PHASE I - Planning To Plan For Successful Implementation

1.0 **Pre-Planning Awareness Activity** - This activity is to bring to the attention of all stakeholders what is possible in the venture to engage *IntelliLearn*® as a strategic process to meet the stated goals and objectives of the school district. This would include disseminating articles and related awareness material for learning about *IntelliLearn*® at the awareness level.

1.1 **Plan-to-Plan** -

1.10 - Awareness Sessions - These awareness sessions are to build understanding and enthusiasm, as well as support from sponsors, for implementing a jointly created plan to achieve the goals and objectives of the district, the individual schools and the personal goals of the various stakeholders. These sessions are held for anywhere from three hours to a full day, depending upon the overall need. Sessions will be held separately for:

> a. The Board of Education
> b. The Administrators
> c. The Faculty and Staff
> d. The Parents
> e. The Students
> f. The Community at Large

1.11 - Determine the Vision, Mission, Goals, Objectives, Values and Community Service priorities of the District. In some cases this work is completed at different levels, but in other cases it is not. This is very important, particularly because it sets the target around which all activity becomes aligned.

1.12 - Conduct an assessment of the district needs determined from the "current reality"; the "future state" and the "things to stop doing, to start doing and to continue to do" which help the district shift from the current state to where it wants to be in the future state. This should be documented with each stakeholder group to obtain consistency of purpose and alignment on strategy, as well as overall "buy in" at the personal level.

.1.13 - Establish a planning and implementation team to review planning prototype and tailor to district resources and timetables. Determine the plan and sequence most agreeable and then assess baseline data from school performance, parent, teacher and student attitudes. (This is a pre-test, baseline data collection process against which process improvement will be both observed and measured.)

1.14 - Based on the Quality Process of Edwards Deming (assess, plan, do, verify), establish an evaluation, assessment and documentation advisory team who will be responsible for both site based and district assessments on progress toward improvement.

1.15 - Determine the cohort for training which best realizes the most visible and measurable success for the district. This might be an entire building or a cross section of curriculum or content areas across the district. These cohorts will proceed together through the core competencies involved in the *IntelliLearn*® process.

PHASE II - Implementation of the Model

2.0 Overview Session for District Staff on Leadership and Learning through *IntelliLearn*®. What can be expected, measured and observed is detailed here in terms of Board expectations. Staff learns skills to improve effectiveness of board meetings, as well as new strategies and tools for leadership.

2.1 Administrators overview session on Total Quality Leadership and Learning. Introduce instructional design and a checklist for school improvement with an effective school's criteria and school-based goals. Obtain support for the model and commitment to success. Students, teachers and staff will employ discovery journals, along with other methods of documenting progress, as well as new rituals for celebrating successes.

2.10 Administrator Booster Training Sessions - depending upon progress and need, booster sessions will be scheduled to continue to support administrators in their success in coaching and supporting teachers. These sessions will include personal skills development, communications styles, learning styles and effective leadership.

2.2 Faculty Instructional Design Session - This is delivered in a series of three, two-day sessions. The purpose of this training is to obtain detailed information about teacher concerns for their students and to coach teachers in an instructional design model that can both meet their concerns and drastically improve student performance and achieve the specific goals outlined by the stakeholders.

2.3 Faculty Design and Development of Curriculum Units. Even though this will occur naturally as a part of the teacher's classroom activity and the graduate credit each might enroll for, there needs to be special time for coaching and facilitation of this process. This can take place after school for a three to four hour session or on a full day basis. Two to three days of this follow-up should be planned and scheduled.

2.4 Classroom Visitations. The coaches and facilitators will visit classrooms and observe, as well as model, where appropriate, class-room instruction based on the new, innovative model. Teachers do find this very helpful and rewarding, as well as reinforcing.

2.5 Faculty Booster Sessions - These sessions usually are of-fered after school for three to four hours or operate over a one and one half day session as needed and requested.

2.5 0- Learning Styles - Gadgets, Gizmos and Contraptions

This session is critical for the use, implementation and moni-toring of learning styles in the classroom where statistically significant increases have been documented in the research.

2.51 - Personal Skills Map and Inventory

This session is essential for faculty and staff to determine how they perform on eleven critical success factors in perfor-mance. Faculty will learn how to implement strategies to im-prove student self-esteem, time management, and goal orienta-tion and so forth through this model.

2.52 - Additional Booster Sessions

Skill development in reading with music, story telling, song writing and "grapple" from text, which creates real life experiences for students. Additionally, the elements of structure are reinforced through the steps to unit design with a selected topic from faculty texts and materials. Art orchestration, peripherals, posters and banners is conducted as a booster, as well as special emphasis on recyclable products for learning. Also special boosters in content areas such as elementary math, science, high school chemistry, music and math are available. Drama and improvisation, thematic unit design and development, Storytelling and Communications effectiveness are also boosters, which have been taught and demonstrated to enhance the *IntelliLearn*® process.

2.6 - Parents Awareness Sessions
(three to four hours)
2.7 - High School Students' "Carpe Diem" Club.
2.8 - Community Awareness, Chamber of Commerce, Business, United Way Sessions

PHASE III - Evaluation, Dissemination and Replication

3.0 - Following the "Assess, Plan, Do, Verify" approach of the Deming Quality Process, this is the Verify phase where post assessments and evaluation occur based on pre-determined goals and objectives established by the stakeholders.

3.1 - Jointly design, develop and facilitate a demonstration conference to "show what we know" as a result of the implementation of *IntelliLearn*® Processes. This will include various aspects of feedback and evaluation, as in determining reactions to the training sessions and processes, assessing the use and effectiveness of the strategies, tactics and tools learned, evaluating the impact of the effort on stated and emerging needs and objectives, and determining the financial, social and educational return on the investment for all stakeholders and contributors.

3.2 - Replicate the Process within the district with another cohort or affinity group and set up a replication team with experienced teachers who can model the process as it cascades outward throughout the school and community.

3.3 - Reward and Recognition - establish a vehicle to reward and recognize outstanding progress toward improvement, which clearly demonstrates the processes, and improvement made by using the processes.

PHASE IV - Utilizing Technology

4.0 - Technology use can be both instructive and supportive of the improvement process. Using Internet and video television in innovative ways can connect people and link together staff in the process in order to create an increase in the order of magnitude of success and implementation when replicating and training others beyond the first cohort group.

Appendix D

A Partial List of *IntelliLearn*® Customers

Education

- ☑ Antioch University Continuing Education Program, Ohio
- ☑ Beaufort County School District, South Carolina
- ☑ Butte County School District, Idaho
- ☑ Cambridge College Graduate Program in Urban Teacher Education, Massachusetts
- ☑ Casa Grande Union High School District, Arizona
- ☑ Celebration Academy, Florida
- ☑ Chama Valley School District, New Mexico
- ☑ Chicago City School District, Illinois
- ☑ Clinton High School, South Carolina
- ☑ Cornell University – Center for Advanced Human Resource Studies, New York
- ☑ Edgewater School District, Ohio
- ☑ Evangeline Parish School District, Louisiana
- ☑ Frederick Douglas High School, Maryland
- ☑ Greece Central Schools, New York
- ☑ Harvard University, Massachusetts
- ☑ Heritage High School, Tennessee
- ☑ Jasper County School District, South Carolina
- ☑ Kapaa Elementary School, Hawaii
- ☑ Kapolei Elementary School, Hawaii
- ☑ Lady's Island Elementary School, South Carolina
- ☑ Lanikai Elementary School, Hawaii
- ☑ Las Cruces Public Schools, New Mexico
- ☑ Lee County School District, South Carolina
- ☑ Leilehua High School, Hawaii
- ☑ Meridian Charter School, Utah

- ☑ National Dropout Prevention Center, South Carolina
- ☑ New York State Department of Education, New York
- ☑ North Syracuse Public Schools, New York
- ☑ Ohio State University – Center on Education and Training for Employment, Ohio
- ☑ Oklahoma State University – Institute for Telecommunications, Oklahoma
- ☑ Osceola High School, Florida
- ☑ Oswego City School District, New York
- ☑ Oswego Vocational Technical School, New York
- ☑ Phoenix, Maricopa County Schools, Arizona
- ☑ Portsmouth City School District, Ohio
- ☑ Rochester City School District, New York
- ☑ Shawnee State University, Ohio
- ☑ Southeastern Illinois College, Illinois
- ☑ Spelman College Continuing Education Department, Georgia
- ☑ Springfield City School District, Ohio
- ☑ Stetson University, Florida
- ☑ Tech Prep – Ohio South Consortium, Ohio
- ☑ Theodore Roosevelt High School, Texas
- ☑ Utica City School District, New York
- ☑ Voyager Charter School, Hawaii
- ☑ Wake County School District, North Carolina
- ☑ Williamsburg County School District, South Carolina

Government Agencies, National and State Organizations

- ☑ American Society for Quality Education Services
- ☑ Georgia Department of Education and Georgia Department of Technical and Vocational Education
- ☑ JROTC – U.S. Air Force
- ☑ JROTC – U.S. Army
- ☑ NASA
- ☑ National Endowment for Financial Education
- ☑ New Hampshire Senate and House Education Committee
- ☑ North Carolina Association of Educators
- ☑ State of California Youth Authority
- ☑ State of North Carolina Governor's Support our Students, North Carolina

- ☑ United Nations Development Program
- ☑ United States Air Force
- ☑ United States Department of Energy
- ☑ United States Postal Service
- ☑ Virginia Education Association

Corporate Foundations Supporting IntelliLearn®

- ☑ Intel Corporation
- ☑ The Eastman Kodak Company

Corporations Who Have Applied the *IntelliLearn®* Processes

- ☑ Alcan-Rolled Aluminum Products
- ☑ Arrow Electronics
- ☑ Gulfstream Aerospace Corporation
- ☑ Intel Corporation
- ☑ James River Corporation (United Kingdom)
- ☑ J. M. Huber Corporation
- ☑ Keene Industries (West Africa)
- ☑ National Education Corporation
- ☑ Sandia National Laboratories
- ☑ Sara Lee Corporation (Knit Products and Fleece Division)
- ☑ Sonoco Products Corporation
- ☑ Support Systems International, Inc.
- ☑ The Eastman Kodak Company
- ☑ The Shell Petroleum Corporation (Asia-Pacific)
- ☑ Xerox Corporation

The
Seven
Secrets
of
Learning
Revealed

Resource Guide

Appendix E

Resource Guide

**One Convenient Location for Resources
Referred to Throughout
*The Seven Secrets of Learning Revealed***

Alderson, Wayne T., Value of Person Consultants, 246 Washington Road, Mt. Lebanon; Pittsburgh, PA 15126. Phone: 412-341-9070; email: info@valueoftheperson.com or www.valueoftheperson.com

Anderson, Jeff, Audio Enhancement, 12613 South Redwood Rd., Riverton, UT 84065. Phone: 1-800-383-9362; Email: jeff@audioenhancement.com or www.audioenhancement.com

Anthony Robbins Foundation, 4888 Carroll Centre Rd., Suite 112, San Diego, CA 92126. Phone: 1-800-554-0619 or www.tonyrobbins.com

Cercone, Donna
Cercone Learning International. www.cerconelearning.com

Dunn, Rita, Ed.D., The Center for the Study of Teaching and Learning Styles; St. John's University, 8000 Utopia Parkway, Jamaica, NY 11439. Phone: 718-990-6161 or www.stjohnsuniv.edu

Fuller, Renee, Dr., President, Ball Stick Bird Publications, P.O. Box 429, Williamstown, MA 01267; or www.ballstickbird.com

Irlen , Helen, The Irlen Institute, International Headquarters, 5380 Village Road, Long Beach, CA 90808. Phone: 562-496-2550 or www.Irlen.com

Nevins, Mike, President, Full Spectrum Solutions,
4880 Brooklyn Rd., Jackson, MI 49201. Phone: 1-888-574-7014 or
www.fullspectrumsolutions.com

Nutritional Ecological and Environmental Delivery Systems (NEEDS),
P.O. Box 580, East Syracuse, NY 13057. Phone: 1-888-634-1380 or
www.needs.com

Batmangheldi, F., M.D. www.watercure.com

FOR MORE INFORMATION

on how you can obtain training products and research, materials, or to request a seminar, please contact Dr. Martel at the following address:

Laurence D. Martel, Ph.D.
President
National Academy of Integrative Learning, Inc.
PO Box 5784
Hilton Head Island, SC 29938
phone: 843-686-4050 fax: 843-686-4519
www.intellilearn.org
martel@intellilearn.org

Additionally, Dr. Martel provides keynote addresses for national and international organizations and is available for your community group or parent or student organizations to speak on a variety of issues related to improved learning performance.

Share the Secrets by ordering additional copies for those you love

**Check with your neighborhood and online bookstores
or order here
Toll-Free: 1-800-662-2394
secured online ordering
www.cameopublications.com**

	#	Price
The Seven Secrets of Learning Revealed by Dr. Laurence D. Martel *What Your Teacher Never Taught You* *Because Your Teacher Never Knew* 336 pages $49.95 ISBN: 0-9715739-8-0		
Order Total		

Shipping:

USA: $5.95 for first item; add $2.00 for each additional book

SC residents please include 5% sales tax

Corporate, School, Church, and Volume discounts are available. Please Call (843) 686-4050

Please Print

Name_____

Company_____

Ship To _____

City/State/Zip_____ Country _____

Phone (   ) _____ Email (optional) _____

National Academy of Integrative Learning, Inc.
PO Box 5784
Hilton Head Island, SC 29938
phone: 843-686-4050 fax: 843-686-4519

credit card # _____ expires_____

please sign _____